ULTIMATE REALITY
AND ITS DISSIDENTS

A PHILOSOPHY OF LIFE

Graeme Donald Snooks

IGDS

Institute of Global Dynamic Systems Books
Canberra

First published 2016
by **IGDS Books**
Canberra

Printed in the United States of America by CreateSpace

National Library of Australia cataloguing-in-publication data
Snooks, G.D. (Graeme Donald)
Ultimate Reality and its Dissidents
Bibliography
  1. Human Nature
  2. Ethics
  3. Good & Evil
  4. Truth
  5. Freedom

ISBN 978-0-9808394-4-9

"What is man, that thou art mindful of him?" **King James Bible** (*Psalm* 8:4).

"What is man, the praised demigod! Does he not lack the powers just there, where he needs them most?" **Goethe** *(Werther, 1774)*.

"Is it possible to imagine anything so ridiculous as this miserable and wretched creature [man], which is not so much master of himself ... and yet dares to call himself master and emperor of this universe in whose power it is not to know the least part of it, much less to command the same?" **Montaigne** (*Essays*, 1580).

"What a piece of work is man! How noble in reason, how infinite in faculty ... in apprehension how like a god! ... And yet to me, what is this quintessence of dust?" **Shakespeare** (*Hamlet*, 1604, First Folio).

"What is great in man is that he is a bridge and not a goal." **Nietzsche** (*Zarathustra*, 1883–85).

Contents

Figures, Tables & Boxes

Figures

Tables

Boxes

"Alpine Heights", © G.D. Snooks

Preface

This book constitutes the pinnacle of my work on the dynamics of life and human society that began fifty years ago. In a series of books published during that time, I have developed a general dynamic theory to explain the origin and development of life over the past 4,000 million years (myrs) and of human society over the past 2 myrs. This theory has been employed also to suggest probable dynamic outcomes for human society during the immediate and distant futures. The most exciting discovery made during this intellectual odyssey has been the hidden universal life-system—which I call the strategic *logos*—that is responsible for the emergence and exponential transformation of life and human society. The strategic *logos* is an entropy-defying, shock-deflecting engine of life that has operated powerfully under the radar until now. An overview of this research program is provided in my recent book *Ark of the Sun* (2015).

The purpose of this new book is to analyse the implications of the recently discovered strategic *logos*—which I argue is the ultimate reality in life—for the way we might wish to live our lives. As will emerge from the following pages, there is a paradox at the heart of life. While the *logos* is the giver of life, it is also life's oppressor. To examine this paradox, I explore the origin and character of human nature, the role mankind plays in the operation and transformation of the *logos*, together with the strategic reality of good and evil, truth, ethics, and individual freedom. Like the solitary pine tree on the misty alpine heights, the meaning of life emerges from the fog of human delusion. This book is only for the "very few" who are prepared to scale the alpine heights.

One should never embark on the highly risky venture of truth-seeking alone, owing to the high casualty rate involved. Fortunately I have had the delightful and supportive companionship of my lovely wife Loma Graham for 46 years of this half-century journey. And for that I am truly grateful.

Once again I wish to express my gratitude to Julie Hamilton for her invaluable professional and personal support in designing the cover (using a photograph I took in the Austrian Alps in June 2011) and formatting the text.

GDS of Sevenoaks
24 January 2016

Chapter One

How Should We Live Our Lives?

The central issue exercising the minds of thoughtful people is how we should live our lives. Should we just accept the world as it is, follow the line of least resistance, and seek pleasure wherever it leads? Should we attempt to change the world, or at least the prevailing set of behavioral standards, if we find it not to our liking? Or should we accept that there is nothing we can do to change the world, but nevertheless refuse to acquiesce in its oppressiveness?

To respond to this challenge, it is necessary to understand the nature of life. Is the world capable of being changed by the exertion of our will power and, if so, how could this be achieved? There are many who believe that significant change brought about by human will power and action is indeed possible. An example we are all familiar with is the issue of climate mitigation. A growing number of scientists, politicians, and ordinary individuals believe not only that human-induced climate change is a reality, but that it can be mitigated through concerted global action. Of course, if something as momentous as large-scale climate mitigation could be achieved, then perhaps even life itself could be transformed. Perhaps self-interest could be replaced by altruism in our interactions with each other. Perhaps human nature could be radically changed, so that harmony would replace conflict in individual, group, societal, and international relationships. Perhaps the lion could lie down with the lamb; perhaps we could create paradise on Earth. And then, perhaps not.

When viewed objectively, idealists who really believe it is possible to create paradise on Earth are very few indeed. Behind most demonstrations against prevailing social and political realities lie fairly crude material interests. The vast majority of people are prepared to accept life as it is, provided it meets a comfortable buffer above their basic material requirements. They see no need to fundamentally change a material system that is meeting their needs. Self-interest rather than altruism prevails. Unreflective indulgence characterizes most people who chase after "happiness".

There is, however, another way. By analysing the nature of life, it is possible to challenge it without attempting to change or destroy it. This approach has always been possible. It began 2,500 years ago—sometime in the fifth century BC—in Athens with the founders of Cynicism, Antisthenes (c.445–366 BC) and Diogenes of Sinope (c.412/403–324/321 BC). This way of life—more than a fully developed philosophy—became one of the most influential branches of the Socratic tradition in the ancient world. Essentially, the Cynics challenged the conventions of Greek and, later, Roman civilisation by rejecting their social rules and materialist objectives. But they did so without philosophising about the nature of ancient society. They had no model of how and why it worked the way it did.

The purpose of this book is to provide not only a model of **ultimate reality** (which I call the "strategic *logos*")—a model that emerged from my scientific research over the past five decades—but also a way of responding to life. This response involves wrestling the strategic *logos* rather than trying to fundamentally change it (something that cannot be successfully achieved) or to destroy it.

WHAT IS ULTIMATE REALITY?

The most significant outcome of my research over the past 50 years has been the discovery of the strategic *logos*, which is the hidden universal life-system that has enabled life forms to take the development of biological and social complexity to a level that could not be predicted by hypothetical observers familiar only with the physical forces of the universe. By inventing the dynamic life-system, organic life forms have, for a relatively brief time, been able to defy entropy and exploit a physical environment extremely hostile to life. Human society, therefore, is an outcome, not of "cosmic self-organisation" as many scholars have argued, but of the emergence of the strategic *logos* (hereafter called *"logos"*), with its own very special laws of life. The *logos,* in other words, is not a physical system, such as a "biosphere" claimed by some physicists, but rather a social system composed of hidden yet powerful forces that have led to order and complexity in life and human society.

It is argued here that the strategic *logos* is the ultimate reality, or the ultimate truth, in life. It is a holistic system that provides meaning for all other systems and truths in life. There is nothing beyond the *logos*. What is essential to realise is that the *logos* is a materialist system composed of visible agents, organisations and capital structures on the one hand and invisible interacting forces on the other. It is *conceptually* similar to other scientifically delineated systems—with which we are all familiar—the cosmos and the human mind.

While the ability of life forms to gain access to energy from the sun (or from the molten core of the Earth in oceanic depths) is usually taken for granted, this is no easy task. Life-forms need to develop either biological or technological methods to access energy to do work, so as to create order and complexity. This is a matter beyond the capability of individual organisms. It can only be achieved through the presence of a dynamic life-system or strategic *logos*. Biological and technological "ideas" do not just emerge spontaneously as do events in the physical world—such as the flow of heat from hot to cold bodies—but rather require the deliberate investment of time and resources in dynamic social structures to generate material outcomes. This is a process I call the "strategic pursuit", whereby materially motivated organisms attempt to maximise the probability of their survival and prosperity through the adoption of "dynamic strategies".

Without a dynamic life-system, individual organisms would be unable to survive, let alone prosper, in a hostile world that is continually running down. These protective life-systems, or strategic *logoi*, need to be dynamic, because the biological and technological methods required to survive and prosper are continually being degraded—what I call "strategic exhaustion". This dynamism is an outcome of the need to continually reinvent ways of gaining access to sources of energy and natural resources.

While the laws of physics determine the conditions under which the *logos* might emerge, it is the internal laws of the *logos*—the laws of life and history—that determine the way in which life unfolds. These laws, which I have derived and discussed in my books *The Laws of History* (1998) and *The Collapse of Darwinism* (2003), can only be understood through the systematic observation of the operation of the *logos* throughout life on Earth over the past 4,000 million years (myrs) and by the construction of a general dynamic theory that can be employed to explain what has been observed.

ULTIMATE REALITY AND ITS DISSIDENTS

We need, first of all, to clarify the meaning of ultimate reality, and then to explain why I have identified it as the scientifically derived strategic *logos*. The ultimate reality is the final source of all life to which all biological and technological activities are related. It is a reality, or truth, that is established empirically rather than metaphysically. This is the case with the strategic *logos*, which was discovered using a systematic inductive method. As shown in chapter 3, the strategic *logos* is the source of all life and material progress, and it can only be explained by examining its empirically determined component parts. It is a self-starting, self-sustaining life-system, beyond which there is no other life principle. It is the alpha and omega of biological and societal existence.

There is, however, a fundamental paradox in life: the *logos* is both life-giver and life-oppressor. Most people implicitly accept the authority of the *logos* in their lives and unknowingly work to sustain it; but there is a minority of people who wish to destroy the *logos* in the mistaken belief that it is responsible for their material difficulties. These dissidents are militant antistrategists, or terrorists. But a case can be made for another group of dissidents, who do not wish to destroy the *logos*, but instead to understand it, wrestle it to avoid being overwhelmed by the grossness of life, and to find ultimate freedom. These are the **"supralogosian" dissidents**—those reaching "beyond the *logos*"—and their approach will be explored in this book.

The central question asked here is: Should we just accept the *logos* and blindly tread the path that it prepares for us, or should we seek freedom from its oppressive dictates? The former path implies accepting, if not indulging in, the apparent motives and objectives of the *logos*. I say "apparent", because these motives and objectives can only be imputed to a life-system that has no *conscious* existence. What are these logosian motives and objectives? Essentially, the *logos* is a system driven by the desire of individuals to survive and prosper, and its objectives are to maximise the material concerns of its self-motivated agents. These matters are responsible for the drive to build complex material institutions and organisations. Our modern civilisation is the outcome.

While this is hardly an edifying way of life, it is an existence that virtually all people accept and seem to enjoy. Otherwise, civilisation as we know it, even life itself, would not exist. Herein lies the great dilemma of existence: to embrace the *logos* with all its material implications is enslaving yet life-affirming; whereas to reject the *logos* is unshackling yet life-denying. To accept the *logos* is to take the path of the materialist strategist, whereas to reject the *logos* is to take the path of the self-defeating antistrategist. Both ways, however, are unattractive to the rational mind. One leads to mindless material indulgence and enslavement to the *logos*, and the other to oblivion. My entire professional career has been dedicated to analysing the materialist triumph of the symbiotic relationship between the strategist and the *logos*; and the destructive impact of the determined antistrategist (for example, Akhenaten, Hitler, Stalin, Mao, al-Qaida, Islamic State) on society and its underlying *logos*.

This analysis has led me to ask if there might be a middle way; a path that steers clear of materialist indulgence and doesn't endanger the *logos*. It is argued in this book that there is indeed a middle way that offers the prospect of freedom from the oppressive forces of life. But it is a solution that involves contradictions and challenges. There are no simple answers, no black and white solutions. This middle path involves acquiring a thorough understanding of the nature of the ultimate reality—its motives, objectives, processes, outcomes, and futures—in order to struggle against becoming enmeshed in its machinations. It involves, in other words, wrestling the *logos*. **What I am suggesting is that the realist thinker be neither a strategic supporter nor an antistrategic opponent; to be instead, a supralogosian participant in life**. By making this suggestion, I wish to make it clear that I am aware of the contradictions involved. To take a combative position against the *logos* is to take a strong stand against life, at the same time that one is living off the benefits provided by the *logos*. The only entirely consistent position would be to take an early exit from life. But that would be taking the easy way out of a complex dilemma, and to put a premature end to an amazing experience that will never occur again. The world is a very messy, but also a very interesting, place; not to be missed for the world!

There have, of course, been other thinkers and groups that have taken a nonstrategic, rather than a supralogosian, stance in life. The distinction I wish to make here is between a superficial turning away from society on the one hand, and the deeper struggle with the underlying life force on the other. In the classical world, "Cynics" was the name for a philosophically inspired movement—consisting of a notorious collection of eccentrics—inspired by the lives and ideas of Antisthenes and Diogenes in Athens in the late fifth and early fourth centuries BC. While the Cynics will be discussed at greater length later, we need to note here that they had no theory about the life-system of Athens or the rest of the Greek and non-Greek world, only a distaste for the prevailing customs of their society. They attacked the superficial characteristics of Greek and, later, Roman society in the belief that by doing so they could make life better. They had no understanding of the unchangeable nature of the *logos* underlying these ephemeral customs and habits. They did not wrestle with ultimate reality—with the *logos*.

Another example of a famous nonstrategic movement was the early community of Jesus of Nazareth. The historical character of Jesus lived at a time when the eastern end of the Mediterranean was dominated by the military force of occupying Rome. This imperial domination resulted in a number of different responses by the local Palestinian population in order to find release from imperial oppression, with all its attendant physical and mental disorders. These approaches ranged from terrorist activities (antistrategic), through religious responses (other-worldism), to the creation, as Jesus did, of nonstrategic groups within the wider strategic society. Once again, this response was not the result of any philosophy about the strategic *logos*, and did not involve wrestling with the ultimate reality. Rather it was an attempt to heal damaged bodies and minds by turning away from the *logos* as represented by Roman imperialism. This movement only became a fundamentally religious movement after the death of Jesus, largely at the hands of Paul, who developed a theology about the figure of Christ the Son of God, something never claimed by the historical figure Jesus.

What I am suggesting is something very different from these nonstrategic movements. What I am suggesting is that we need to understand the nature of the life-system and to wrestle against it to prevent the *logos* from swallowing up our lives and denying us our freedom as thinking individuals. You have to know your opponent in order to wrestle successfully with him. Neither the Cynics nor Jesus were involved in challenging ultimate reality, because they didn't know what it was. What I am suggesting is that the realist thinker should struggle with life rather than being absorbed into it, or attempting to destroy it, or turning away from it. Only by testing the limits of the *logos* is it possible to discover the greatest freedom life has to offer; a freedom that transcends the type granted to strategists within the confines of even the most democratic strategic *logos*. Such a wrestling match has implications only for the thinking individual, not the society generated by the *logos*. What I am suggesting is an individual search for truth and freedom. These values are not anti-*logos*, but supra-*logos*—beyond *logos*.

In order to understand ultimate reality we need to explore a number of central issues with which thinkers have grappled for thousands of years. These issues include the nature of man, ethics, evil, truth, freedom, and the system that makes sense of it all—the strategic *logos*. By the end of this book we will have an appreciation of ultimate reality—that paradox at the heart of life—and its supralogosian dissidents.

Ultimate Reality

Chapter Two

What is Man?

What is man? This is a question asked repeatedly down through the ages. And it is a question that has elicited different answers at different times and in different places. The type of answer given has depended upon the strategic aspirations of the societies framing the question. It is argued in this chapter that our conception of human nature has not evolved progressively from early ideas, but, like all other influential ideas, reflects the type of dynamic strategy pursued by human societies. Yet, despite mankind's changing conception of itself, the underlying reality is that, fundamentally, human nature is unchanging. And this unchanging nature of humanity—which can reveal different aspects of itself in different strategic circumstances— could only be fully understood once the strategic *logos* had been discovered. **The strategic *logos* is the shaper of man.**

CHANGING PERCEPTIONS OF HUMAN NATURE

Widely accepted ideas about the nature of humans and their role in life have changed markedly over the past 150,000 years, as the dynamic strategies pursued by human society have changed. Elsewhere I have identified four universal dynamic strategies, namely family multiplication (procreation and migration), conquest, commerce, and technological change. Each of these dynamic strategies has given rise to not only different ecosociopolitical systems, but also different perceptions of the nature and role of mankind. To illustrate this, I will briefly sketch the changing self-portrait of mankind from early hunting society through early conquest society, Greek commerce society, Roman and medieval conquest societies, early modern European commerce society, modern technological society, to our contemporary transitional society. It will become clear that mankind's image of itself has waxed and waned, rather than evolved, in response to the dynamic strategy pursued by the *logos*.

Early Hunting Society

Early hunting society is interesting because it provides a clear insight into the real relationship between man and the strategic *logos*; a relationship less easily detected in later more sophisticated societies saturated with elaborate systems of metaphysical thought. As discussed fully in my earlier book *Dead God Rising* (2010), early hunting societies were vitally concerned to maintain their hunter-gatherer life system, which was an expression of the family-multiplication strategy that they pursued for tens of thousands of years. To ensure the longevity of their life-system, the early hunters attempted to seek the favour of strategic guardians, who, they thought, were responsible for bringing the climatic conditions required to maximise the number of wild animals available for hunting and the plants, bushes and trees for gathering. In the process, members of these societies saw themselves as an integral part of their life-system. This is often expressed by Indigenous peoples around the world as belonging to the "land" (rather than the land belonging to them) that sustains them. What they really mean is that they belong to the underlying Indigenous strategic *logos*, of which the land is the most obvious visible component. According to this world view, man is just part of a larger organic system. In more technologically sophisticated societies this integral relationship between mankind and a larger organic system—the strategic *logos*—has been largely overlooked, except by mystical writers such as the Romantics or modern followers of Gaia with whom this work has nothing in common.

Ancient Conquest Society

With the neolithic technological paradigm shift, which occurred in the Old World around 11,000 BP and in the New World around 8,000 BP, new agricultural communities emerged, with people forming villages and, later, cities (30 to 50 thousand people) for economic and military reasons. In order to defend these cities and the accumulated resources they contained, semi-professional military organisations were developed. Before too long, these military forces were employed to raid and loot other urban communities nearby. This was the origin of the dynamic strategy of conquest, by which levels of both population and living standards could be raised above those made possible solely by agricultural activities. At the same time, a smaller number of societies pursued commerce rather than conquest, owing to their favourable location, enabling then to exploit regional trading patterns. But, while commerce societies experienced a more aesthetic life-style, they were always in danger of being overrun by neighbouring conquest societies.

New conquest societies in Mesopotamia and Mesoamerica emphasised team work based on the principle of division of labour according to comparative advantage. Accordingly, some members of society specialised in economic activities such as pastoral and/ or agricultural pursuits, urban craft work, and construction; others became soldiers, priests and scholars, bureaucrats, and politicians. Of course, this process of specialisation emerged gradually, as the society became larger and technologically more sophisticated; in the beginning the same people did a number of different jobs, for example, working on their farms during the growing season, going on campaigns of conquest during the quieter times of the year, and doing craft work during winter.

The point I wish to make is that the growing specialisation of the population in economic, military, intellectual, administrative, and leadership roles meant that members of society saw themselves increasing as part of a larger system rather than as individuals in small family or tribal groups. In addition, the establishment of a professional class of learned priests, led to the transformation of the simple concepts of strategic ideology and strategic guardians into formal religion and austere gods. This meant an increasing divergence of thought and attitudes from strategic reality. According to this world view, in say Mesopotamia or Mesoamerica, man was an integral part of a larger military economic structure supported by the city's gods.

Ancient Commerce Society

For those fortunate societies—such as ancient Greece or Phoenicia—located at key crossroads on international trading routes, the less brutal and ruthless dynamic strategy of commerce was adopted. The city-states of Greece successfully pursued the commerce strategy between 800 and 500 BC, which resulted in the colonisation of the Mediterranean. Commerce involved the active entrepreneurial participation of a much larger proportion of the population and a greater strategic role for the ordinary individual. As a consequence, old authoritarian institutions and organisations gave way to more democratic ones in which economic, social, and political decisions were decentralised. This led to the development of the world's first democracy—even if limited to free, adult male citizens—in the commerce city-state of Athens.

The outcome of the growing democratisation of Greek society that interests us here is the new focus on individualism. This individualism began in competitive commercial activities and spread throughout the entire society and culture of Greece. Male Greek citizens viewed themselves as individuals capable of playing a positive role in a progressive society. This attitude extended to the world of ideas and the arts, and is seen reflected in the moral philosophy of Democritus (c.460–370 BC), Protagoras (c.490–421 BC), Socrates (c.470–399 BC), Plato (c.430–347 BC), and Aristotle (384–322 BC); as well as in the remarkable development of figurative sculpture and decorated pottery. Greek philosophers focused on human reason in attempting to understand reality, while Greek artists focused on a realistic exploration of the human form. Most memorably, Protagoras summed up this new attitude to man, when he wrote evocatively: **"man is the measure of all things"**. With greater subtlety, the classical Greek sculptors Myron (fl.c.480–440), Polycleitus (5th century BC), Praxiteles (4th century BC), and Lysippus (4th century BC) were inspired by the human form and transformed Greek sculpture into a realistic, life-size, intimate portrayal of the athletic human body. Even the gods were made in the image of man, not man in the image of the gods. In this way, the ancient Greeks saw man as the centre of the Universe, rather than as a cog in the military machine of life. Herein lies the origin of the intellectual outlook later called humanism.

Conquest in the Greek, Roman, and Medieval Worlds

No matter how brilliant were the commerce societies of the Egyptians, the Greeks, the Phoenicians, and the Carthaginians, when they came into conflict with emerging conquest societies they were always swept away. Alexander the Great conquered the Egyptians and destroyed the Phoenicians on his way to invade Persia and western India; and the Romans destroyed Carthage and conquered the Greek empires in Egypt and the north-eastern Mediterranean. These developments saw the re-emergence of more authoritarian economic, social, and political institutions in the Mediterranean world. Once again, life became more regimented, more corporatized and, with it, the creative individualism that had existed in the Greek world (before the rise of Alexander) was finally extinguished. The fact that Rome imitated the artistic Greek forms, as a type of cultural camouflage—a wolf in sheep's clothing—does not lessen the radical nature of this change in intellectual and social outlook. Man was viewed as a small cog in the machinery of the conquest state; unless he was the emperor, in which case he saw himself as a god.

With the exhaustion of Rome's conquest strategy toward the end of the second century after Christ, the Western Empire collapsed and was replaced in Western Europe by a large number of conquest societies that had formed around militarily powerful local leaders, who initially offered protection, in exchange for bonded service, from a failing predatory state, a marauding Roman army, and, finally, from "barbarian" invaders. In contrast, the Empire in the east, centred on Constantinople, survived by pursuing a commerce rather than a conquest strategy, located as it was at the crossroads of trade between Europe and Asia.

In Western Europe during the thousand years between 476 and 1478, as many as twenty highly-competitive feudal kingdoms waxed and waned. The borders between these kingdoms, which adopted conquest strategies, changed constantly throughout the millennium. Unsurprisingly, these societies were characterised by authoritarian economic, social, and political structures, and were dominated by a very small military/aristocratic elite that rallied around a kingly leader. The military elite owned all productive land, which was worked by a coerced population; the strategic ideology was provided by the Christian church, inherited from the late Roman Empire; and the Church was controlled by the same families who operated their societies' military activities. Leadership of a secular and a sacred nature was a family business in medieval Europe.

Throughout this medieval millennium, life in Western Europe was dominated by an intensely competitive struggle to survive and even to prosper, as living standards of the strategists rose and fell with the success of the surging waves of conquest. This intense struggle to survive also led to the subjugation of the individual to the requirements not only of society's military machine, but also the supporting strategic ideology. Man was a servant of both the militarist state and a demanding Old Testament God. In this brutal strategic environment, individualism was largely extinguished. **God rather than man was the measure of all things.**

Yet, even in this savage strategic environment, the urge for creativity found expression in art, architecture, and music, all dedicated not to man as the Greeks had done, but to the divine strategic guardian—or God—who offered the hope of profit in this world to the fortunate few, and of joy for the elect in the next. It is wrong, therefore, to call this period the "Dark Ages", as the uninformed have been accustomed to do. As all ages are a response to the life-giving strategic *logos*, all ages are equally enlightened or unenlightened. Perception is a matter of subjective preference.

Early Modern Commerce Society

By the fifteenth century, the conquest strategy was showing signs of widespread exhaustion in Western Europe. Further economic expansion in societies such as England, the Low Countries, and the Italian city-states, could only be achieved through the adoption of the dynamic strategy of commerce. Doing so enabled European societies to exploit growing trade opportunities throughout the Mediterranean/ Aegean/Black Sea region, and in the Baltic and, later, the Americas, Africa, India, China, Japan and the East Indies. The commerce age from the mid-fifteenth to the mid-eighteenth centuries was a time of great prosperity for Western European states, which established strategic colonies and empires throughout the world.

With this early modern commercial expansion, came a transformation of the institutional and cultural constitution of West European society. This was an outcome of the growing prosperity of a much larger proportion of their populations. The burgeoning middle classes demanded greater political control over the sources of their new wealth, which in turn generated a growing effective demand for an unprecedented range of luxury goods and services. In this new economic and social climate, scholarship and the arts flourished, and the role of the individual in society came to the fore, just as it had during the last great expansion of European commerce in the classical age of Greece. Searching for precedents for their new life style, Western Europe focused on the aspirations and achievements of that earlier "golden age".

Yet, although the Renaissance may have gained inspiration from Classical Greece, it was driven not by the desire to imitate earlier ideas, but by the dynamic strategy of commerce that both cultures had successfully embarked upon. This common cultural response to the requirements of the mercantile *logos* was called humanism—the view that man and human reason were central to progress in life. Similarly the later "scientific revolution" (mid-16th to mid-18th centuries) and the "enlightenment" (18th century), both of which reflected the renewed focus on human reason and individualism, were pragmatic responses to the requirements of the dynamic strategy of commerce, and were not self-starting, free-standing intellectual movements (see *Dead God Rising*, 2010, ch. 7).

Needless to say this world view overlooked the many millennia when man and reason were subordinated to the more brutal dynamic strategy of conquest. And it failed to take heed of the experience of the ancient Greeks once their commerce strategy had been exhausted (by 500 BC) and they were forced to return once more for survival to the conquest strategy. This was an experience that Western Europe nearly repeated when, by the mid-eighteenth century, their commerce strategy had exhausted itself. During the second half of the eighteenth century, former commerce societies such as Britain, Holland, and

France began reverting to conquest in the Mediterranean, North America, the West Indies, Africa, and the East Indies. Only the circuit breaker (more accurately the strategic-sequence breaker) provided by the Industrial Revolution (beginning in Britain in the 1780s), which was made possible for the first time in history by the exhaustion of the "neolithic" (or agricultural) technological paradigm, prevented the return of the dynamic strategy of conquest on a global basis. The reason that the technological strategy prevailed is that its net economic returns on strategic investment were significantly greater than those generated by conquest (see my books *The Dynamic Society* [1996] and *Ark of the Sun* [2015]).

The Industrial-Technological Strategy

Had the Industrial Revolution occurred a century later (owing to a delayed "neolithic" technological paradigm exhaustion), the returning conquest strategy would have led to a reversal of all the democratic achievements of the previous 300 years, and to the reemergence of a darker ideology (as occurred in Nazi Germany). This would have resulted in a renewed subjugation of the individual to the corporate structure of a militarist society. The ancient view of man as a cog in the military machine would have reemerged, humanism would have been abandoned in favour of a darker more irrational ideology, the legacy of the "enlightenment" would have been aborted, and the scientific "revolution" would have foundered. But fortunately, owing to the timing of global dynamic structural change, this was not to be.

Instead, with the emergence of the Industrial Revolution—a true revolution, unlike the so-called "scientific revolution"—the humanistic attitudes to the role of the individual and human reason continued to develop and flourish. Why? Because the new industrial technological paradigm progressively embraced a growing proportion of the citizens of the societies it transformed, until virtually entire populations were involved. Accordingly, social and political institutions became increasingly, indeed thoroughly, democratic, and, **by the early twenty-first century, the individual achieved a status and position of influence unprecedented in the entire history of humanity**. But this position is currently being challenged by the radical ecologists—one of the new antistrategic movements—who want to dethrone mankind in favour of nature.

The fortuitous coincidence of the exhaustion of both the European dynamic strategy of commerce and the "neolithic" technological paradigm, has given the false impression that there is an evolutionary principle embedded in human society: an evolutionary principle that is falsely claimed to lead to the steady and sustained emergence of democratic political and social institutions; to the evolution of scientific ideas; and to the final triumph of man as the measure of all things. But as suggested earlier and demonstrated elsewhere, all these modern developments have been a response to the dynamic demand generated by the structurally changing (not evolving) strategic *logos*. Without the Industrial Revolution, there would have been no continuity of change in societal institutions and ideas between the early modern and the modern eras.

For the same reasons, it should be recognized that the continued sustainable development of scientific ideas and of humanism into the future are not inevitable; not guaranteed. It is possible to envisage a realistic scenario in which the future development of these matters is imperiled. My dynamic-strategy theory suggests that the current industrial technological paradigm will exhaust itself by the middle decades of the twenty-first century. If the global economy is going to continue growing rapidly, rather than stagnate and collapse, a new technological paradigm—which I call the Solar Revolution (a radical accessing of the Sun's energy, **not** through existing solar panel technology)—must be embarked upon during the second half of the century. It is possible that a successful attempt by global antistrategists to hijack the major world strategic societies (just as the Bolsheviks hijacked the Russian Revolution), on the pretext that, without their radical interventions, the world will not be able to negotiate the problem of climate change, could derail the normal transition from Industrial to Solar Revolution. If this became a long-standing state of affairs, the global economy would collapse, anarchy would reign, and the conquest strategy as the only dynamic alternative would reemerge. In turn this would throw the focus on individualism and humanism into reverse (see my book *The Coming Eclipse* [2010]). Even if the climate-mitigation interventionists were only partially successful, the outcome for humanism would be bleak.

The Real and Universal Role of Man in Life

This historical survey demonstrates how the general self-perception of man and his role in both society and life has changed over time. My thesis is that man's perception of himself has not evolved, but has changed structurally in response to the dynamic strategy pursued by human society as the *logos* has continually transformed itself. Now I wish to argue that this changing *perception* has failed to capture the true nature of man. Man is neither the "measure of all things", nor slave to divine beings, nor a mere cog in a societal machine beyond his influence.

In reality, the "measure of all things" is the strategic *logos*, which is a self-starting, self-sustaining, entropy-defying, shock-deflecting life-system; and man is an integral part of this larger system of life. As we will see in chapter 3, the strategic *logos* is a materialist system that is responsible for the generation of both life and human society. It consists of a strategic interaction between visible agents, physical structures and organisations on the one hand, and invisible dynamic forces on the other. Conceptually it is akin to other systems explored by scientific research, such as the cosmos and the human mind.

Mankind plays an essential role in the composition and the operation of the *logos* in two main ways. First, mankind provides the driving force that motivates and provides the kinetic energy for the strategic *logos*. This driving force is what I call "strategic desire"—the desire to survive and prosper. Second, mankind responds creatively to the strategic demand generated by the *logos*, through the employment of the "strategic cerebrum", which helps in the supervision of strategic activities. Therefore, while man is an active participant in the strategic *logos*, he is not the controlling agency. **The strategic *logos*, not man, is the measure of all things.**

It might help to explore this issue further by considering what mankind is *unable* to do. First, individuals, whether in nature or humanity, are unable on their own to develop biological or technological methods to extract energy from the Sun (or from the molten core of the Earth) so as to do work in order to create order and complexity. This can only be achieved through the strategic *logos*, which is the vehicle of life. Second, only the *logos* can provide life and society with continuity and sustainability, as this is beyond the capability of individual life forms. Third, while the series of transforming biological and technological paradigm shifts has been critical to the progress of both life and human society, no individual or group of individuals has even recognised or understood (until now) these transformations, let alone been able to engineer them. No one has the ability or foresight to do so.

This argument, which is based on a half-century of empirical research, is further supported by the confusion of intellectuals and the practical impotence of political leaders concerning the future negotiation of technological paradigm transition, together with what role, if any, will be played by climate change. The future technological transition will be resolved not by the forward decision-making of mankind, but by the unseeing, unknowing operation of the strategic *logos*. Without the hidden existence of the strategic *logos*, life, let alone mankind, would not have developed any further than ephemeral single cellular life floating in the primeval seas. **Man would be nothing without the *logos*.** Hence, while perceptions of the role of man have changed throughout history, our real role in relation to the *logos* has remained unchanged. We now turn to an examination of the real nature of man.

WHAT IS HUMAN NATURE?

My argument is that human nature can only be fully defined by exploring its relationship with the strategic *logos* of which it is an inseparable part. Man is a flexible strategic agent possessing considerable life-force qualities in order to be able to respond to the requirements of the *logos*. This is what underlies our material success. While driven by an ever-present "strategic desire", man displays a range of secondary characteristics that are expressed in different ways in different places and different times in response to the changing dynamic strategies pursued by society. Different facets of a many-sided human nature are required to respond effectively to, say, the conquest *logos* in contrast to the commerce or technological *logoi*. What doesn't change, however, is the driving force in life—the desire to survive and prosper—which dominates all other aspects of human nature. For this reason, when explaining human dynamics, rather than discussing the complexity of human nature, I focus on "strategic desire" as the overriding motive in life. To understand human nature in the round, however, it is necessary to recognize and explore the complex interaction between man and the strategic *logos*.

The Concentric Spheres Model of Behaviour

What is human nature? Does it amount, as many commentators appear to believe, to the sum total of observable human characteristics, such as aggression and gentleness, selfishness and altruism, meanness and kindness, love and hate, friendship and betrayal, honesty and dishonesty, justice and injustice, greed and generosity? Just what type of nature does such a list of opposing characteristics suggest? Surely it is impossible to sum up the nature of a species in this way, other than to say it must be variable and contradictory. How can we possibly predict what such a creature might do in the future?

It is this descriptive-list approach that has generated so much confused debate about human nature. Some observers focus selectively on the "attractive" or "positive" characteristics, such as gentleness, altruism, kindness, love, friendship, honesty, justice, and generosity; while others see only the "unattractive" or "negative" characteristics of aggression, selfishness, meanness, hate, betrayal, dishonesty, injustice, and greed. Of course all these characteristics (and more) can be observed in any society at any given point in time, and in any individual during the course of his life time. Hence, the descriptive approach has nothing to tell us about why individuals and societies have acted as they have in the past, or how they will act in the future.

A more fruitful approach might be to suggest that while all these descriptive characteristics can be observed in mankind, some sort of hierarchy between them must exist. The problem here lies in determining the theoretical basis for such a hierarchy. Elsewhere I have suggested a model for determining the relative importance of the individual, or "self", and all other individuals and groups in society.

It is called the "concentric spheres model of human behaviour". This model is developed in a general way, and then used to explain that most perplexing of human emotions called love.

The general model

In this model (see Figure 2.1) the "self" lies at the centre of a set of concentric spheres that define the varying strength of cooperative relationships between it and all other individuals and groups in society. The strength of the material relationships and, hence, the behavioural response between the "self" and other individuals and groups, will depend on how essential they are to the self's maximization of the probability of survival and prosperity. These relationships and behavioural responses are a function of the "economic distance" between them. Those aspects of the self's objective function that require the greatest cooperation and display the most "attractive" characteristics of human nature—the generation of love, companionship, and children—are located on spheres with the shortest economic distance from the centre.

Figure 2.1. The Concentric Spheres Model of Behaviour

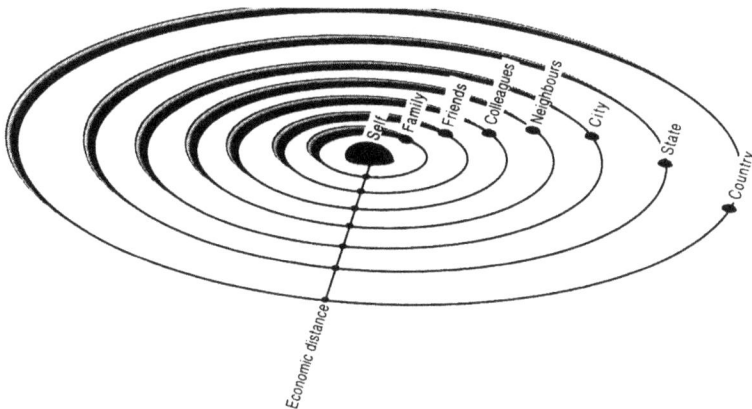

Source: Snooks 1997: 30.

For the typical individual, spouse and children occupy the sphere closest to the centre, with other relatives, friends, work mates, neighbours, members of various religious and social clubs, other members of their socioeconomic group, city, state, nation, and group of allied nations occupying those concentric spheres that progressively radiate out from the centre. As the economic distance between the centre and each sphere increases, the degree of cooperation and display of "attractive" characteristics in behaviour diminishes.

Underlying the concentric spheres model are two opposite and balancing forces: one centrifugal and the other centripetal. The centrifugal force is the incessant desire of the self to survive and prosper—a desire that leads the typical individual (but not all individuals) to place himself before all others. It is this force—which I call "strategic desire"—that provides individuals with ambition and competitive energy. The centripetal force—or economic gravity holding society together—is the need of self to cooperate with other individuals and groups in order more effectively to achieve its materialist objectives, through the pursuit of a joint dynamic strategy. It is through this interaction between competition and cooperation that the individual maximizes the probability of its survival and prosperity, and that social order is created from primitive chaos. The balance between these forces, and hence the expression of positive and negative personality characteristics, will depend on whether the social environment favours individual or group action. The outcome depends on the nature of strategic demand generated by the *logos*.

But exactly what is it that enables self-seeking individuals to cooperate with each other? The usual answer is that it is something called "trust". It is a response, however, that merely begs the further question: What generates trust? The naive response is that trust is generated by a general faith in the basic goodness of human nature. A more sophisticated response, usually made by economic institutionalists, is that trust is an outcome of the evolution—through some sort of Darwinian mechanism—of formal and informal social rules that shape predictable and cooperative conduct. Yet, as I show in *Ephemeral Civilization* (1997), no one has proposed an evolutionary model that can convincingly explain the changing nature of societal rules, particularly when major institutional reversals occur, as they regularly do in history. And finally, game theorists claim that trust is something that emerges from "strategies" (actually they are tactics) adopted by interactive individuals playing reiterative games. This, however, is a supply-side approach that employs arbitrary rules which totally ignore the wider social context (particularly the key force of strategic demand).

My dynamic-strategy theory tackles the problem from a different and more realistic perspective. It suggests that the reason chaos— which results from a breakdown of the centripetal force—does not emerge in a viable society, is that such a society is still pursuing a successful dynamic strategy. This viable dynamic strategy generates a network of competitive/cooperative relationships, together with all the necessary supporting rules and organizations to sustain a progressive society. Individuals in this society, who draw confidence from the success of the prevailing dynamic strategy, are able to display trust as well as the other positive characteristics of human nature in their dealings with each other. It is not a matter of mutual trust as such—of having confidence in the nature of other people—but rather having confidence in the wider dynamic strategy in which they are all participating and thriving. "Strategic confidence", therefore, is the economic gravity of the concentric-spheres model of behaviour as well as the liberator of the positive characteristics of human nature.

Strategic confidence, however, lasts only as long as the success of a society's dynamic strategy. Once a dynamic strategy has been exhausted and cannot be replaced, strategic confidence declines and in extreme cases, collapses completely. And as strategic confidence falls, social trust, cooperation, and the display of all those positive characteristics of human nature evaporate. The outcome is the fragmentation of society as families turn in on themselves in order to survive, and as they display selfishness, aggression and all those other negative characteristics towards their neighbours (such as the Taliban in Afghanistan or ISIS in Iraq and Syria). Under extreme pressure, individuals abandon even their families to form marauding bands of males, and cease to display any positive personality characteristics. In terms of the concentric spheres model, this implies the stripping away of the concentric spheres, one by one, until the "self" is left isolated, attempting to live by its wits alone, or as part of a group of desperate and self-serving males.

What the concentric spheres model shows is that the various positive and negative traits of human nature are employed opportunistically by individuals to exploit the prevailing material conditions of their society. While there is a constant driving force (strategic desire) to survive and prosper—a driving force associated with selfishness and aggression—it is overlaid with the more positive personality traits during the prosperous exploitation phase of the strategic pursuit. But once the prevailing dynamic strategy has been exhausted and a more individualistic and explicitly competitive approach is required to survive and prosper, these dispensable positive traits are stripped away to leave the fundamental nature of mankind exposed—the desire to survive at any cost.

While the concentric spheres model is useful in sorting out the role and relative importance of the various positive and negative characteristics of human nature, it is a **static** model and can only be regarded as a method of ordering the usual descriptive list and of explaining the resulting hierarchy. It does not actually explain human nature. To understand the nature of species in general and of human beings in particular, we need to employ a realistic **dynamic** theory of life and human society. The dynamic-strategy theory provides the answers we are seeking.

This theory shows that the individual organism has emerged through the selfcreating process of "strategic selection" in response to changes in demand generated by the strategic *logos*. While each species possesses a defining set of innate "personality" traits, the essence of its nature is not captured by these changing characteristics. Instead, the dynamic-strategy theory suggests that the real nature of a species resides in what I call its "strategic power", which is its capacity to engage in the strategic pursuit. This capacity has been developed over vast periods of time in response to the strategic *logos*. Human nature, therefore, is the expression of the way our species employs strategic power through its instinctual, emotional, and intellectual faculties in response to strategic demand. Hence, while the particular set of personality characteristics that *describe* human beings in a given society will change over time, the essence of human nature—its strategic power—is always the same. Essentially, personality characteristics are ephemeral, whereas strategic power is eternal.

One final point about the personality traits of man. We have talked about positive and negative—or attractive and unattractive—personality characteristics. Why do we prefer the least fundamental of these in the people we deal with? Not because they are morally superior, but because they threaten us less, and are easier to deal with. It is not the meek that will inherit the Earth, but those who manipulate them. The real answer is strategic not moral, despite the ethical rationalization we usually employ. Now let us turn to love!

A theory of love

Love is part of a range of human emotional responses to other human beings (and even other animals). It is part of a spectrum that includes love, friendship, fellowship, community feeling, patriotism, and nationalism. These emotions, which are expressed with varying intensity, can be viewed as facilitators in the concentric spheres model of behaviour. Accordingly, this behavioural model can explain the emotional response required at the various concentric levels of organisation radiating out from the self.

Love is the emotional response needed to create and sustain the strategic organisation of the family. The family is the original and core organisation operating under the strategic *logos*; and love makes living in a close and intense strategic relationship possible. It makes the close union of two people and their resultant offspring not only bearable but also potentially pleasurable and enjoyable. Love helps to keep the family together. But even this emotion is far from perfect, as is quite clear from problems experienced by modern families, both in terms of domestic violence, and the increasing failure-rate of marriages. The intense relationship involved in people living so closely together often breaks down. In some cases it even turns to hate, resulting in physical violence and sexual abuse. These families become dysfunctional and impose a cost on the rest of society. While a given society is progressive and prosperous, this problem is minimal, as prosperous families experience less tension and stress; but when economic conditions deteriorate, stress and tension increase and the rate of family disintegration increases. Yet, as seen over the past couple of generations, family breakdown also occurs because, in an increasingly affluent society, couples can afford to leave difficult relationships without having to work through their problems. They break up because they can economically.

It should be realised that while the family is facilitated by the emotion of love, it is not a response to love. Rather, the family is a response to the demands of the strategic *logos*. It is a central organisation in the struggle to survive and prosper. While the family plays a central role in all forms of the strategic *logos*, it is most fundamental in the "hunting *logos*" pursuing the dynamic strategy of family-multiplication. Love is the emotional material that oils the machinery of family, which in turn is a response to the requirements of the *logos*. In other words, human love is the outcome of the interaction between human nature and our life-system.

In a similar way our emotional relationships with friends, community groups, and the nation as a whole are elicited by the requirements of the *logos*. And the nature and intensity of these emotional states can be explained by the concentric spheres model of behaviour. The emotional bond with friends is less intense than love felt for family, but more intense than that felt for members of the various community groups we come in contact with. This reflects the declining importance of these concentric levels to our material wellbeing as we move outwards from the "self" in our model. In exceptional circumstances, such as during war-time, these relationships can be changed temporarily owing to the change in perceptions of what is in the individual's best interest. Some individuals will experience all emotional relationships, including patriotism and nationalism more intensely, while others will see their best interest in betraying family, friends, and nation, and focusing solely on "self".

Something should be said about another form of love: "love for humanity". This is a concept that goes back at least to the ancient Greek philosophers. In attempting to express their disdain for Athenian society of their time, the early Cynics claimed to be not Athenians, but *kosmopolites* (cosmopolitans)—citizens of the universe. This is an artificial concept employed by the Cynics in a rhetorical manner. "Humanity" is a collective term for something that has no strategic existence. Where is the holistic societal system, with all its integrated economic, social, and political interactions that corresponds to "humanity"? It does not exist. There is no point in referring to international organisations such as the UN, the IMF, the World Bank, or the International Court of Justice (the judicial branch of the UN), as these organisations, which emerged for the first time as recently as the twentieth century, are not a response to a global strategic *logos*, but to the various national *logoi* in order to facilitate their individual national interests. As humanity is a metaphysical rather than an existential concept (it is not an entity), there can be no "love for humanity", which is an expression that derives from the ancient Greek word *filanthropia* or philanthropia.

Then why does this concept exist in the modern world, when the Cynic movement that gave rise to it is long dead? The answer is that it is part of the armoury of "existential schizophrenia"—the separation of self-image from reality. Today, philanthropy is a cover for the unlimited greed of the wealthy. It is estimated that the "ultra-high net worth (UHNW) philanthropists", who on average have a net worth of $240 million, set aside about 10 percent of their wealth for "charitable" activities (2014 report of World-X and Arton Capital Philanthropy). Traditionally this has been distributed through family trusts, which are not only controlled by these philanthropists, but are a means of obtaining tax concessions. More recently, these funds have taken the form of "venture philanthropy", which attempts to earn profits that are supposed to be ploughed back to make the fund self-sustaining. These activities are increasingly in areas that are thought to provide benefits to "humanity", such as education, health, science, and climate-mitigation. What is clear is that these "philanthropists" are not "giving" their money away, but are controlling it closely, and using it to enhance their moral standing in their own eyes as well as in the eyes of a gullible world. Having made their fortunes (the average UHNW individual is 64 years old!), they want to save their "souls"; just like the aging Spanish conquistadors, who, having destroyed entire civilizations in the New World for a hoard of gold, sought redemption from their God. But times have changed. Today one has the impression that college drop-out billionaires are attempting to control research programmes they are insufficiently educated to understand, with the questionable objective of winning that ultimate accolade for guilty fame-seekers, the Nobel Prize.

Box 2.1 *Why There Is No Such Thing As "Humanity"*

As a workable life force, "humanity" doesn't exist. It is only a collective noun for the sum of all human individuals living and working in a large number of strategic *logoi* throughout the world. "Humanity" could only be a workable dynamic entity if the total human population on planet Earth was an integral part of a single global strategic *logos*. There has to be an integrated relationship between the *logos* and its strategic agents for the "agent-collective" to have a meaningful life-force identity. But such a dynamic relationship has never existed at the global level—currently there are in excess of 190 strategic *logoi* of varying size and economic viability—and will never exist in a sustainable way.

The reason there will never be a successful global strategic *logos* is because of the ruthless competition needed to drive the dynamic process of technological paradigm shifts that have been transforming human society over the past 2 million years. The Industrial Revolution, for example, was the outcome of more than 1,300 years of intense competition between a large number of European societies. China, which, owing to its location, was able to isolate itself from this competition, failed to negotiate the Industrial Revolution until the present century, despite its technological superiority during the Song dynasty (960–1279). China went from being the largest economy in the world in the mid-eighteenth century to a relatively small economy following the Industrial Revolution in the West. And, accordingly, the West dominated China for a century from the mid-nineteenth century. Similarly, Aboriginal Australia, which was effectively isolated from the rest of the world for 60,000 years, experienced no external competition and, as a result, missed out on two global technological paradigm shifts—the Neolithic (or agricultural) Revolution about 11,000 years BP in the Old World and 8,000 years BP in the New World, as well as the Industrial Revolution—and were unable to resist invasion from an industrialising Britain in 1788 (see Snooks, *Ephemeral Civilization*, 1997: 465–86).

Owing to an absence of external competition, isolated societies pursue the strategy of stasis (what I call "dynamic equilibrium" involving minor fluctuations around a horizontal time trend) rather than one of the four types of dynamic strategy aimed at achieving exponential growth (see Snooks, *Dead God Rising*, 2010: 36-37 & Snooks, "Dynamics Downunder", 2006). If, for the sake of argument, the world were able to merge all its societies into a single strategic *logos*, it would automatically cease growing exponentially and enter the holding pattern of "dynamic equilibrium". Why? Because without intense external competition there would be no economic incentive to pursue the dynamic strategy of technological change or to generate further transforming technological paradigm shifts, which involve huge risk and an immense investment of effort and resources. A single global strategic *logos* would be the ultimate end game for the human race, as we would be unable to survive the collapse of our solar system billions of years in the future (see *Ark of the Sun*, 2015: ch. 1).

But this is unlikely to ever happen; at least for very long. The establishment of a global strategic *logos* would always be vulnerable to defections by regional war lords. As soon as one region of the Earth saw an economic advantage in breaking away and adopting the more profitable dynamic strategy of conquest—as the alternative dynamic strategy of technological change would be defunct under a global command system—other regions would follow, and the global strategic *logos* would collapse. As there will never be a sustainable global strategic *logos*, the idea of "humanity" will never be more than an abstract concept; certainly never a dynamic life force. Instead there will always be competing strategic *logoi* driven separately by their own human strategic agents.

Strategic Dualism

While human nature is a reflection of our capacity to respond to the strategic *logos*, that capacity possesses a destabilizing potential for some individuals. This problem is an outcome of the tense relationship between the "unconscious organism" and the "strategic cerebrum" in man. The unconscious organism is driven by "strategic desire", while the strategic cerebrum, which initiates and supervises our participation in the strategic pursuit, is ruled by reason. It is this strategic dualism that has created man's biological dilemma.

Strategic dualism has nothing in common with Cartesian dualism. René Descartes (1596–1650), as is well known, made a distinction in his philosophy between "extended substances" or matter/bodies, and "thinking substances" or minds/souls. Only bodies, he claimed, are subject to the mechanical laws of natural science. Bodies, according to Descartes, are machines. Minds or souls, which remain beyond the reach of scientific laws, are subject only to divine laws and are released when machine-like bodies die. Cartesian dualism, therefore, involves a distinction between the material body and the non-material mind.

Strategic dualism, by contrast, does not draw this mystical distinction. The strategic mind, which is an outcome of the material brain, has no independent existence. It is subject to the laws of natural science and is extinguished when the body dies. Strategic dualism arises from the different roles played in life by the body and the brain. While the body is the embodiment of strategic desire—the fundamental driving force in life—the brain, and hence the mind, is the instrument employed by the unconscious organism to satisfy this desire through successful participation in the strategic pursuit.

The relationship between body and mind in man is complex. This, however, has not always been the case. Indeed, the body and the mind have very different development histories. The body has developed over the past 4,000 million years (myrs) from a single-celled organism into the complex structure we are and know today. From the very beginning, unconscious organisms were driven by strategic desire—a biochemical force that maximizes the probability of survival and prosperity—without the benefit of brains. Even these simple organisms were able to pursue the full range of dynamic strategies required to achieve their "objectives". Supervision of the unconscious organism's strategic pursuit was invested in what I have called the "strategic gene". It should be realized that the role of the strategic gene was limited to facilitating the objectives of the unconscious organism—by turning on and off the strategic pursuit of its host—and that it had no agenda of its own, as claimed by the neo-

Darwinists. The unconscious organism, or dynamic strategist, was always in full control, because it alone was driven by strategic desire.

There came a point in the development of life when some unconscious organisms found that in order to continue the successful pursuit of dynamic strategies, which were becoming increasingly complex, they required a more effective strategic instrument. This turned out to be the brain, or strategic cerebrum, that emerged in animals with central nervous systems through the "autogenous" process of strategic selection in response to the requirements of the strategic *logos*. Those able to take this step, a mere 500 myrs ago, demonstrated considerable success in life, at first in the sea and later on the land. To participate in this success, growing numbers of vertebrates possessing the necessary central nervous systems substituted the strategic cerebrum for the strategic gene. In the process, the relationship between body and brain became increasingly complex, culminating in its very close association in man. Yet, despite this high degree of body–brain integration in man, there remains a tension that reflects the different roles played by these two entities. It is a tension that causes mental disorders in susceptible individuals.

What are the main implications of strategic dualism? Essentially, it suggests that human nature is the outcome of a complex dialogue between body and mind, strategist and strategic instrument, strategic desire and reason. It is this dialogue that defines our strategic power and, hence, our nature. This contrasts with the rationalist view that reason is the "governor" of the passions; with the neo-Darwinian view that the body and mind are *both* instruments of the selfish gene; and with the sociological view that the body and mind are fashioned by society. Strategic dualism is also the source of tension within individuals that sometimes leads to the breakdown of the psychic unity that normally prevails in human beings.

The dialogue between the different sources of human nature operates at a number of different levels. The first and most commonplace of these takes place at the level of body and mind. It is the level most familiar to the layperson in all societies. Most people are aware of the interaction and tension that exist between the body and mind in daily life. Culture, both popular and refined, is based on the obvious unequal conflict between the passions and the intellect. The dominance of sex and aggression in our daily lives is the staple fare of news programs, television melodrama, and grand opera.

The second level of tension is the philosophical dialogue between reason and desire. In contrast to popular commonsense, the dominant philosophical view of this dialogue is the Platonic one in which reason dominates desire. If reason failed to govern desire, Plato argued, the ideal society would unravel and descend into chaos. The "guardians"—Plato's moral police—were to ensure that this did not happen. Even Aristotle, who was less disturbed than his teacher by the passions, still viewed the rational mind—the self or *kyrios* ("dominant one")—as the core of individual personality. While this philosophical tradition has its critics, it remains the mainstream.

By contrast, the dynamic-strategy theory shows that strategic desire is the driving force in life, while reason is employed to facilitate and rationalize our acquiescence in a role we share with the rest of life. While other life forms are not bothered by the desires that drive them, mankind has achieved such a degree of selfconsciousness and intellectual sophistication that it is difficult for us to accept our true nature. While we are able to see and understand what we are, we invariably do not like what we see, and we look the other way.

It is in order to live with ourselves—to cope with our dual nature—that we have learnt to "look the other way". We pretend to ourselves that we are not like other animals—that we, being intellectual beings, are not driven by desire. We have even developed complex arguments to convince ourselves not only that we are dominated by positive personality traits but that we have somehow transcended the rest of life. This self-deception is, as discussed in my earlier work, a survival mechanism. If we were forced to see ourselves as we really are—to acknowledge our true nature—many more people would not only develop debilitating disorders but also take their own lives. As this would prevent us achieving our objective in life of maximizing the probability of survival and prosperity, we have adopted strategic mechanisms (such as "existential schizophrenia", discussed in detail in Chapter 6) to prevent it.

The third level of tension is between the strategist and the strategic instrument. It is a perspective involving a number of important issues. Human nature—indeed the human individual itself—is the product of a symbiotic relationship between the unconscious organism embodying strategic desire, and the strategic cerebrum embodying the facilitating function of reason. As we have seen, until some 500 myrs ago the unconscious organism was an independent entity and, unlike the brain, was able to exist on its own. But over the intervening years the strategist and its strategic instrument have developed together and become so interdependent that neither can survive on its own, at least not without artificial life-support systems. There is no going back. They survive or perish together.

Unfortunately, the emergence of strategic dualism has made it possible for the mind to hijack the strategic pursuit and endanger an otherwise healthy organism. There are numerous examples. Individuals willing to destroy themselves for an idea have been as numerous in the past as they are today. No one in the early twenty-first century needs reminding of the suicide bombings around the world that culminated in the terrorist attack on New York on September 11, 2001; and which continue today (2015) as Islamic extremists pursue their antistrategic mission. It is strategic dualism that makes suicidal terrorism possible.

Suicide is the hollow triumph of the confused strategic instrument over the materialist strategist. The strategic cerebrum, which is supposed to facilitate the desire of the unconscious organism to survive and prosper, breaks the historical "contract" with its "employer" and terminates their symbiotic existence in the pursuit of an abstract idea that owes nothing to existential reality. It is an idea that emerges deductively rather than inductively—from rational rather than strategic thinking—in the minds of individuals alienated from their bodies. Other examples of the mind hijacking the strategic pursuit include the self-destructive quest for cerebral sensation through the use of chemical substances, the imposition of starvation owing to extreme views of body image, and the suicide of depressed individuals who have lost touch with reality. In all these cases, the mind forces the body to abandon strategic desire by employing its drive and energy against itself.

To sum up: The strategic power, or capacity, of the individual to survive and prosper, which finds expression in human nature, is the outcome of strategic dualism; which in turn is a response to the demands of the strategic *logos* over vast periods of time. Our ability to participate in the strategic pursuit depends on the strategic desire that drives the unconscious organism, together with the control and ideas generated by the human brain that facilitate this participation. In contrast, the wide range of personality characteristics is changeable, reflecting the dynamic nature of the strategic pursuit. The interaction between body and mind gives rise not only to mechanisms of a cognitive nature but also to those of an instinctual and emotional nature. Instincts are associated with our reptilian brain (the brain-stem and cerebellum), while emotions are an outcome of the mammalian brain (the limbic system). Any exploration of human nature, therefore, must focus on these aspects of strategic dualism in our species. These matters are dealt with in the next section.

What is Strategic Desire?

Strategic desire, which animates the strategic *logos*, is the driving force in life. It is the strongest and most persistent force fashioning the nature of all species, including that of mankind. And it is responsible for the development of all other instincts that influence animal and human behaviour. In the dynamic-strategy theory, this driving force is embodied in what I have called the "materialist organism" in nature and "materialist man" in human society. Many, as we shall see, are reluctant to acknowledge this essential aspect of human nature.

Strategic desire is the most fundamental force in life. Without it no form of life on this or any other planet could exist. It is the force that drives all organisms to struggle with each other to survive and prosper—something that has been happening on Earth for some 4,000 million years (myrs). Quite clearly it is a force embodying great strength and endurance. It is a force that arises from the biochemical foundations of life. To sustain life the first simple cells had to be able to maintain an internal metabolic process to meet their energy requirements. Once an individual metabolic system is established, the simple cell generates a continuous demand for fuel to feed this biochemical process. If this "metabolic demand" for fuel is not met, the cell begins to starve and its structure starts to break down. Impending starvation, therefore, leads the cell to frantic efforts to discover new sources of fuel. This is the source of strategic desire that leads all life forms, no matter how simple or complex, to struggle to survive and prosper.

Table 2.1 The Differential Impact of Dynamic Strategies on Human Physical and Instinctual Characteristics

Dynamic strategy	Physical	Instinctual
1. Genetic change/ technological change	Increased ability to access new and existing resources	Drive for curiosity and knowledge
2. Family multiplication	Increased fertility and mobility	Sexual drive and drive for adventure
3. Commerce (symbiosis)	Monopolizing and "bargaining" abilities	Drives for acquisition and adventure
4. Conquest	Abilities to wage war and to "administer" a larger resource base	Drives of aggression and power

Source: Snooks, *Selfcreating Mind* (2006: 62).

In order to maximize the probability of survival and prosperity, individual organisms adopt the most effective of the quartet of dynamic strategies generated by the strategic *logos*. Each of these dynamic strategies has a different, yet characteristic impact on the physical (including intellectual) and instinctual traits of organisms in any species. This is reflected in Table 2.1. The dynamic strategies of genetic and technological change generate a demand for physical abilities that provide greater access to new and existing natural resources, together with the instinctual drives of curiosity and thirst for knowledge. Family multiplication requires increased fertility and mobility together with greater sexual and adventure drives. Commerce needs increased abilities to monopolise and trade in scarce resources, together with acquisition and adventure drives. And conquest demands the abilities to wage war and to administer a larger captive resource base, together with the drives of aggression and power.

In responding to these different types of strategic demand generated by the *logos*, the selective organism will ignore any mutation that does not possess the required physical and instinctual characteristics in favour of any mutation that does possess them. Individuals possessing the characteristics required by the strategic demands of the *logos* in any population will become desirable as comrades and sexual mates, whereas the rest will be regarded as undesirable, even freaks. The desirable will be feted, whereas the undesirable will be boycotted, attacked, and even destroyed by parents, siblings, and neighbours. Through this autogenous—or self-creating—process of "strategic selection", strategic desire operating within the *logos* shapes the physical and instinctual characteristics of individuals in any given species.

Secondary Instincts

From the discussion of Table 2.1 it is clear that there exists a marked difference between strategic desire and animal instincts. Strategic desire owes its origins to the basic metabolic needs of all organisms, both plant and animal, whereas animal instincts have been originated and shaped by strategic selection in response to the strategic demand of the *logos*. If we think of strategic desire as an instinct, then it is the **primary** instinct and all the others are **secondary** instincts. Strategic desire, which is the driving force of the *logos*, is the progenitor of all other instincts.

While there is a hierarchy between strategic desire and the secondary instincts, there is none within the group of secondary instincts. The instincts that come to the fore in any historical era are those that respond to the strategic demand generated by the *logos'* prevailing dynamic strategy. Accordingly the importance that society might place on the various instincts depends upon which dynamic strategy is dominant. In other words, the importance of individual instincts is relative and ephemeral. There is no absolute or long-term hierarchy among the secondary instincts.

Box 2.2   What Are Animal Instincts?

The usual definition of instincts nominates those innate bodily impulses that increase the survival prospects of animals, including humans. While these unlearned impulses obviously influence behaviour, in more advanced animals they can be controlled, sublimated, and redirected by the higher functions of the brain. It should be realized that some scientists are unhappy with the word "instinct", probably owing to the debasement of the concept by William McDougall, who, at the beginning of the twentieth century, applied the term loosely to all forms of motivation. Alternative terms such as "neurobehavioral", however, are rather vague and do not convey the idea of innate reactions as succinctly and precisely. If handled in a discriminating way, the instinct concept is a useful one.

As shown in Table 2.1, there is a limited range of instincts, which has emerged in response to, and been shaped by, the dynamic strategies that organisms have relentlessly pursued for the past 4,000 myrs. Its purpose is to assist in the strategic pursuit, particularly in organisms that do not possess advanced brains or conscious minds. Indeed, the original reason for the emergence of instincts was the absence of conscious minds that could direct the strategic behaviour of organisms.

Man, however, inherited instincts as well as a conscious mind. Clearly, instincts under the supervision of the strategic gene were not sufficient for hominids to successfully pursue their increasingly sophisticated dynamic strategies. More precise and complex control over self and the social and physical environment was required; and this type of control could only be attained through the development of a more sophisticated brain. Conversely, the fact that we still possess powerful instincts, such as the aggressive and sexual urges, suggests that they still play an important role that cannot be taken over by the conscious brain. Instincts appear to provide organisms with a proactive character that is missing in the conscious mind. Instincts arise from an interaction between the body and the reptilian brain, which includes the brain-stem and the cerebellum (or little brain). The reptilian brain, which is mechanical and unconscious, closely monitors the body and controls the instincts, which have been called "genetically encoded memories". We are now in a position to discuss the main human instincts.

The sexual instinct

Sex and fertility are central to the human family-multiplication strategy, which involves procreation and migration to enable the extended family to bring more of nature's resources under their control. The adventure instinct, discussed below, is also involved in this dynamic strategy as new territories have to be explored and occupied. Owing to its strategic role, the sexual instinct is clearly a secondary driving force in the human survival arsenal. It was shaped in the distant past by the unconscious organism to exploit specific strategic opportunities. In fact, until about 1,000 to 600 myrs ago— only the last 25–15 per cent of life's time on Earth—all reproduction occurred asexually. *Hence, the sexual instinct has been an influence for only a small proportion of the time that strategic desire has been driving life.*

In *Selfcreating Mind* (2006), I argue that sexual reproduction emerged, not in response to any pre-existing sexual drive, but because it gave organisms, which had long been driven by strategic desire, greater control over the process of physical and instinctual change in response to strategic demand. Individuals were able to influence the genetic constitution of their offspring through informed mate choice. And the characteristics that are desirable in a mate during the family-multiplication strategy are high fertility and an adventurous spirit. **Why sex? Because it facilitated the strategic pursuit for those species negotiating increasingly complex dynamic strategies.**

While the sex drive is an important asset during the unfolding of the dynamic strategy of family multiplication (and during the phase of colonial expansion under the commerce or conquest strategies), it can be a liability under the technological strategy. While the other three dynamic strategies require an expansion of territorial boundaries through population increase in order to bring additional resources into the strategic process, technological change is independent of population growth. Larger surpluses are generated in the technological society by employing *existing* resources in a more *intensive* way. Technology dispenses with the need for population growth. This is the fundamental reason for changing societal attitudes to homosexuality and same sex "marriage".

Not surprisingly, powerful sexual drives in modern technological societies generate more costs than benefits. For the first time since its emergence, the sexual instinct has lost its strategic purpose. Beyond the need to replace the existing population of an advanced technological society, sex is indulged in merely for its own sake—merely for self-gratification. This change in the role of sex is reflected in the changing size of the average family. Between the mid-nineteenth and early twenty-first centuries, the average household size in the United States and Australia declined dramatically from 9–10 people to 2.5 people, as these societies substituted the dynamic strategy of technological change for that of family multiplication during frontier expansion.

Social problems arising from the sexual instinct—rape, incest, and other forms of sexual abuse—have always existed, but in the past the individual cost was measured against a social benefit. In advanced modern societies, where additional population is not necessarily an economic asset, that is no longer the case. Also this loss of strategic role has led to a massive increase in the sexual "culture", centered on pornography, to justify and exploit an instinct without strategic purpose in the modern world. The aggressive way in which this sexual culture promotes itself merely reflects the reduction in strategic demand for the sexual instinct. The pornography industry, which dominates the Internet, is supply-driven not strategy-driven. This problem will be exacerbated if, as seems likely, artificial forms of sexual reproduction are employed more routinely in the future to replace existing populations.

What then is the future of sex? With rapid advances in biotechnology generating IVF births and cloning, it is highly likely that the sexual instinct will become largely redundant in a strategic sense. And when we are able to control our genetic structure through technological means, the original reason for sexual reproduction will no longer exist. But even when the strategic purpose of sex has been completely eliminated, we will still be left with the obsolete sexual instinct. No doubt even pleasure associated with this instinct will be subject to technological control.

A major implication of this strategic analysis is that existing theories about human nature based on the primacy of the sexual drive are both superficial and wrong. Such theories include those by the younger Sigmund Freud in psychoanalysis, and by the neo-Darwinists in evolutionary biology, sociobiology, and evolutionary psychology. The reason for this widespread fundamental flaw is that the pioneering thinkers in these fields failed to develop a realist dynamic theory of life and human society. Consequently they have not been able to place the sexual instinct in its proper context. Their analyses are based on guesswork, partial observation, and *ad hoc* theorizing.

The aggression instinct

In a world wracked by wars, both general and civil, territorial conflicts, terrorism, social unrest, crime, and domestic violence, it is hardly necessary to demonstrate that aggression is one of the most powerful instincts in human nature. While its consequences are regrettable, the aggressive drive has been, and is, essential for the survival and prosperity of individuals in a world characterized by scarce resources.

As with sex, the aggression instinct was developed through strategic selection to facilitate the strategic pursuit by the *logos*. During an era when early man was pursuing the family-multiplication strategy into new and dangerous territory, those individuals displaying aggressive tendencies were much in demand. This was a time when our species was developing non-biological weapons and refining the instincts needed to become the world's leading predator. Of course, this development was based on a process that had its origins in our earlier mammalian and reptilian ancestors. There is also a gender dimension here, with male hormones, such as testosterone, enhancing the innate aggressive drive possessed by the species as a whole.

More specifically, the aggression instinct was essential to the successful pursuit of the conquest strategy, to the colonial phase of the commerce strategy, and to the conduct of wars needed to protect the other strategies from hostile takeover. It is a role reflected in the entire history of mankind. Conquest was the dominant dynamic strategy of the ancient world, and even for the favoured few societies that pursued commerce—such as Egypt, Phoenicia, Carthage, and Greece—wars were employed to extend and maintain their trading empires. Even in the modern world, the instinct of aggression has been employed by societies defending their technological strategies through war aimed at securing strategic resources (such as oil) or strategic territories (military bases).

Aggression is also employed as a strategic instrument within modern technological societies in peace time. Even in sophisticated corporations, which are engaged in bloodless warfare, there is a role for the "hardman", who employs aggression and bullying tactics to achieve corporate objectives by eliminating internal competition and sweeping aside market competitors; or to secure the objectives of labour unions. While this may be inevitable in the corporate and union worlds, problems arise for modern society—they always plague individuals who suffer from these exercises in aggression—when the aggressive tactics of large corporations and large unions are employed in more creative or cultural organizations like the public service and universities. The recent appearance of hardmen, who in some instances are borderline psychopaths, in cultural institutions owing to funding cutbacks, threatens to terminate the flow of creative ideas that can only flourish in liberal environments. Cultural institutions should not be run as if they were corporations. They are, and should remain, centres of strategic thinking rather than instruments of strategic desire.

The aggression instinct also plays a more subtle role in human society. In sublimated form it enables mankind to take a proactive stance in life. It provides the drive to make effective decisions and to execute plans for the future. Rational abilities on their own are not sufficient to achieve these things. Patients with brain damage that prevents communication between the frontal lobes and the more ancient parts of the brain are incapable of making the right decisions in life or in undertaking them effectively. It is now established that both instincts and emotions are essential if man is to successfully participate in the strategic pursuit. And the reason is that strategic desire, the driving force in life, is located in the body and is communicated to the conscious mind through the reptilian and limbic systems in the brain. Once again we are brought to the conclusion that "desire drives and reason facilitates", which is the central maxim of the dynamic-strategy theory.

What will be the future role of the instinct of aggression? It is unlikely that highly competitive situations will ever disappear, owing to the intensity of strategic desire. But the era of systematic, as opposed to accidental or irrational, conquest has passed, owing to the emergence and widespread adoption of the technological strategy. In the premodern world, the most economical dynamic strategy was usually conquest, sometimes commerce, but in the modern world, owing to the exhaustion of the former "neolithic" (agricultural) paradigm, technological change in industrial production generates higher returns than conquest. Hence, conquest in the modern world will always fail. In the mid-twentieth century, Germany, Italy, and Japan found this out the hard way. Their objectives were economically irrational and were based on racial rather than materialist issues. The Thousand-Year Reich, for example, lasted a mere twelve years.

At the beginning of the twenty-first century, the major global conflict is the so-called "war against terrorism" conducted by the leading technological nations against international terrorists and those societies that harbor them. It is a major example of the aggression instinct let loose. In terms of my dynamic-strategy theory, it amounts to a struggle between strategists and "antistrategists", not a "clash of civilizations" (both of which would have to be strategic). This type of struggle has been experienced throughout history, both at the "national" and global levels.

Despite a recent overflow of aggression and violence, mainly in less developed parts of the world, contemporary society is not an easy environment for those individuals with more than their share of the aggression instinct. In the premodern world such individuals were much in demand owing to the predominance of the conquest strategy, and many of these were highly successful in war, and were regarded as heroes. But in modern technological societies their talents go unappreciated and unrewarded, except on the sporting field. Those unable to sublimate this drive are likely to fall foul of the law, face social censure, and spend some of their lives in prison. Many are likely to experience considerable frustration, depression, self-destructive urges (resulting in the use of drugs and fast cars) and other psychological disorders. All because of a mismatch between primeval instinct and the strategic demand of the modern *logos*.

A number of philosophical and psychological theories are based on the assumption that mankind is driven by aggressive and self-destructive drives. Friedrich Nietzsche popularized these instincts and Alfred Adler and, later, Sigmund Freud, used them in their versions of psychoanalysis. What none of these thinkers realized is that aggression is not a primary instinct, but rather a strategic response to the true driving force in life — strategic desire. They too failed to develop a realist dynamic theory of life and human society.

The curiosity instinct

Curiosity is a universal characteristic of the animal kingdom. Individual animals continually explore their environment, seeking new sources of food and delight, and attempting to discover how their world works. While this basic instinct contributes to participation in all dynamic strategies, it is particularly important for involvement in the genetic and technological strategies.

Under the dynamic strategy of technological change the curiosity instinct is central and indispensable. Individuals with an insatiable curiosity are continuously exploring new gadgets, new technical possibilities, and new ideas of all conceivable types. They wish to know how things work, and how they can be made to work better. Most are interested in practical matters. In our formative past for example, man needed to achieve a sharper edge on, or better balance in, stone tools. Some were even interested in esoteric matters, such as how to account for the rising and setting of the sun, or the regular movement of the bright lights in the sky at night, or the success of their own clan over their neighbours, or even the meaning of life. This curiosity of both a practical and theoretical nature enabled mankind to escape the limitations of the "genetic option" by replacing it with the "technology option", partially at first (about 2 myrs BP) and then totally (about 150,000 years BP)—see *Ark of the Sun* (2015).

The genetic option also required curiosity. Individual organisms have always been curious about who might be more successful than they, and why this might be so. It is this curiosity that underlies the "autogenous"—or selfcreating—process of strategic selection by which gifted and successful individuals seek out each other in order to maximize their probability of survival and prosperity. In this way—as I discuss in *The Selfcreating Mind* (2006)—they increase their chance of joint success and pass on their physical and instinctual characteristics to their offspring. Curiosity is essential to the process of "biotransition" (a term I use in preference to "evolution").

Despite the central importance of the curiosity instinct, it is not *intensely* felt by the average person, nor does it provide an effective power base in human society. Those people, in whom the instincts of aggression and power are more strongly expressed, always gain the upper hand in the strategic struggle. The thinkers and dreamers are always outmanoeuvred and exploited by the practical strategists, who are driven more strongly by strategic desire. It is for this reason that there are more effective property rights in material property than in intellectual property. Of course, the best way to ensure a steady flow of ideas is to adequately reward curiosity.

A central finding in my work is that the existential curiosity instinct examined here has nothing in common with the metaphysical "will to truth" postulated by Plato and his followers. There is no "will to truth" in life for the simple reason that it would endanger the strategic *logos* by exposing the unmitigated and unbearable horror of existence. In other words, there is no gene for truth in general, because the *logos*, during its emergence over billions of years, had no use for truth. What then of science? First, the *logos*'s demand for science is a demand for a very constrained and utilitarian form of truth, not truth in general; and second, even this demand is very recent and, hence, is part of the "technological option", not the "genetic option" in life's history (see *Ark of the Sun*, ch. 3). In chapter 6 it is shown that **truth and truth-seeking are accidental outcomes of an underactive "existential schizophrenia" mechanism in a very small number of individuals who also have an overactive curiosity instinct.**

The adventure instinct

The adventure instinct is the drive to explore unknown parts of the physical environment: as the old cliché would have it—"to go where man has never gone before". It is this instinct that has driven our explorers to risk their lives over the deepest oceans, on the slopes of the highest mountains, and across the widest deserts of ice and sand in order to discover new lands and resources. And once we had seen all that there was to see on Earth we began to explore the Universe.

While the instinct for adventure is significant in one form or another to all four dynamic strategies, it is essential to the family-multiplication and commerce strategies that require constant access to new land and resources. The family-multiplication strategy, for example, depends on migration as well as procreation. It was this dynamic strategy that led to the diaspora of early man. Without the adventure instinct our forefathers would have remained in the rainforests, as did our closest living relatives, and would never have developed large brains and sophisticated civilizations. More recent and better-known examples of the role of the adventure instinct in the family-multiplication strategy include the great westward-moving frontier in North America throughout the nineteenth century, and the equally great eastward-moving frontier in Northern Asia—now Russia—from the seventeenth century. While the great frontier movements were driven by strategic desire, these unfolding dynamic strategies depended on the secondary instincts of sex and adventure. In both North America and Russia, the sexual instinct responded to the strategic demand for increasing family size, while the spirit of adventure contributed to millions of people leaving their homes in Europe and the eastern American seaboard to explore new lands in the hope of greater security and prosperity for themselves and their children.

Pursuit of the commerce strategy is also driven by strategic desire and facilitated by the instinct of adventure. Ancient Greece was a great commerce society—or, more accurately, a closely interacting group of commerce societies—that employed the adventure instinct to pursue their commerce strategies throughout the Mediterranean world. Without this instinct the Greeks would have remained at home and become a society of poverty-stricken, illiterate, dirt farmers and fishers. The same could be said of the Venetians, whose society began with a handful of small marshy islands at the head of the Adriatic but became a great commerce empire that stretched throughout the

Mediterranean and Aegean seas. While driven by strategic desire, the expansion of the Venetian commerce empire was facilitated by the instinct of adventure as its merchants set out on the seas and across the land in search of new resources, commodities, and markets.

Clearly this secondary instinct will also be important in the future as mankind explores the possibilities of colonizing space. In the distant future—possibly in 2 or 3 billion years—when we will have exhausted the strategic possibilities of this planet owing to the predicted expansion of our dying sun, we will need to colonize the outer planets of the solar system and, eventually, to depart for outer space. This will occur not only because of our technological development, but also because of our unquenchable thirst for adventure. It is this adventurous part of our nature that is driving the current exploration of the solar system, well before the predicted exhaustion of the sun and without any immediate prospect of economic return. But there is always a materialist element in even the most adventurous investment. The case of space exploration is similar to the nineteenth-century rush for Africa—the need to control territory to prevent one's competitors closer to home gaining the upper hand in the global strategic struggle. Explorers, rather than their financial and political backers, care little for these strategic considerations, as they are driven by the spirit of adventure.

The acquisition instinct

The acquisition or hoarding instinct plays an important role in human society. We habitually hoard resources, particularly food, as insurance against difficult future times, such as severe winters, drought, earthquake, war, and other natural and man-made crises. It is interesting to speculate that while this instinct existed in our primate forebears it would not have been well-developed until hominids began deliberately leaving the well-stocked rainforests for the drier savannah and, much later, for regions with extreme climates. This instinct, therefore, would have been shaped by the strategic demand generated by our forebears' more sophisticated dynamic strategy.

It is also interesting that while many mammals—the most familiar being squirrels and hamsters—hoard food, reptiles do not. This probably arises from the fact that warm-blooded mammals tend to migrate to regions with extreme climates, whereas cold-blooded reptiles remain in their formative environments, which are well-stocked with food. Man, however, is the only species to occupy regions in numbers that far exceed the normal carrying capacity of the land. Accordingly, we have acquired the most developed hoarding instinct, through the interaction between strategic demand and strategic selection.

Humans hoard objects of all kinds. The wealthy collect a wide variety of prestigious objects, such as paintings, sculpture, expensive furniture, rare cars, boats, houses, an endless range of expensive and useless consumer durables, and precious stones and metals. They also "collect" artists, writers, designers, architects, intellectuals, and mystics. Even the less wealthy collect commonplace objects—stamps, bottles, toy trains, cameras, knives, fishing rods and reels, smoking pipes (if they are politically incorrect!), porcelain objects, children's dolls, and so on. The list is endless. While some people hoard objects in the vain hope that this will make them rich, most do so merely for the pleasure of indulging their instinct of acquisition.

While the acquisition instinct was, as already suggested, developed in our hominid forebears as an insurance policy for a more risky version of the family-multiplication strategy, at a later time it played a significant role in facilitating the commerce strategy. Merchant princes in the ancient and medieval eras were great collectors of art and other fine objects, and they were great patrons of the arts. This provided an incentive for merchants to cross the seas and deserts in search of expensive and exotic goods, obtain a monopoly over their distribution, and earn the supernormal profits required to keep a generous proportion for themselves.

The acquisition instinct exploits the success of other dynamic strategies, such as conquest and technological change, but it is not an integral part of their dynamic mechanisms as it is in commerce and family multiplication. Nevertheless during the reign of each dynamic strategy the acquisition instinct ensures that surpluses will always be spent. This is why successful dynamic strategies create full employment and prosperity. There appears to be no end to the consumption of luxury goods and services. While a poor man will have to be content with a bonsai garden, a wealthy man will want to own a forest, an estate, a village, a town, a country, or even the world.

The power instinct

One of the most characteristic features of human and animal society is the struggle between dominant individuals for the control and leadership of their society. In effect they are attempting to control their dynamic strategy because this is the source of their society's income and wealth. I have called this the "strategic struggle". While this struggle is a response to strategic desire, it is facilitated by the instinct to power—an innate desire to control other members of one's group or society. Power is the means, not the end of human striving as many thinkers (for example, Friedrich Nietzsche) believe.

The positive side of this power struggle is that whoever wins, has to provide their society with strategic leadership as well as enriching themselves. If they fail in this they will be soon eliminated, because strategic leadership involves assisting the society's dynamic strategists to achieve their material objectives. Most leaders in the past have understood what was required of them in this respect, largely because they emerged from the very group of strategists that look to them for leadership. In medieval Venice, for example, the Doge was a member of the wealthy merchant class, which pursued the dynamic strategy of commerce. He understood that his role was to facilitate his brother merchants' pursuit of commerce through the provision of commercial infrastructure (docks, navy, armory), the negotiation of favourable international trade deals, and the establishment of sufficient trading posts and colonies throughout the Mediterranean and Aegean world to maximize the returns from trade. Similarly the leaders of Republican Rome were members of the patrician class of warrior-landowners, who knew they were expected to invest their society's surpluses in the instruments of war and empire, and to provide military leadership in order to facilitate their conquest strategy.

Only since the late twentieth century has strategic leadership failed, largely because in advanced democracies the political and material returns to leadership have fallen so low that those driven by the power instinct have abandoned politics for the corporate sector.

Today, society's real power lies in the hands of fabulously wealthy corporate bosses. This has serious implications for the progress and liberty of the advanced democracies, as discussed in my book *Global Crisis Makers* (2000).

There is a significant difference between the role of the power instinct and all other instincts discussed so far. The first five instincts—sex, aggression, curiosity, adventure, and acquisition—are required to facilitate the unfolding of the various dynamic strategies, whereas power is the instinct underlying the **mechanism** of the strategic struggle. This mechanism plays an important role in human (and animal) society, by facilitating the transformation of a country's institutions and organizations as the old, exhausted dynamic strategy is replaced by a new, vital one (see *Ephemeral Civilization*, 1997).

The instinct to imitate

One of the most remarkable mechanisms in both nature and human society is the way that the successful activities of leading individuals are transformed into dynamic strategies pursued by entire societies, species, and even dynasties. I call it the mechanism of "strategic imitation". At the heart of this mechanism is the instinct to imitate. But to imitate what? To imitate those in our society who are conspicuously successful materialistically. While this is an effective way to survive and prosper, it is also the way that individual actions are coordinated to build rapidly growing and wealthy societies, and the way that organisms are able to transform their biological structure through strategic selection. Recent emerging societies—such as Japan, China, and India—have even employed imitation as a strategic strategy.

The issue here is how organisms make strategic choices. Essentially, the method of strategic choice employed throughout the animal world economizes on the Earth's scarcest resource, namely intelligence. This is as true of humans as it is of all other animals. Despite mankind's relatively large brain, we employ the same basic method of decision-making used by the rest of the animal world. As our species began emerging 2.4 myrs ago, it continued employing the decision-making methods inherited from earlier mammals. The reason for this is that rationalist decision-making—the collection of large quantities of benefit–cost information on a range of options, the use of intellectual models of reality, and the employment of rapid processing techniques—is very costly in terms of intellectual energy and its success rate is not high. Hence, mankind, like all other animal species, employs a more pragmatic and effective method of decision-making.

A systematic examination of the history of both nature and human society suggests that the decision-making process is imitative rather than rationalist as the worldly philosophers claim, or genetic as the neo-Darwinists insist. It is also dualistic rather than holistic: decision-making can be divided into the pioneering and the routine phases, with each part of the process being dominated by a different type of decision-maker—the strategic pioneer and the strategic follower. This dynamic-strategy theory of choice is briefly outlined in the remainder of this section.

The investment of energy and resources in new genetic/technological ideas, or new activities, is risky because little information of any kind about likely outcomes is available to **strategic pioneers**, and because the probability of failure for new ventures is high. It is all a matter of trial and error, with the pioneers operating largely on intuition about outcomes and on faith in their own abilities. These pioneers, who are few in number, work at the frontier of the unfolding dynamic strategy, and they are more perceptive than all the rest to the changing incentives it generates. In essence, the pioneers provide the drive and enthusiasm to propel their ventures into the marketplace, and it is the marketplace of competing ideas and activities (shaped by strategic demand) that determines the outcomes. A few succeed and many fail.

The successful pioneering "few" initially earn "monopoly profits" on their new strategic activities. Their prosperity provides the first positive information for the "many"—the **strategic followers**—about rates of return on the investment of energy and resources in alternative ventures. The pioneers, in other words, provide "imitative information", which satisfies the key questions asked by the strategic followers: Who and what are successful, and why? Armed with this simple, almost costless information, the vast number of risk-averse, intellectually constrained organisms, ranging from simple to advanced (including mankind) animals, are also able to invest in the demonstrably successful strategies, and to share the rewards of better access to natural resources.

The method of imitative choice, therefore, requires no more than a minimal amount of intellectual capacity. All animals, including humans, have a remarkable ability to mimic those around them. And mimicry, which arises from the instinct to imitate, is all that is required. Animal studies are replete with examples of the way mimicry is employed in discovering new food sources and new mates. Quite clearly animals are not the automatons that Descartes and the neo-Darwinists claim and, in this respect, are very similar to humans. Fashions covering all aspects of life that sweep through human society are well known. Finally, it must be emphasized that the imitation instinct, like all other instincts, emerged in response to, and was subsequently shaped by, the strategic demands of the *logos*. And the driving force in this dynamic process was, and is, strategic desire.

To sum up: My argument is that strategic desire is the driving force in life. It is the force responsible for organisms seeking to survive and prosper through the pursuit of the most effective of the universal quartet of dynamic strategies and multitude of substrategies. The unfolding dynamic strategy of the *logos* generates a changing strategic demand for a variety of inputs including physical and instinctual characteristics, which are supplied through the autogenous process of strategic selection. The instinctual characteristics of human nature— of sex, aggression, curiosity, adventure, acquisition, power, and imitation—are required to facilitate the unfolding of the prevailing dynamic strategy and to drive a number of central dynamic mechanisms of the *logos*. If strategic desire is thought of as the primary instinct in life, then the others, which owe their origin and intensity to it, must be regarded as secondary instincts. They all, however, contribute to the strategic power—which is the essence of human nature—of our species. Human nature, in other words, embodies the personal characteristics required to respond successfully to the requirements of the *logos*, of which man is an integral component. This theory provides the basis for a discussion of emotions in the next section.

A GENERAL THEORY OF EMOTIONS

Emotions, which help to define human nature, are essential to our ability to make decisions and to undertake planned action. This is now widely understood. What is not known is why emotional systems emerged in mammals or what their wider role is in life. There is, in other words, no general theory of emotions. This is openly acknowledged by leading researchers on emotional systems. Joseph LeDoux, for example, tells us in an interview with J. Horgan (*Undiscovered Mind*, 1999: 31-32) that:

> We have no idea how our brains make us as we are. There is as yet no neuroscience of personality … In short, we have yet to come up with a theory that can pull all this together. We haven't yet had a Darwin, Einstein or Newton.

He even goes on to say, in a defeatist way, that a general theory may not even be required:

> Maybe what we need most are lots of little theories … The field of neuroscience is in a position to make progress on these problems [anxiety, depression, fear, love], even if it doesn't come up with a theory of mind and brain.

It is interesting that LeDoux believes that the study of emotional systems has yet to be explained by "a Darwin, Einstein or Newton"— someone, that is, who can provide a theory about the big picture. It is interesting because he clearly believes, quite rightly, that Darwin's theory of natural selection is not a general theory of the human emotions. Actually he is quite explicit about this in *The Emotional Brain* (1998:178), where he writes: "We clearly need to go beyond evolution in order to understand emotion, but we should get past it by understanding its contribution rather than ignoring it". This is a damaging admission for a Darwinist, because had Darwin's natural selection hypothesis been a general theory about the dynamics of life—even if it could be generalized for this purpose—LeDoux and his colleagues would already possess a general theory of emotions. In contrast, my dynamic-strategy theory, which *is* a general theory of life, is able to explain the emergence and wider role of emotions.

The Emergence of Emotions

The dynamic-strategy theory shows that emotional systems emerged in mammals to enable them to engage more effectively in the strategic pursuit determined by the *logos*. Emotions, in other words, were part of a developing strategic instrument that enabled mammals to exploit their strategic opportunities. This theory not only provides a general explanation of the emergence and role of emotional systems, it also integrates it into an explanation of the human mind, human nature, and the dynamics of human society and of life in general.

The forcing ground for improvements in the mammalian strategic cerebrum was the struggle of early mammals with their dinosaur counterparts, possibly *Stenonychosaurus*. As argued in my book *Collapse of Darwinism* (2003), their dynamic strategy was pursued with "finesse rather than force", because it was in finesse—requiring a relatively larger brain—that they had a comparative advantage over the dinosaurs. In this way they managed to survive on the margins of dinosaur society until the dinosaur dynasty had exhausted its sequence of dynamic strategies—of genetic change▶family-multiplication▶conquest—and gone extinct some 65 myrs ago. With the removal of this intense competition, the mammals pursued the same strategic sequence and took over the world. Yet they only just missed following the dinosaurs into oblivion, because their timely discovery of the "technology option" enabled them to avoid a repetition of Armageddon.

What is important here is that the mammals continued to pursue their dynamic strategies with "finesse rather than force". It was this strategic approach that led to the growing size and complexity of the brains of mammals. Enlargement of the mammalian brain occurred during speciation; that initial phase in the existence of a species when individuals pursue the genetic strategy to gain favourable access to abundant natural resources. And its size and complexity increased from species to succeeding species as they attempted to outwit their opponents. The modern jaguar, for example, has a brain twice the size of the sabre-toothed cats some 30 myrs ago; and, among the hominids, modern man has a brain twice the size of that of *H. habilis* about 2.4 myrs ago. This did not happen among succeeding species in the dinosaur dynasty. Sheer crushing force, which was the norm under dinosaurs, was replaced, by degrees, with a more subtle and skilful execution of the same strategic pursuit by the mammals.

The growth of the primate/hominid brain between *Proconsul* (18 myrs BP) and modern man (150,000 years BP), as shown in *Ark of the Sun* (2015), traced out an exponential growth path. How can we relate this increase in brain size to the development of emotional systems in man? The growth of cranial capacity was an outcome of total brain development that included not only the neocortex but also the limbic system and its connections with the cortex. The growth of total brain size, in other words, was due to the expansion of both the cognitive and emotional systems. Naturally, the relative importance of these two systems in the strategic cerebrum changed over time. In the early stages the emotional systems dominated, giving way to the cognitive systems in the later stages.

The key point to understand is that human cognitive systems were only able to develop through strategic selection because of the prior or parallel development of the emotional systems. Why? Because the brain was developed as a strategic instrument. In these circumstances, cognitive systems are of no use unless they enable organisms to make proactive decisions and to implement strategic plans; and it is the emotional systems in the brain that make this possible. As always, it is essential to remember that the human brain is a strategic instrument—a device employed by the strategist to successfully pursue its dynamic strategy.

But while the human cortex could not have developed without the prior emergence of the brain's emotional systems, this is not why the limbic system developed. The reason is strategic demand generated by the *logos*. Early mammals began developing the limbic system to give them an edge over the dinosaurs that relied more heavily on the reptilian brain, despite their warm-bloodedness. With a range of emotional mechanisms, the early mammals were able to respond more quickly, changeably and, hence, effectively to threats from dinosaurs that were driven largely by inflexible instincts. The emotions of fear, hate, anger, and disgust, although not experienced consciously, enabled the early mammals to pursue their dynamic strategies with greater finesse.

Essentially, the role of emotional responses was to make the existing system of instincts more flexible and effective. They injected a passion, volatility, and unpredictability into the way mammals behaved. Yet, like instinctual behaviour, emotional responses are driven by strategic desire, the driving force in all organisms. In *The Selfcreating Mind* (2006) I discuss the importance of changing bodily states to the operation of emotional systems, and of the importance of emotions to cognitive systems. In a meaningful sense, emotions provide the link between instincts and thinking.

While emotional systems did not emerge in the early mammals to facilitate the development of cognitive abilities, their prior presence did enable those abilities to develop when the *logos* generated a strategic demand for them. In particular, as we have seen, it was the need for even greater finesse in the face of dinosaur force that provided this demand for cognitive abilities. The early mammals survived not only because they responded more flexibly to danger but also because they were able to outwit their opponents. It is for these reasons that the emotional and cognitive systems of the mammalian brain are *integrated* rather than being largely autonomous as neo-Darwinian scholars claim. Further changes in the mammalian brain after the collapse of the dinosaur dynasty 65 myrs ago, witnessed the integrated development of both systems until, when the emotional system had achieved all that the *logos*' strategic demand required of it, the cognitive system continued to develop to its full potential. The ceiling for this cognitive growth was in turn determined by the minimum brain size required to enable the full substitution of the "technology option" for the rapidly exhausting "genetic option" (see *Ark of the Sun*, 2015).

The Strategic Theory of Emotions

Emotions, according to the dynamic-strategy theory, are shaped by strategic selection in response to strategic demand generated by the *logos*. In this way the organism is able to cope effectively with an increasingly complex social environment. To understand the nature and role of these emotional systems, we need to briefly review the main elements of the dynamic-strategy theory. The dynamic-strategy theory, it will be recalled, comprises a driving force, a quartet of dynamic strategies, and a number of key dynamic mechanisms. To exploit this dynamic reality to the full, the organism employs a strategic instrument called the strategic cerebrum. Initially the strategic cerebrum was responsible for supervising the strategic behaviour of the organism via the instincts. But as the social environment became more complex, strategic behaviour needed to become more subtle and flexible. Greater finesse was required. This was where emotions and, later, cognition came in.

Table 2.2 The Strategic Origins of Emotions

Elements of dynamic-strategy theory	Emotional states
Driving force (strategic desire)	selfishness/greed
Dynamic strategies	
• family multiplication	lust/love/acquisitiveness
• conquest	hate/anger/fear/disgust
• commerce	greed/acquisitiveness
• technological change	exhilaration
Dynamic mechanisms	
• strategic imitation	envy/admiration/disgust
• strategic struggle	greed/hate/fear
• strategic leadership	admiration/disgust
• strategic confidence	exhilaration→depression

Source: Snooks, *Selfcreating Mind* (2006: 90).

Each of the elements of the dynamic-strategy theory is associated with different emotional states. In reality these emotional states enhance strategic behaviour. Table 2.2 illustrates the different emotional states associated with the various elements in the dynamic-strategy theory. An important point to note is that these dynamic elements are not exclusively associated with a single emotional state. In other words, emotions are not outcomes of autonomous, domain-specific brain modules as one would expect if Darwinism were true. Instead they are interactive. The reason being that emotional mechanisms were developed together in response to the demand of the strategic *logos* for an integrated and flexible strategic instrument.

This developmental process is explained in greater detail in my book *The Selfcreating Mind* (2006).

We need to consider briefly the emotional states associated with each of the *logos'* dynamic elements in Table 2.2. First, the driving force, here called strategic desire, is responsible for generating the mechanisms associated with the emotions of selfishness and greed. These are the most fundamental of all emotions, because they ensure that the organism strives to survive and prosper. As characterized by the concentric spheres model of behaviour, the "self" lies at the very centre of all animal and human relationships. With increasing competitive pressure placed on the individual, the outer spheres of relationships and emotions fly off under the relentless centrifugal force of strategic desire, which is served by the emotions of selfishness and greed.

Second, there are a range of emotions associated with the quartet of dynamic strategies employed to meet strategic desire. In order to survive and prosper, organisms must adopt the most effective of the four available dynamic strategies and of the more numerous substrategies. Strategic behaviour is enhanced by the possession of emotional mechanisms that produce automatic responses to external stimuli. In the case of **family multiplication**, the emotion of lust enhances the sexual instinct that leads to reproduction; parental love increases the survival prospects of the offspring; and acquisitiveness encourages territorial expansion through migration. While other emotions can be used to support this, and all other, strategies, it is lust, love and acquisitiveness that are the distinctive emotional states driving family multiplication. The point is that the pursuit of any dynamic strategy requires the parallel development and exercise of a larger number of emotional mechanisms to create a single and integrated strategic instrument that we call the human brain.

Conquest calls upon those emotions that many regard as negative, such as anger, hate, fear, and disgust. These emotions, which act in conjunction with the instinct of aggression, are essential to a species or society that is engaged in systematic warfare to promote its growth and prosperity. While all the other emotions required in the creation of a sophisticated and workable society—love, generosity, altruism—

exist within a conquest society, just as in any other, they are always subordinated to those needed to generate wealth through killing and plunder. This subordination of the gentler emotions produces a very different civilization—one possessing a darker spirit—to those generated by the commerce and technological strategies—which embody a more humane and lofty spirit. We should never be tempted to regard these cultural differences as a reflection of the people who inhabit these civilizations; which is the trap of unintentional racism that most cultural theorists fall into. Rather it is an outcome of the nature of the dynamic strategy they are compelled to pursue if they are to survive and prosper. Any group of people, including ourselves, would display the same general characteristics when placed in conquest circumstances. The dominant emotions as well as the culture of the people are shaped by strategic demand of the *logos*.

Commerce relies largely on the emotions of greed and acquisitiveness. This dynamic strategy involves the monopolization of desirable tradable commodities, key trading routes, essential forms of transport, and/or the most effective forms of finance and exchange, in order to extract supernormal profits from those that need to trade to survive and prosper. Greed and acquisitiveness have driven merchants to risk their lives by trekking across parched deserts, sailing on dangerous waters, and attacking those who have the goods and services they require but will not relinquish. It is greed that drives merchants to risk their lives, and acquisitiveness to acquire new territories and to collect fine goods, works of art, and even artists of all types. But, underlying this are the darker emotions—anger, hate, fear, and disgust—because when bargaining fails, force prevails. Nevertheless, owing to the different strategic demand generated by commerce societies, a loftier spirit, that allows philosophy, literature, and art to flourish, usually emerges. This was the emotional and cultural basis of the great commerce empires constructed by the Egyptians, Phoenicians, Greeks, Venetians, Dutch and British.

The **technological strategy** draws heavily on the emotion of exhilaration. It is the joy of making discoveries and doing things in new ways. It is the emotional return to the instinct of curiosity, which would have developed as early man began to investigate the technology option. Indeed, this emotion is vital in a technological society, because those who generate the ideas that facilitate growth and prosperity have no property rights in those ideas, only in the means by which they are expressed. The technological society, more than any other, highlights the distinction between the desires that drive it and the ideas that facilitate its progress. In other words, the technological strategists, who are dominated by greed, are the ones that produce and supply the goods and services in high demand, but they are only able to do so by employing the ideas of imaginative thinkers. It is those dominated by greed who hold the property rights in material assets and who deny the thinkers any property rights in ideas. The usual, self-serving argument is that property rights in ideas—as opposed to the medium in which they are embodied—are unworkable. But what they really mean is that property rights in ideas will reduce the supernormal profits of successful strategists. In such circumstances, ideas only continue to be supplied because of the exhilaration experienced by the insatiably curious few amongst us. It can be argued that the supply of ideas could be increased by granting property rights in ideas *per se*. This could well be the substance of a future strategic struggle between the old materialist strategists and the new intellectual strategists; a strategic struggle that will find expression in the next great economic revolution or technical paradigm shift—the Solar Revolution—which will take place later this century.

Finally, we need to consider the emotions associated with the main dynamic mechanisms of our theory. The first of these is **strategic imitation**, in which the successful strategic pioneers are followed by the rest of society. It is the mechanism by which successful individual behaviour of either a biological or economic kind is transformed into successful strategic behaviour for the entire species or society. The emotions most closely associated with this mechanism are *envy*, *admiration*, and *disgust*. It is the envy or admiration of those who are conspicuously successful that motivates other people to imitate their behaviour. And it is disgust that leads the many to reject the behaviour of those who are unattractive and unsuccessful. These emotions, therefore, help to reinforce the underlying instinct to imitate.

The **strategic struggle**, as analysed in my dynamic-strategy theory, is another central dynamic mechanism in animal as well as human society. It is the mechanism by which those championing a new dynamic strategy are able to wrest political control—control of the sources of income and wealth—from those defending the old, exhausted dynamic strategy. Participation in this struggle is motivated by *greed*, *hate*, and *fear*. Greed motivates involvement in this materialist struggle, whereas hate and fear are required to employ the brutal and cruel methods needed both to defend and to plunder the major sources of society's wealth, and to dispose of strategic opponents. Greed, hate, and fear are a powerful combination of emotions that are employed not only to motivate but also to justify our brutal ways.

To the victors of the strategic struggle go not only the spoils, but also the responsibility of **strategic leadership**. It is far better for modern leaders to dazzle than to coerce. For the strategists to voluntarily support a new leader, they must be given the opportunity to participate in and profit from the prevailing dynamic strategy. It is the role of strategic leadership to facilitate the material interests of the strategists. But successful leaders are assisted in this endeavour if they possess the ability to inspire in their people the emotion of *admiration*. The admired leader can, for a time, even transcend his strategic deficiencies or antistrategic proclivities. But only for a time: modern examples include Peron in Argentina, Mao in China, and Castro in Cuba. Admiration works in strategic leadership in a way similar to its role in strategic imitation. In contrast, a leader who inspires disgust, even if he possesses strong strategic qualities, will be unable to provide effective leadership (as in the 2015 coup against Prime Minister Tony Abbott, discussed here in chapter 4).

Finally, we consider the mechanism of **strategic confidence**, which is generated by a successfully unfolding dynamic strategy. As the dynamic strategy is effectively exploited, strategic confidence increases owing to the high returns on society's investment in the dynamic process. This confidence produces a feeling of *exhilaration*, which in turn leads to even more adventurous investment. Prosperity will continue until the prevailing dynamic strategy is finally exhausted, after which the returns to further investment along old lines falls to unprofitable levels. Initially this outcome leads to a shift of investment funds from strategic projects (profit-seeking) to speculative (rent-seeking) activities in order to maintain the previously high returns. In the process, strategic confidence is replaced by gamblers' confidence, which also feeds on exhilaration. Ultimately, however, a widespread realization that paper assets are massively overvalued leads to a collapse even of gamblers' confidence. Exhilaration gives way to *depression* among individual investors.

Strategic depression, however, is a positive rather than a negative emotion, because it acts as a spur to find a new dynamic strategy. *Depression*, as shown in *Selfcreating Mind* (2006), is an indication to the individual that the old ways constitute a danger to his survival and prosperity, and that the time has come to explore and develop new ways. Once those new ways—in the form of a new dynamic strategy—bring a renewal of high returns on investment, strategic confidence and exhilaration return and feed, in an interacting way, into a new process of prosperity. Strategic depression is very different to the debilitating mental condition of pathological depression.

An important implication of the dynamic-strategy theory of emotions is that there are more than a dozen "primary emotions". These include greed, selfishness, lust, love, hate, anger, fear, disgust, acquisitiveness, exhilaration, envy, and depression. They are primary emotions because they have been shaped by strategic selection in response to the strategic demands of the *logos*, so that the individual organism might survive and prosper in an increasingly complex social environment. All other emotions, which can be called "secondary emotions", are a combination of these and are constructed by the conscious mind for its own pleasure or pain. These secondary emotions have considerable cultural significance, as they are essential for the creation of sophisticated forms of art.

It is clear from the dynamic-strategy theory of emotions that the human brain cannot be characterized as an "emotional brain" as some scientists have done. As we have seen, the human brain consists of a number of historically determined sections that control our instinctive, emotional, and cognitive behaviour. Instead of viewing the brain as being dominated by any of these three secondary functions, it should be seen in terms of its overall or primary function, which is strategic. All parts of the brain are highly integrated and directed towards providing man with a highly flexible strategic instrument capable of supervising our participation in a strategic pursuit that is growing increasingly complex. The human brain, therefore, is a "strategic brain", not an emotional brain or a rational brain. And it has emerged over the past 500 myrs through the "autogenous" process of strategic selection in response to strategic demand generated by the *logos*.

MAN IS THE AGENT OF THE STRATEGIC *LOGOS*

What is man? The dynamic-strategy theory shows that, while the strategic *logos* is the vehicle of our aspirations, we are the agents of the strategic *logos*. Owing to the desire to survive and prosper, human beings have been shaped by, and have been responsive to, the requirements of the *logos*; not in any slavish way, but as an integral part of the dynamic process of life. Human nature is complex and flexible in order to meet the *logos*' constantly changing requirements. Owing to this causal relationship, **the *logos* is the measure of all things**. Indeed, the only constant in human nature is strategic desire, which is essential if man is to survive and prosper. Strategic desire is mankind's dominant or primary characteristic; all other facets of his nature change in relative significance as the dynamic strategies unfold, stagnate, and are replaced by new dynamic strategies; and as the nature and intensity of societal competition changes.

While strategic desire ensures the survival of the species, it imprints on man an unshakable darker character. In the final analysis, individuals, on average, will do anything it takes to survive and prosper. If this was not so, our species would have gone extinct millions of years ago. Many, particularly those who have highly functioning "existential schizophrenia" mechanisms (see Chapter 6), find this difficult to accept. But if one is to live truthfully, it is the central issue in life that must be squarely faced. This reality is central to my attempt in this book to demonstrate the need to wrestle the strategic *logos*. Having explored the nature of man, it is time to consider the nature of the strategic *logos*—life's ultimate reality.

Chapter Three
Ultimate Reality

One of the abiding mysteries of life is how human society emerged from the mists of time and how it has been sustained over thousands of years. Clearly this has not been an easy venture, as attested to by the ruins of numerous past societies and civilizations unearthed by archaeologists and historians. Nevertheless, the impetus to social formation has been persistent and, in the medium term at least, highly successful. There have been many attempts to explain both the success and failure of human societies, but, until now, none of these explanations has been persuasive. In this chapter it is argued that the emergence and fluctuating fortunes of human society are outcomes of the dynamics of the strategic *logos*—a self-starting and self-sustaining system of hidden forces driven by the desire of humanity to survive and prosper. The *logos* is the vehicle of life in a hostile physical world; the *logos* is the ultimate reality.

EXISTING EXPLANATIONS OF HUMAN SOCIETY

Before outlining the main existing explanations of human society, we should consider whether there is such a thing as human society. The contemporary scientific position is that society exists not in its own right, but only as a consequence of the interactions of a large group of individuals; in other words, as an emergence phenomenon. While societal organisations and institutions clearly exist, it is claimed by some that they have no inherent driving forces. More extreme scholars, particularly neoliberals, go so far as to assert that society has no independent existence, and what we call society consists only of a loose collection of self-interested individuals and their interacting relationships. In consequence, the state, as self-proclaimed agent of society, has no claim over individuals, except where these claims are freely granted and revokable. In contrast, socialists make a greater claim for the existence both of society and the state, which is to protect workers from capitalists. What do these very different approaches have in common? They all take a supply-side approach to society; they attempt to explain societal relations as emerging from the inherent qualities of human participants.

Currently, the dominant intellectual fashion is that of complexity theory. These theorists argue that order and complexity in both nature and human society are the outcome of an interaction between large numbers of agents (or particles). It has its origins in **physical models of self-organisation**, such as the Abelian sand-pile model (published by Bak, Tang & Wiesenfeld in 1987), and, as such, is a form of social physics. While this simplistic physical model is easily refuted as an explanation of the origin and development of human society, some complexity theorists have developed a seemingly more realistic version known as the "agent-based model" (or ABM). While ABM theorists have largely abandoned the laws of physics in their explanation of the local interaction of agents, they have been forced to impose a set of artificial rules on computerised "living" systems in order to mimic orderly patterns observed in the real world. These artificial rules about agent decision making, however, are still based on the central assumption of social physics, that order and complexity are the outcome of agent interaction. By manipulating these rules, ABM theorists are able, through computer simulations, to generate the real-world patterns in which they are interested. In other words, they develop computerised "artificial societies" (their term) based on the insights of complexity patterns generated by physical systems. They claim that these systems can actually "explain" the regularities in human society. This research program is not only methodologically flawed—the underlying supply-side physics model is just not applicable to human society—it has also led to the distortion of reality. While this intellectual effort may be entertaining, it has nothing to do with reality.

There is a second approach to the emergence and evolution of society based on the natural sciences, which comes from biology rather than physics. It is as if social scientists have no confidence in their own field of study. **The biological approach**, which also involves supply-side theorising, employs arguments from Charles Darwin's work. There are two main strands of social Darwinism—neo-Darwinism based on the idea of kin selection, and "Darwinian deviationism" based on the more heretical idea of group selection.

First, what of the neo-Darwinists or sociobiologists? Social organisation in the animal world—and by extension the human world—is, according to the sociobiologists (such as J.M Smith, W.D Hamilton, and R.L. Trivers), genetically determined through natural selection. They argue that institutions (informal rules and conventions) emerge from the genetic basis of "kinship", and from "reciprocal altruism". By kinship, sociobiologists mean not the socioeconomic bonds between members of the extended family, but rather their "genetic relatedness". They argue that the social relationships experienced by individuals depend on the degree of "genetic relatedness" between them, and that the probability of this genetic relationship can be measured by the "generation distance".

Genetic relatedness can be simply mapped. For example, in the case of identical twins the genetic relatedness is equal to unity; for siblings it is, on average, 0.5; for parent and child it is also 0.5; for grandparents and grandchildren, aunt/uncles and nieces/nephews it is 0.25; for first cousins it is 0.15; for second cousins 0.03; and for third cousins (as with a random selection of the population) it is 0.008. With perfect information and a copy of this genetic table, individuals can not only maximise the spread of their genes (the driving force in life for neo-Darwinists), but are able to construct an orderly and complex social structure! Social structure in this model is merely kinship structure. The limitations of this model are obvious. Even if animals had perfect knowledge—which clearly they do not—kinship relationships extend only to about second cousins, and so the reach of this model is highly restricted. There are many higher levels of social organisation that are beyond the scope of kinship theory, because they involve interactions between unrelated individuals and strangers. Kinship theory, therefore, is a particularly myopic type of supply-side theory. These matters are discussed in greater detail in my book *The Collapse of Darwinism* (2003).

The difficulty experienced by Darwinists attempting to explain higher levels of social organisation has led some sociobiologists to develop group-selection theories, whereby individuals evolve to devote themselves to the higher good of the wider social group or species. They argue that group selection leads to a widespread, genetically determined altruism (or cooperation) that can provide a basis for explaining wider forms of social organisation. Clearly this is another variant of the supply-side approach—social structures being spun out of the genetic proclivities of individuals—which would lock humans and other animals into inflexible decision making processes. Where future change must be predicted accurately in advance, this inflexibility would prevent a species responding successfully to the radical structural changes experienced by life and human society throughout their histories.

Needless to say, the neo-Darwinists are quick to brand the group-selectionists as heretics. Neo-Darwinists such as Richard Dawkins and R.L. Trivers claim that the "fallacy" of group-selection theory is based on a misunderstanding of evolutionary theory. It would take, we are told, only one selfish rebel determined to exploit the altruism of the rest of the group to provide the genetic basis for his progeny to eventually overwhelm the entire community. Essentially, the entire field of sociobiology completely lacks any persuasive explanation of the emergence of order and complexity. So much for the claim of Edward Wilson, a leading sociobiologist, that his discipline will ultimately take over the social as well as the biological sciences. Indeed, all supply-side theories arising from physics and biology in an attempt to explain order and complexity in human (or even animal) society are just not up to the task.

What, then, about the explanatory power of **the social sciences**? The sorry fact that most social scientists have adopted either physics-based complexity theories or neo-Darwinian evolutionary theories to explain social structures, immediately suggests that the social sciences do not possess convincing theories of their own. We are, however, able to detect two different approaches arising from the social sciences. First, there is the rational approach to human society often favoured by philosophers. This tradition goes back at least to Plato (c.428–347 BC) who, in his famous books *The Republic* and *Laws,* argued that the ideal society could be fashioned by the philosopher king, by returning to early Greek tribal society ruled by wise and just warrior leaders. This would recreate the "best state" where corrupting change is eliminated by asserting reason over desire. Imperfect reflections of this "best state" could, he believed, still be seen in Sparta and Crete, which unlike Athens retained their kings and primitively pure military structures. Plato thought this could be best achieved through the formation of a state police force called the "guardians", which would follow reason and keep desire (embodied in the poets of Athens) under control. He believed that change had led to the corruption of the original perfect state, owing to a biological deterioration of the ruling class which, in turn, corrupted human nature and resulted in material and political conflict between the noble factions. Plato, therefore, believed that human institutions, whether perfect or corrupt, emerged from the prevailing aspect of human nature, which was changeable. Clearly this is a supply-side approach that has continued to today (see my book *The Laws of History* [1998]).

The second main approach to society in the social sciences is that of institutionalism. Institutionalism has a long, but not very distinguished, history. It can be traced back to the German and English historical schools of economics in the nineteenth century (see my book *Economics without Time* [1993]), which employed an ineffective form of induction. While the historical schools did not survive competition, with the newer deductive school of economics, into the twentieth century, it did give rise to two more robust offspring—the British economic and social history tradition and the North American school of institutional economics, which includes T.B Veblen (1857–1929), J.R. Commons (1862–1945), and W.C. Mitchell (1874–1948). Veblen adopted a Darwinist evolutionary approach, while Commons emphasised property rights and transaction costs. Both schools, however, were contemptuously dismissed by the mainstream deductive tradition, particularly during the "golden age" of academic economics from 1950 to 1973. With the growing difficulties experienced by the deductive tradition in explaining issues of stagflation and structural change in the 1970s and 1980s, institutionalism experienced a renaissance. Particularly influential was the "new institutional economics" of Friedrich Hayek (1899–1992) and Douglass North (1921–2015). Both Hayek (from the neo-Austrian deductive economics) and North (from neo-classical deductive economics) emphasised different aspects of the earlier institutionalist school: Hayek, like Veblen, focussed on a Darwinian evolutionary process; and North, like Commons, opted for an historical process initially involving an interaction between institutions (rules) and organisations (social networks), but more recently also employing an evolutionary model (see my book *Ephemeral Civilization* [1997]. Like all other society theorists, the institutionalists adopted a supply-side approach—they view societal change as arising from the nature of institutions. This begs the question: what determines the nature of institutions. The institutionalist answer is: culture. Which begs the further question: what determines culture? Unfortunately for the institutionalist cause, the only answer to this question is: race. All supply-side theories, therefore, are unintentional racist theories; despite the best intentions of their supporters.

WHAT IS SOCIETY?

A new conception as well as a new theory concerning human society is required if we are to properly understand its origin, role, development, and future. We need to be able to definitively answer the question: What is society? The truth differs fundamentally from all earlier answers to this deceptively simple question.

Society is a self-starting, self-sustaining system that is greater than the sum of its visible parts—its people, organisations, institutions, and capital assets. At its core is the strategic *logos*, which comprises not only what we see around us every day, but also a set of invisible forces that determine the relationships between people, organisations, institutions, and capital assets, together with how they change structurally over time. The strategic *logos* is a hidden life-system that is both entropy-defying and shock-deflecting, that enabled the emergence of life some 4,000 million years ago and has been responsible for the transformation of life from simple single-cell organisms to sophisticated human societies. This remarkable transformation has taken place via a series of biological and technological paradigm shifts, made possible only by the strategic *logos*. It is beyond the capabilities of man alone.

The people, organisations, institutions, and structures that we can see and experience are, therefore, but the external manifestation of the hidden life-system called the strategic *logos*. All four visible components of society are a response to logosian demand. In society, **the people**, who are driven by "strategic desire"—the desire to survive and prosper—are responsive to the requirements of the hidden life-system. They attempt to maximise the probability of survival and prosperity by adopting the most effective of the four-fold "dynamic strategies" of family-multiplication, commerce, conquest, and technological change in any particular circumstance. In the process, the people build houses, villages, towns, and cities; they adopt facilitating ideas (technological, organisational, cultural, religious, intellectual); they build workshops, factories, and power stations; they fashion facilitating organisations and institutions; and they increase their number, their human capital, and their prosperity. Even the genetic makeup of the people is the outcome—the very longrun outcome—of the strategic demands of a very longrun succession of former *logoi*. But all this depends on whether their strategic *logos* is successful in a world of competing *logoi*. Many societies have failed at some critical stage in their development, usually when encountering more successful societies. Without the *logos*, man could do nothing; indeed he wouldn't even exist.

Human institutions are those rules, customs, and laws designed to achieve designated outcomes required by the strategic *logos*. They include constitutions, political systems, judicial systems, market regulations, property rights, insurance, welfare, criminal and civil law, arbitration, and small claims regulations. These institutions are developed in response to logosian demand so as to facilitate the strategic pursuit of society. Hence, these institutions differ according to the type of dynamic strategy being pursued. Societies pursuing the same type of dynamic strategy will develop functionally similar institutions, even though their cultural expression—which depends on different geographical, climatic, and historical conditions—will differ, but only in superficial ways. (See my book *Ephemeral Civilization* [1997]).

The emergence and development of **organisations** (social networks) in any society is also a response to the requirements—communicated via strategic demand—of the strategic *logos*. Once again, it is the type of dynamic strategy pursued by any society that determines the nature of society's organisations. Society is not an outcome of a supply-side interaction between institutions and organisations as Douglass North claims. Societal organisations facilitate production, trade, and military activities, together with social, educational, training, and cultural activities. And these organisations change in response to changing strategic demand as a dynamic strategy unfolds, exhausts itself, and (in successful societies) is replaced by new dynamic strategies. This process of change is driven by a self-transforming strategic *logos*. Unlike the unidirectional requirements of evolutionary theory, strategic demand of the *logos* can and does reverse itself, thereby reversing the development of organisations.

An excellent example of strategic reversal is the development of democracy in the ancient world. Ancient Greece experienced three main phases of political organisational development for a millennium in direct response to the dynamic strategies they pursued. The very longrun Greek strategic sequence consisted of: conquest from 1100 to 800 BC; commerce from 800 to 500 BC; and conquest again from 400 to 100 BC. This was a dynamic process, driven by the strategic *logos*, involving the exploitation of one dynamic strategy until it was exhausted, then its replacement with a new dynamic strategy, and so on. Each of these dynamic strategies were worked out over periods of about 300 years; and each of these strategies had a characteristic impact on the nature and development of political (and all other) institutions in Greece. The conquest strategy pursued by the tribal Greeks between 1100 and 800 BC generated an authoritarian political structure dominated by kings and a warrior elite. With the exhaustion of conquest opportunities (where marginal *strategic* costs were equated with marginal *strategic* benefits), the Greeks turned to commerce. Between 800 and 500 BC the urban Greeks developed a limited form of democracy (excluding females, foreigners and slaves) in which assemblies of male citizens made all the important political decisions. With the exhaustion of the commerce strategy, Athens turned once more to conquest around 400 BC, and in the process they replaced their former democratic form of government with the more authoritarian structures required by a military *logos*. A similar political reversal was experienced by other pre-modern societies—such as Carthage and Venice—by pursuing the same circular conquest▶commerce▶conquest strategic sequence.

The only reason that the institution of democracy in England/ Britain appeared to "evolve" between Magna Carta (1215) and today (2015) is that over these 800 years, this society experienced a strategic sequence not of conquest▶commerce▶conquest, but of conquest▶commerce▶technological change. The dynamic strategy of technological change generated strategic demand for even more radical democratisation than commerce, owing to the need for a wider injection of enterprise in the dynamic process. Britain was the first society ever to have undergone this historically unique strategic sequence, and it only did so because the exhaustion of its commerce strategy coincided with the exhaustion of the underlying "neolithic" technological paradigm (based on agriculture), which had prevailed ever since about 11,000 years BP. The central point here is that, had the neolithic paradigm lasted another century, Britain would have turned to conquest again as the only available dynamic strategy when its commerce strategy ground to a halt in the mid-eighteenth century; and its political institutions would have been thrown into reverse, becoming autocratic and militaristic. There were signs in the second half of the eighteenth century that this was already happening, but was cut short by the Industrial Revolution. Democracy like all other institutions does not evolve; it responds to the changing requirements of the strategic *logos*.

The contemporary world seems to have discovered the secret of preventing the strategic reversals of the pre-modern world. And that secret is technological change. Since the Industrial Revolution, which began in Britain in the late eighteenth century, the old dynamic strategy of conquest has become obsolete. While this may not stop some economically irrational societies attempting to pursue the conquest strategy—such as Nazi Germany, Fascist Italy, and Imperial Japan—they will never succeed because in the modern era the dynamic strategy of technological change is significantly more economical, in the medium- to long-run, than conquest. While the Roman Empire lasted 800 years, the "Thousand-Year" Third Reich lasted for only 12 years. Only a collapse of the global technological economy could lead to the re-emergence of the dynamic strategy of conquest, together with the replacement of democracy with authoritarian political structures. One possible scenario that could bring this cataclysm to fruition is the emergence of a serious and successful attempt to impose a global climate-mitigation command economy on the world. Such a structure would badly damage the strategic *logos*, and prevent it from effecting a new technological paradigm shift this century—the forthcoming Solar Revolution (see my book *The Coming Eclipse* [2010]).

Finally we need to ask ourselves: What was the probability of human society even getting started some two million years ago, let alone being able to progress materially since then at a constant geometric rate—what I call the "logological constant"—unless the strategic *logos* actually existed. The probability is zero. It is not something that could happen entirely by chance. It would be like arguing that the cosmos could exist even in the absence of the invisible forces of dark energy, dark matter, and black holes. Behind the people, organisations, institutions, and capital structures is a dynamic engine of life that has established human society as a self-starting and self-maintaining system. That dynamic system, as I have shown in a series of books, is the strategic *logos*.

What is the Strategic *Logos*?

Life is the most profound mystery in the Universe. Although scholars take great pride in their major scientific achievements, they don't really understand how life emerged on our planet, how it was able to generate complex genetic and institutional forms, how it was able to sustain itself over some 4,000 million years, what the future might bring, or whether intelligent life exists on worlds other than our own. The fundamental reason for these critical uncertainties in human knowledge is that the underlying life-system is a hidden system, which, until recently, has eluded the objective methods of science. Accordingly, the shadowy life-system has, over thousands of years, become the subject of much speculation, myth, and religious veneration. It has been the objective of my recent work (since *Dead God Rising* [2010]) to dispel the mystery of millennia by uncovering the real but hidden life-system. This has been achieved by introducing the strategic *logos*, which provides the key to understanding not only life and human society, but also the origin, role, and dynamics of mythmaking and religion. **The *logos* is the shaper of life**.

While I have elsewhere attempted to model the materialist life-system called the strategic *logos*, I anticipate that some readers may have difficulty coming to grips with this concept; not because it is difficult to conceptualise, but because it is unfamiliar. New ideas take time to make their impact on the popular consciousness. It may help, therefore, if I draw comparisons with a number of conceptually similar concepts that have been part of the conventional wisdom for some time. I can suggest three analogous concepts with which most of us are familiar: the cosmos, the atomic world, and the self-conscious human mind. In each case, a hidden dynamic system has emerged owing to a complex and invisible interaction between its physical components; an interaction that ceases forever when those physical components are destroyed. So it is with the strategic *logos*.

- In **the cosmos** we can observe planetary motion, but not the force of gravity that shapes the solar system. We can observe the dynamic outcomes of solar systems and galaxies, but not the forces that drive them, such as the appropriately named dark matter (a pull factor), dark energy (a push factor), and black holes. Yet, scientists claim that these invisible forces exist because they can be indirectly and theoretically recognised. The cosmos, therefore, is a hidden dynamic system consisting of visible physical objects on the one hand, and invisible interacting forces on the other. Without this cosmos of invisible forces, the observed Universe would not exist. Further, as a dynamic system, the cosmos can last only as long as the physical bodies that inhabit it. Our solar system, for example, will last only until the Sun exhausts its fuel supply.

This is a useful analogy for the strategic *logos*, which is also a hidden system consisting of visible agents, organisations, institutions, and capital structures on the one hand and invisible interacting push and pull forces that can be indirectly and theoretically recognised on the other. And like the cosmos, the *logos* is ephemeral; it disintegrates with the destruction of its physical components.

- In **the atomic world**, it is possible to observe the patterns of atoms, sub-atoms, and molecules, but not the invisible yet powerful nuclear and electromagnetic forces that determine these patterns. Nevertheless, scientists tell us that these forces do in fact exist, despite being unable to observe them directly. There is, they claim, a hidden atomic system of interacting microscopic particles. And we believe them because it has been demonstrated that by disrupting the nuclear and electromagnetic forces through a process we've all heard of called "splitting the atom", a subset of the atomic world can be forced to breakdown violently (nuclear fission) releasing a large amount of energy.

  In a similar way, the strategic *logos* can be made to break down violently by disrupting the core "strategic demand-response" mechanism (discussed below) through the dictatorial controls of a centralised command economy, such as the now defunct USSR or, possibly, a future even more destructive command-mitigation (climate) economy. Societal breakdown of this type is indirect evidence of the existence of a hidden life-system holding human society together; just as nuclear fission resulting from deliberate intervention in the atomic world is evidence of an atomic system holding matter together. *In the ruins of chaos we recognise the invisible structure of order.*

- Another suggestive analogy concerns that complex strategic instrument we call **the human brain.** We can observe the brain's physical composition, but not the complex and detailed interactions (only their reflections recorded on special electronic equipment) taking place between its various component parts—invisible interactions that create **the hidden mind**. The selfconscious mind is invisible and cannot be directly observed by scientists, only experienced existentially by its host, or explored analogously through metaphor. The metaphor I have in mind is the metropolis, in which we can fortuitously observe the interaction between agents and organisations, and even the resulting modes of "self-awareness" (a generalised form of self-consciousness). Both the mind and the metropolis last only as long as their physical building blocks retain their integrity. Irreversible damage sustained by the brain or urban structure will terminally disrupt the network of strategic interactions, and will lead to the demise of the mind or the metropolis as a dynamic system. So it is with the strategic *logos*.

THE VEHICLE OF LIFE

Nature of the Cosmos

Some natural scientists are fond of telling us that we inhabit a peculiarly "life-friendly" Universe. By this they mean that the laws of physics and the values of the "fundamental constants of nature"—including the cosmological constant, gravity, the velocity of light—are just what is required to enable the emergence of carbon-based life in the Universe. These scientists usually have some sort of teleological theory—either the "Mind of God" or a form of superintelligence—that they are promoting. In contrast, those scholars studying life-systems in either the natural or human domains are keenly aware that the physical world is extremely hostile to life.

Because the Universe is so hostile to life, all its forms are dominated by the overriding desire to survive and prosper. For example, life forms only exist because they have found ways to defy the second law of thermodynamics. This law tells us that while heat flows *spontaneously* from hot to cold bodies, this inevitable process cannot be reversed, at least not *spontaneously*. The upshot of this law is that all *closed* physical systems are trapped in a one-way trip towards the final state of thermodynamic equilibrium, or "heat death". Stated in slightly different terms, this equilibrium is the outcome of increasing entropy. Hence, all closed systems are moving inevitably from a state of order to a state of disorder.

Of course, while the entire physical system may be closed—such as the Universe as a whole—any part of it may find ways to decrease its entropy (or increase its order) by absorbing heat released by other parts of the larger system. This, in physical terms, is how order and complexity can be achieved by open biological systems, without violating the laws of physics. It happens when ways and means are found to convert energy from a body like the sun (or from the molten core of a planet in the ocean depths) into work—a less than fully efficient process that loses energy to the environment in the form of heat.

The Universal Life-System

While all of this appears straightforward in physical terms, the trick—and it is not an easy one to master as far as life forms are concerned—is to develop techniques that provide continuous access to energy and other natural resources. These techniques, which can be both biological and technological, are generated by investment of time and energy in new "ideas". Much of my work—generated by metabolic energy derived both directly and indirectly from the sun—over the past few decades has been devoted to showing how this has been undertaken. What should be realized is that biological and technological "ideas" do not just emerge spontaneously in a way similar to the flow of heat from hot to cold bodies. While *disorder* is a spontaneous physical process, the creation of *order* requires considerable energy, effort, and *creative* impulse to be achieved. In other words, life forms need energy not only to survive and prosper, but also to develop a continuous supply of techniques to gain long-term access to sources of energy and other natural resources. But the survival "trick" requires more than this. Energy is also needed to develop "dynamic life-systems" in order to protect and sustain this extremely difficult process of survival and prosperity in a hostile world that is continuously running down. This protective life-system—which I call the "strategic *logos*"—has to be dynamic because it is necessary to continuously reinvent itself in order to gain access to the resources required. A static system would quickly perish in a world running down. The strategic *logos* is the vehicle of both life and human society, which is fueled by solar energy.

Once established, a strategic *logos* operates according not to the laws of physics but to its own internal laws—the laws of life and history. The laws of physics merely provide the background against which agents of the strategic *logos* play out the game of life. While the laws of physics make it possible to play the game of life, it is the players—the individual organisms driven by strategic desire—who decide whether or not to play the game and, if so, how it should be played. And we play this exacting game in the self-contained world of the strategic *logos*; a world which defies the hostilities, difficulties, and mindlessness of the physical world. Because the strategic *logos* operates according to its own internalized rules, scientists are unable to employ the laws of physics to explain life. This is why self-organizational and complexity theory—currently popular supply-side models—which emerged from the natural sciences, are not capable of conveying an understanding of life and human society. To comprehend these amazing entities we must first understand the strategic *logos* and the internal laws by which it operates.

Once a viable strategic *logos*—or dynamic life-system—has been established, it is necessary to defend it against a wide range of external threats. These threats come from both the physical and organic worlds. Physical threats include asteroid attack, volcanic eruptions, earthquakes, tsunamis, floods, typhoons, droughts, fires, and rapid climatic change. Most viable strategic *logoi* are able to withstand these physical threats precisely because they have been shaped over millions of years to do so. There will be times, of course, when extreme events will force a dynamic life-system into a temporary decline, with recovery taking time, energy, and the employment of accumulated wealth. These random events temporarily distort the more cyclical pattern that has been detected in human and other life-systems.

In contradiction of the claims of most natural scientists and environmentalists interested in this issue, the strategic *logoi* of life and human society are remarkably resilient to the onslaught of random physical shocks. Massive volcanic eruptions can tear holes in a society—such as the Roman cities of Pompeii and Herculaneum in AD 79—but viable societies just repair these holes and continue on with life; major changes in climate—such as those in Egypt from the prehistoric to the Old Kingdom—can provoke viable societies to respond creatively through the introduction of new technologies (irrigation systems) and the adoption of new economic activities (riverine agriculture in place of hunting), but they are not responsible for the collapse of those societies. This is merely a myth propagated by natural scientists and their Green followers, who have not constructed the dynamic theory required to analyze complex living systems. As I have shown in my earlier work, the collapse of dominant species, societies, and dynasties is the outcome not of random physical shocks, but of the exhaustion of dynamic strategies and of biological and technological paradigms. The same will be true of human-induced climate change, as discussed in my recent books *The Coming Eclipse* (2010) and *Ark of the Sun* (2015).

More problematical are the threats posed by other life-systems. These more serious threats arise from other strategic *logoi* within the same species and from other species. In our own species, the greatest threat comes from competing strategic *logoi*, particularly those pursuing the dynamic strategy of conquest. For example, Phoenicia was swept away by Alexander the Great; Carthage was finally completely destroyed by Rome; Egypt was seriously challenged by Assyria, Persia, and Macedonia, and finally extinguished by Rome; Venice was challenged by the Ottomans and ultimately felled by Napoleon. Ironically, even the victorious societies in these conflicts eventually collapsed owing to their very success—ultimately they exhausted their dynamic strategies of conquest. And an exhausted, irreplaceable strategic *logos* does not survive for long.

Less challenging for the human strategic *logos* are the attacks of other species. Wild animals are annoying because they take human life and generate minor economic loss, but microbiological life forms have had a greater impact. In the past, diseases like bubonic plague—which eliminated between one-third and one-half of the populations of viable societies—and the great influenza pandemic—which killed 20 million people world-wide just after the First World War—have been devastating. But the fascinating thing is that these societies continued as if nothing had happened. In Europe during the mid-fourteenth century, the Hundred Years' War between England and France hardly missed a beat, even when bubonic plague first struck Western Europe; and Europe was ready to engage in a Second World War less than a generation after the great influenza pandemic. The point is that the strategic *logos* is a very effective mechanism for throwing off even large-scale effects of exogenous shocks. And it will be the same with any viral pandemic—whether "bird flu" or "swine flu"—in the future. Individuals are highly vulnerable to the attack of virulent new diseases, but the strategic *logos* is remarkably resilient. It has to be, if life is to survive in a hostile world.

The resilience and success of the strategic *logos* are reflected in the "logological constant" of life discovered in my book *Dynamic Society* (1996) and elaborated in *Ark of the Sun* (2015). What it measures is just as remarkable and unchanging as the fundamental constants of the physical world. It shows that over the past 3,800 myrs the global biomass/GDP has not only increased at an exponential rate, but that in geometric (or compound growth-rate) terms it is a *constant* with a coefficient value of approximately 3.0. This suggests that each biological/technological transformation (taken as a whole) occurs in one-third of the time taken by the previous one. This fundamental constant of life is ample proof of the resilience and effectiveness of the strategic *logos* in the face of both the second law of thermodynamics and the hostile physical and biological worlds (including a series of major episodes of climate change over the past 100,000 years). Hence, it is the strategic *logos* rather than the brute physical facts of the Universe that is "life-friendly". It is the strategic *logos* that confounds the gloomy predictions of the crisis exaggerators, who are antistrategists fearful of change.

The strategic *logos* is a dynamic engine that generates a largely invisible process of interaction between human agents and their society. It is a self-generating and self-sustaining life-system that not only protects its members from a hostile world but enables them to progress both technologically and culturally. In the absence of overwhelming external shocks—such as the invasions of the New World in the early sixteenth century and of the Great South Land in the late eighteenth century—the strategic *logos* continues to flourish until its entire sequence of dynamic strategies is completely exhausted. In the case of the world's most successful societies, such as ancient Egypt or Rome, this can last anywhere from one to three millennia. During this time, the *logos* is driven and shaped by its own internal laws—the laws of history—that are independent of the laws of physics. Ultimately, however, the laws of history run their course, the strategically exhausted society enters into terminal crisis, and the strategic *logos* collapses. The heart of this particular human society throbs no more. But, in time it will be replaced by another *logos* and society.

The strategic *logos*, therefore, is ephemeral rather than eternal. It exists only as long as the society with which it came into the world. While a particular *logos* accounts for the rise and fall of a client society, it is also the creation of that society—or, at least, of the collectivity of individuals in that society, who are integrated by their common strategic pursuit. The strategic *logos*, as will be demonstrated, is both the outcome of, and reason for, the creative interaction between the people and their society, which I have called "strategic exchange". Hence, the *logos* is born with the emergence of a particular society and the *logos*, together with its mythical strategic guardians, dies with that society. It is this close and essential relationship that has led human societies to worship the unknown strategic *logos* and to call its strategic guardian God. As each society unknowingly creates, and is created by, its own strategic *logos*, it is not alone; many *logoi* exist at any point in time. It was for this reason that human societies in both the Old and New Worlds had their own home-grown gods. Each society created its own god or gods in order to protect and sustain its own strategic *logos*. Further, it should be realised that while each society has its own strategic *logos*, there is no overarching *logos* for humanity as a whole. Earth's human race is the outcome of the interaction between competing *logoi*.

Perceptions of A Hidden Life-System

While the "strategic *logos*" is invisible and its meaning hidden, all ancient societies have been aware of its shadowy presence, and based their mythologies and religions on it. They referred to it as: harmony, order, stability, cosmic balance, security, truth, law of the Universe, unity of nature, and "sacred circle" (Sioux).They saw this shadowy reality as the changelessness beneath the superficial flux of everyday life. (In fact, the strategic *logos* is ever-changing.) And they personified the various perceived characteristics of this underlying reality as gods. We can even see the longing for order, balance and stability today in the inflation-targeting policies of economists and central banks, and the climate-mitigation policies of environmentalists, each serving their own gods of Mammon or Nature.

Some ancient and pre-modern societies even had names for this hidden system of order, balance and stability. The Greeks called it *Logos*; but, in addition, this mystery of mysteries was called *maat* by the Egyptians, *Asha* by the Persians, *Rta* by the Vedic Indians, *Nelli* by the Toltecs, *Wakan-Tanka* (or "Great Mystery") by the Sioux, and the "Dreaming" by Australian Aborigines. All these societies, as well as those who had no special name for this mysterious system underlying life, were extremely concerned to sustain it, together with all its life-giving powers. They were convinced that their life-system would be disrupted by inappropriate behaviour, either of omission or commission, and the result would be disorder and chaos. Without understanding the scientific concept of entropy, they had a strong sense of the world running down. Hence, it was essential in their eyes to undertake the appropriate sacrifice and ritual, and to live according to the laws of the *logos*. In this they looked to their wisemen and their kings. This was the real origin and purpose of religion.

A Diagrammatic Model of the Strategic *Logos*

In an effort to make visible what has for many thousands of years remained hidden, a diagrammatic model of the strategic *logos* is presented in Figure 3.1. This model is based on the dynamic-strategy theory, which in turn was constructed inductively from the close and systematic observation of living systems in both the human and non-human worlds. Needless to say, this figure is merely a simple, two-dimensional representation of a complex, three-dimensional process. What Figure 3.1 clearly shows, however, is the fundamental circular nature of interaction between man and society—the selfcreating process of strategic exchange—that lies at the heart of the strategic *logos*. This pattern of concentric circles—this complex mandala—bears a close resemblance to the dominant role that circles and concentric circles played in the sacred art of the paleolithic era.

Figure 3.1 The Strategic *Logos*

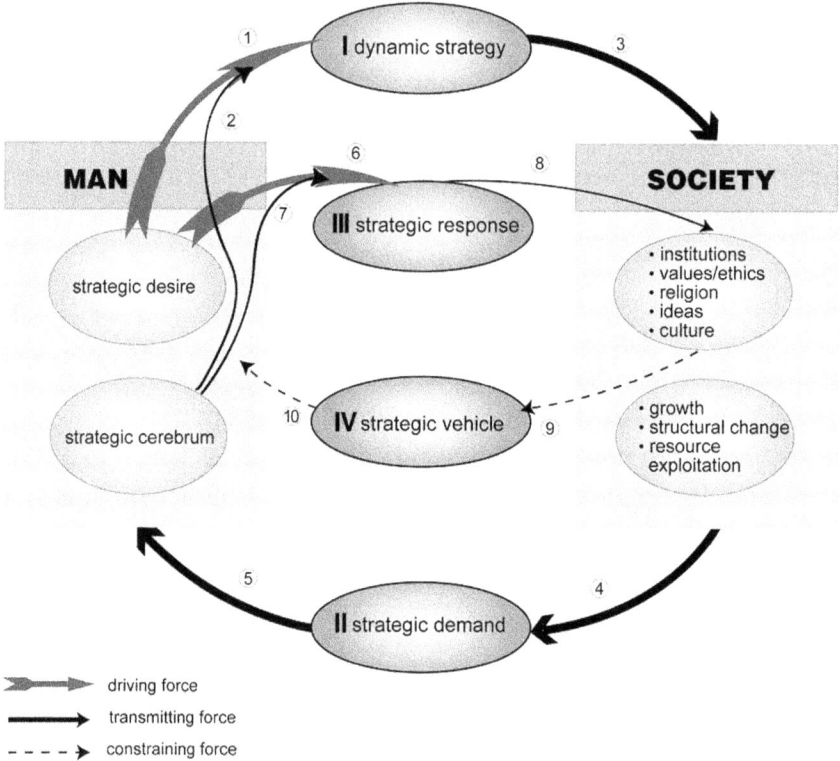

Source: Snooks 2010b: 322.

The circular process of strategic exchange occurs at four main levels. These include: **I** the dynamic strategy pursued by society; **II** the strategic demand that this unfolding process generates for a wide range of strategic inputs; **III** the individual and collective response to strategic demand; and **IV** the resulting strategic vehicle that carries society forward in its "strategic pursuit". These forces also generate the laws of history (and of life).

The strategic *logos* is driven by "strategic desire", which is the motive force that powers the dynamic circle, or mandala, of life. It is the centre of life's pulsating heart, and it provides this dynamic engine with its self-starting and self-sustaining character. Strategic desire, which is fed both directly and indirectly with energy from the sun, operates primarily by driving both the dynamic strategy being pursued by society together with its "strategic response". In both cases this activity is facilitated by the supervisory and planning role played by the "strategic cerebrum".

The great *directing* force in human society is "strategic demand", which continually changes as the dominant dynamic strategy unfolds in response to a transforming *logos*. This directing force provokes a necessary response from the people, thereby providing the institutional, organizational, and cultural vehicle required to engage successfully in the strategic pursuit. This societal vehicle also provides the medium for natural-resource exploitation, as well as for economic growth and the structural change required to meet the people's strategic objective of survival and prosperity.

Just as the laws of physics are derived from observing physical relationships in the cosmos, so the laws of life and history have been derived from observing societal relationships in the strategic *logos*. These laws shape and regulate the dynamics of life, human society, and civilization. In *Laws of History* (1998) and *The Collapse of Darwinism* (2003; ch. 15), I derived nine general and universal laws from the operation of the strategic *logos*. These "primary" laws, which are merely listed here, include:

- The law of motivation in life
- The law of competitive intensity
- The law of strategic selection
- The law of strategic optimization
- The law of strategic imitation
- The law of strategic struggle
- The law of diminishing strategic returns
- The law of strategic crisis
- The law of societal collapse.

These laws define the entropy-defying nature of the strategic *logos*. Other laws—"secondary" (four in life and five in society) and "tertiary" (four in life and nine in society)—applicable to the major historical eras, have been derived from these eight primary laws by introducing different initial conditions from these eras. They are discussed in detail in my earlier books.

With this overview in mind, we can investigate the operation of the strategic *logos* in Figure 3.1. We begin with "Man" in the left-had box. Man is dualistic in his strategic nature. Not only driven by strategic desire to achieve his fundamental joint objective of survival and prosperity, Man also possesses a highly sophisticated instrument— the strategic cerebrum—employed to plan and supervise the strategic pursuit. This was achieved through the adoption and exploitation of one of a quartet of dynamic strategies—family multiplication, conquest, commerce, technological change—available to that society. As the chosen dynamic strategy unfolds, society increases its access to natural resources, grows economically, and changes structurally. In the process, the "Society" generates strategic demand for an extensive range of strategic inputs, including land, labour, capital, ideas (technological, strategic, other), institutions (societal rules), organizations (societal networks), values, ethics, religion, and culture. The nature of these inputs bears the stamp of the particular dynamic strategy being pursued. All human values, in other words, are initiated outside (although with the participation of) man by the strategic *logos*, not purely by the mind of man as most scholars claim. The *logos* is the measure of all things.

The drive behind the strategic response to "logosian demand" is, once again, provided by strategic desire, and is facilitated by the strategic cerebrum. A major outcome of this strategic response is the creation of an institutional, ethical, religious, cultural vehicle capable of carrying the strategic pursuit forward and, thereby, delivering the material success that meets the needs of strategic desire, which initiated the entire process. The completion of this circular interaction, however, doesn't lead to equilibrium, because strategic desire is never satisfied. Accordingly, the circular interaction becomes an upward spiral that continues until the strategic *logos* collapses, sending the whole process into reverse.

While this diagrammatic model of the strategic *logos* provides a convenient two-dimensional sketch of a complex dynamic engine of society, its limitations are obvious. First, Figure 3.1 is merely a cross-section of the entire circular process of "strategic exchange". The missing third dimension is time, which is needed to show how the *logos* allows a society not only to exploit the founding dynamic strategy, but also how its exhaustion, which threatens the continuing viability of the *logos*, opens the way for the adoption and exploitation of a further dynamic strategy from its four-fold armoury.

By adding time, a three-dimensional model would demonstrate the strategic sequence, which would burrow into the surface of the page at level **I**. Such a sequence would show how a changing strategic demand impacts on the strategic vehicle we call civilization. One need only reflect, for example, on how different was Greek civilization under the conquest strategy (400–100 BC) from that under the commerce strategy (800–500 BC). Of particular interest in this example, is how the circular strategic sequence of conquest▶commerce▶conquest led ancient Greece to advance toward and, later, retreat from democratic ecosociopolitical forms. This unfolding strategic sequence was presided over by the Greek *logos*, which was recognized but misinterpreted as the divine *Logos* by Heraclitus around 500 BC.

Secondly, the strategic *logos* should not be thought of as being confined by fixed dimensions as Figure 3.1 probably suggests. By adding the missing variable of time, the *logos*, as a dynamic engine, grows larger (or smaller, if in decline), more complex (representing a spiral rather than an ellipse), and it generates greater (or lesser) levels of population, GPD and GDP per capita. In a more partial and ad hoc manner, these issues can be dealt with by employing conventional "timescapes" that show changes in the variables by which the success (or failure) of societies and civilization are usually measured. What is important to note here is that these performance variables feed back into the decisions made by agents through "strategic confidence". Also we need to remember that all three outcomes are generated by the strategic *logos*, which is not to be simplistically confused with the crude representations of it made in Figure 3.1.

Finally, it is important to realize that in life, dynamics—or, in the words of Heraclitus, "flux"—is deep and abiding, not superficial and intermittent. Not only is life in constant flux, but the system of life that generates this flux is also dynamic in itself. In other words, the dynamic engine that is the strategic *logos* acts upon itself as well as on life and society. The *logos* is not absolute, eternal, and changeless in the way that gods are supposed to be—or in the way Plato thought about the Forms—but rather it is ephemeral and in a state of continuous change. The strategic *logos* changes as its dynamic strategy unfolds; and it is transformed as the global genetic/technological paradigm shifts occur. Both the moved and the mover are dynamic. This reality is in stark contrast to the theological idea that arose to explain this mystery of mysteries—the fanciful idea of the unmoved mover.

The strategic *logos* depicted in Figure 3.1 can be generalized to embrace all "societies" in life. They would differ largely in terms of degree of sophistication of the strategic cerebrum (or, in its absence, the "strategic gene"), of complexity of the strategic vehicle, or of the type and magnitude of material outcomes. As discussed in *The Collapse of Darwinism* (2003), even simple, single-cellular life adopts and pursues the generalized quartet of dynamic strategies available to human society. Hence, the strategic *logos* accounts for the origin and growing complexity of the entire "society" of life. The *logos* is, in other words, the dynamic machine responsible for the selfcreating—or autogenous—process that can be detected in all species of life.

It is the strategic *logos* which provides the protective environment that life and human society require to flourish in a difficult environment. It is the vehicle of life, the **ark of the Sun**. But to undertake this critical function, the *logos* requires above all else, sustained loyalty and dedication by society's members to the cause of survival and prosperity. It can only do its work if there are no serious divisions in society—if the inevitable emergence of antistrategic elements is restricted to a tiny minority in a sea of enthusiastic strategic supporters. The vast majority of the population are required to support the strategic ideology of their society. In the past, the strategic ideology may have been pagan, Zoroastrian, Christian or Islamic, but today it is "scientism"—the belief in the role of science and technology in the successful strategic pursuit. While the *logos* is blind to colour, race and creed, it demands complete support for the prevailing strategic ideology. Those antistrategists working against the *logos* from the inside include, most obviously, local terrorists involved in destructive activities in support of the conflicting ideologies of external organisations and societies; but also include, less obviously, those internal groups supporting ideologies that surreptitiously and seriously undermine the viability of the *logos* in the name of a pseudo scientism known as the science of climate mitigation (as distinct from the more reputable science of climate change). In the immediate future, the latter will be of greater danger to our civilization, as they are becoming a significant and influential minority in societies that have failed to understand the nature of the strategic *logos*.

HISTORICAL REALITY AND ULTIMATE REALITY

What are we to make of the strategic *logos*? There are, in my philosophy of life, two forms of reality. First, there is "historical reality", which consists of *objects* and physical relationships between objects that can be perceived through the senses over time. And, second, there is "ultimate reality", or the strategic *logos*, that is the outcome of a complex set of invisible relationships between *forces*—such as strategic desire and strategic demand—that cannot be perceived through the senses, despite having materialist origins. Only the agents (or "strategists") and outcomes (institutions, organizations, infrastructure, and material wealth) generated by these invisible forces can be detected by the senses. As suggested earlier, the relationship between invisible forces and visible objects in the social world is similar conceptually to that in the physical world explored by physicists, or the world of the mind examined by psychiatrists. The discovery of the strategic *logos* is similar in nature to these discoveries in science.

The strategic *logos* is the only source of hope for life in a hostile world. It is the meaning of life. This existential fact clearly has been understood by all societies in the past for which evidence is available. All societies have been only too aware of their precarious circumstances in this world. The ruins of former, once flourishing, societies and civilizations are there for all to see. In Mesoamerica for example, the Aztecs saw their life-system as the Fifth Sun, as they were acutely aware that four other life-systems, or "Suns", together with their gods, had flourished in their region for a time, and then collapsed. And in Egypt, every night was a time of potential crisis, as the sun god Re and his divine retinue passed through the underworld, for the ancient Egyptians believed that as their ordered world (*maat*) had emerged from a watery chaos (*nun*) so it would end in a watery chaos. Today there is a widespread fear that climate change will irreparably harm our own life-system. Such concern can be appreciated, because, if our strategic *logos* were irreparably damaged, there would be no hope for societal progress or individual survival. But unfortunately, in an attempt to "save" our life-system—without understanding what it is or how it works— so-called "experts" are advocating massive intervention that, ironically, will destroy the focus of their concern. Only by arming himself with a knowledge of the strategic *logos*—the ultimate reality of life—can man can look forward confidently to the future.

Chapter four
Ethics

To answer the question, "How should we live our lives?", we need to consider the issue of ethics. The study of ethics is a study of rules of conduct operating in human society. Confusion about the origin and role of "moral rules" characterises the writings of many ethicists. It is a confusion caused by the emergence of metaphysical philosophy from the time of the Greek philosopher Plato. In pre-Socratic philosophy, ethics was a practical rather than a theoretical subject. Questions of how one should conduct one's life and what was considered "good" and "virtuous" were questions about how the material life could be pursued most successfully. They wanted to know what habits of mind and action would lead to personal success in a materially progressive society.

With the emergence of a prosperous and leisured class in Athens in the fifth century BC, however, ideas about rules of conduct became divorced from the strategic activity that generated their wealth. A new class of philosophers, who were at arms-length from the commerce strategy that provided their privileges, sought more "noble" origins of what was "good" and virtuous". After all, commerce was an activity pursued by cunning calculators and sharp dealers, while the competing strategy of conquest was pursued by brutal and ruthless men. Only philosophers could aspire to more aesthetic and divine realms of existence. It is hardly surprising that these men of ideas turned their backs on the world of base desires, and sought the origins of ethics in metaphysical concepts. From the time of Plato, metaphysical ethics began to diverge from existential ethics.

METAPHYSICAL ETHICS

While it is not my intention to provide a formal history of Western ethics, it will help the argument to sketch the strange relationship between strategic and metaphysical ethics over the past three millennia—from early Greek society to the present. This is necessary because there is, and always has been, much confusion in the minds of philosophers and lay people alike about the difference between what they *actually do*, and what they think (or are told) they *ought to do* in life.

In the heroic age of Greece—the time of Homer (c.800–700 BC)—ethics were strategic in origin. The Greek word for "good"— *agathos*—was used to describe a Homeric nobleman; an individual who was courageous, talented, capable of endurance, successful in both war and politics, and wealthy. In other words, the "good" Greek was strategically successful, whereas the "bad" Greek was strategically unsuccessful. The Greek word for "bad"—*kakos*— means an individual who is base born. Moral language in early Greece, therefore, was used to describe specific functions in society undertaken by strategists—those who were considered to be contributing to society's material progress. Women and slaves were considered outside the moral order. So, Greek ethics asks: "What should I do if I am to be successful in life?"; while modern ethics asks: "What ought I do if I am to do the right thing?", where the "right thing" is independent of strategic success.

While strategic pragmatism was the main thread in the early Greek approach to ethics, there was a hint of tension. That other great poet of the age, Hesiod (c.700 BC), provided a counterpoint to the Homeric tradition by warning against arrogance and excess. Against this literary background, the pre-Socratic philosophers— such as Xenophanes (c.540–500 BC), Pythagoras (c.560–500 BC), Heraclitus (c.500 BC), Protagoras (c.490–421 BC), and Herodotus (c.485–425 BC)—advanced philosophical ideas about how men should live their lives. They suggested that standards of right and wrong could vary between different societies and yet be equally valid for leading a civilised life (Protagoras and Herodotus); that nature (the ordered cosmos) was the appropriate model for truth and virtue

(Heraclitus and the Stoics); that balance should be achieved and retained between desire (*physis*) and law (*nomos*); or alternatively, that as *physis* reflects reality (freedom and self-interest) and *nomos* reflects artificial restraint (temperance and justice), the latter should be swept away to enable strong, capable men to achieve a monopoly of wealth and power and to provide strategic leadership (the anti-moralist Sophists and all practical men).

While ethics had a long history in ancient Greece, it was Socrates (469–399 BC), Plato (c.428–347 BC), Aristotle (384–322 BC) and their followers who were the first to employ systematic deductive reasoning to investigate how men ought to lead their lives. They were the first writers to develop a theory of ethics divorced from its strategic origins. **Plato** was confident that, in contrast to earlier thinkers, he knew what the human qualities of goodness and justice really were, and was prepared to suggest (in *Republic*) the best political means of imposing them on others. He claimed that, through a process of logical reasoning, it was possible to detect the reality lying behind these and all other human concepts. He called this static ultimate reality the "Forms". By doing so, Plato drew a distinction between the eternal realm of the Forms and the ephemeral human world of sense perceptions.

According to Plato, the highest of these Forms—which could be employed to understand all other Forms—was the "Form of the Good", which existed beyond the boundaries of everyday life. It was conceived as a transcendent entity that acted as the measure of all things. For Plato, the Forms not only provided an understanding of human conduct, but also represented an eternal divine reality free from change and decay. This changeless divine "reality" contrasts with the dynamic existential reality explored throughout my work. Unfortunately for this metaphysical philosophy, Plato, in his later work (*Laws*) lost confidence in the reality of the Forms and experienced a crisis in his thinking. But what he did achieve, which has caused endless confusion ever since, was to provide the methodological means of separating ethics from strategic reality.

Aristotle's ideas differ in many respects from those of Plato. In particular, while Plato viewed ethical criteria as transcendent (the

Forms), Aristotle saw them as defining an ideal rational society. What they have in common is a view of the cosmos in which *timeless* virtues (particularly truth in Aristotle) is superior to human society subject to endless change and dominated by sense experience and faulty rationality. Like Plato, Aristotle separated metaphysical ethics from strategic rules of conduct. He argued that the "good life" revolved around a rational life (where desires were transformed) in which happiness is the "supreme good". The rational life was supposed to give rise to the intellectual virtues of intelligence, wisdom, and providence; together with the moral virtues of liberality and temperance. These were the virtues characterising the "great-souled man", who was independent, self-sufficient, proud, feared no one, placed little value on worldly things, rejected honours offered by the common people, but who, nevertheless, was tolerant of inferiors. Aristotle advises his peers to be virtuous, courageous, and liberal. Clearly he was addressing his remarks to the wealthy, educated, leisured elite; in other words, to Athens' strategic leaders.

Of particular interest to the thesis in this book are the works of the **Cynics**, who trace their ideas back through Diogenes (c.410–c.320 BC) to Socrates. The Cynics reject all contemporary values and look to the natural world for inspiration. To the Cynics—as well as the Stoics and Epicureans who were influenced by them—virtue consists in the rejection of desire. In this they resemble the oriental philosophy of Buddhism. As all evil emanates from human desire, goodness can be achieved by eliminating this human failing. Also if you desire nothing, you have nothing to lose and, therefore, can achieve a negative form of happiness. Cynics also claimed to be citizens of the cosmos—hence coining the term "cosmopolitan"— rather than citizens of the Greek city-state. In their approach to life, the Cynics emphasised the practical aspects of Socrates' philosophy— which they expressed in a crudely outlandish way—rather than the theoretical aspects that were developed further by Plato and Aristotle. In this way they were far more influential in the ancient world than the intellectual Socratic school. Clearly, the ethics of the Cynics were an outcome of a rejection of Greek strategic rules of conduct, rather than a search for their transcendent origins as in Plato.

In the **medieval world** there was a clear separation between metaphysical and existential ethics. This was an outcome of combining the ideas of Jesus of Nazareth and St Paul on the one hand, with the ancient Greek philosophers on the other. It is important here to note the differences between the ideas of Jesus and Paul; and between these foundational ideas and those of the medieval church. This is discussed in depth in my book *Dead God Rising* (2010). Jesus of Nazareth attempted to form a nonstrategic community as a personal and psychological defensive strategy in an era of Roman imperialism, while Paul was responsible for developing a theological philosophy about Jesus as Christ the Son of God. While Jesus emphasised the practical virtues of love, equality, charity, and community service, Paul's metaphysical philosophy extolled the virtues of faith, salvation through Christ, brotherly love, and hope for deliverance from the sins of the world through the second coming of Jesus. These combined virtues formed the basis for the theology of the early Christian church.

Everything changed, however, when Christianity was adopted as the ideology of the Roman conquest strategy in the fourth century AD. This change of Roman strategic ideology began with Constantine's rise to power through civil war conducted under the banner of Christ in 312 AD, and culminated in the Edict of Thessalonica in 380 AD, when Christianity became Rome's state religion. Instead of being a spiritual and psychological defence against the oppressive strategic world, Christianity became a supporter of the strategic world by providing a new and, it would seem, more effective strategic guardian than the old failed pagan gods of war, together with a new strategic ideology. In the medieval world, the strategic role of Christianity, which was inherited from the Romans, can be seen reflected in the careers of aristocratic families, in which older sons became knightly warriors engaged in the strategy of conquest, and younger sons went into the church to intercede with the strategic guardians of God the Father, God the Son, and God the Holy Ghost. But owing to the nonstrategic origins of Jesus' teachings, there was a tension within a Christianity that served the strategic *logos*; a tension that was not resolved until after the Industrial Revolution, when "scientism" replaced Christianity as the strategic ideology of technological societies.

Intellectuals employed by the Church—in contrast to clerical scions of aristocratic families—were, unsurprisingly, more interested in ideas than in dynamic strategies and their outcomes. Theologians such as **Augustine** (354–430) and **Thomas Aquinas** (1225–1274) preferred to theorise about metaphysical rather than strategic ethics; and they did this by combining ideas about Jesus and his Father the Jewish God Yahweh, with the philosophical divinity of the Greeks. Earlier church philosophers like Augustine were influenced indirectly by Plato, and later philosophers like Aquinas were influenced by the growing availability of Aristotle's writings.

Generally, medieval thinkers employed a Greek framework for ethical theory, which they extended and modified to render it compatible with the Christian scriptures. The main features of this Christianised Greek philosophy were its rational nature, its metaphysical foundations, and its focus on virtue as a measure of human thoughts and actions. In this theoretical framework they discussed sin, grace, divine commands, and union with God. Needless to say, none of this was compatible with the strategic rules of conduct that dominated the fluctuating fortunes of medieval society. Where medieval strategists took any notice of these metaphysical ethical standards, it was only to obtain God's forgiveness for enthusiastically pursuing the dynamic strategy of conquest of which He was the patron! Intellectual contradictions, however, have never worried materialists.

The **early modern period** from the late-fifteenth to the late-eighteenth centuries—the era of the commerce strategy in Western Europe—exhibits two major strands of theorising about ethics. One was metaphysical and the other strategic, but both were conducive to business. With the Reformation, metaphysical ethics were asserted rather than argued, and they became the responsibility of the individual in commerce societies that were becoming more democratic, as the ownership of economic resources became more widely distributed. **Luther** (1483–1546) and **Calvin** (1509–1564) asserted fundamental and absolute ethical values devoid of rational justification, but left it up to the individual to apply to his own life. And they made no claim over the actions of secular leaders, who were ethically free to pursue their strategic objectives in the light of their own rules of conduct. While secular leaders had no intention of being diverted from their pursuit of self-interest, they still looked to the Christian God as a strategic guardian and to Christianity to provide their strategic ideology. This strategic guardian also proved useful in forgiving their strategic successes!

A more sophisticated, and immensely more interesting, metaphysical approach to ethics was provided by **Baruch Spinoza** (1632–1677), the great Dutch theologian and philosopher. For Spinoza, the love and pursuit of truth is the highest human goal; and his method of pursuing it was highly rational. He developed a deductive system of thought that he believed mirrored the nature of the Universe, which he claimed was a single web in which the whole determines every part. Any part of the system can only be understood within the context of the whole. Spinoza called this system "Deus, sive Natura"—God or Nature. Accordingly, the individual is an integral part of this system and cannot consider himself to be an independent entity. But to have achieved this self-knowledge is to have achieved a sense of freedom and happiness. Because of this intellectual liberty, we no longer blame ourselves or others for our situation, and, as a result, former feelings of frustration, envy, hate and guilt fall away. Virtue, therefore, resides in the realisation that we are one with the universe and that this realisation leads to freedom and happiness. In this way, Spinoza believed, human nature—with all its dark emotions and desires—is able to be transformed. The role of the state is to provide the framework needed to enable men to pursue rationality and freedom. Spinoza's system of thought is not only metaphysical but also transcendental.

What is more interesting and relevant about the early modern period is the appearance of philosophers who, for the first time since the early Greeks, provided a theoretical framework for *strategic* rules of conduct. These thinkers include Niccolo Machiavelli (1469–1527), Thomas Hobbes (1588–1679), John Locke (1632–1704), and Jean Jacque Rousseau (1712–1778). **Machiavelli** argued that men act as they do because of their human nature, which is timeless and unchanging. Human nature, therefore, generates the natural laws that govern human actions—actions that cannot and should not be constrained by social bonds. His argument centres on ends and means. The ends of social and political life are dominated by a desire for power, which results in political leaders attempting to maintain societal order and community prosperity for self-survival. Ethical rules, enshrined in agreements and promises, are just means to this end; and they can and should be broken when they block the way to this end. He insisted that men should not act according to an abstract set of principles, but according to their own self-interest.

While Machiavelli takes the existence and role of the state as given, **Hobbes** theorises about the rise of the state and the nature of its justification. He begins in a similar way to Machiavelli by claiming that the individual is motivated by a desire to achieve power (to dominate) and to survive (to avoid death). Any display of altruism is merely a form of disguised self-interest. Hobbes asserts that in order to escape the brutal state of nature, where the individual is trapped in a war against all other individuals, enlightened people transfer their individual power to a common power, which becomes sovereign to them. That sovereign power is the leadership of the state. In other words, in order to achieve their objective of survival, men develop a social contract that frames the more civilised rules of conduct. This scenario is established by Hobbes mythically rather than historically. A more rational argument in the Hobbes tradition was developed by **Locke**, who outlined the nature of a social contract—which he called "tacit consent"—whereby consent is given by the people to a political elite so that they can govern society. This bargain between people and leader is the outcome of mankind's "natural right to liberty", which, Locke claimed, can be derived from a moral law apprehended by reason. Locke believed that moral distinctions are derived by reason in a similar way to the derivation of mathematical theorems. Clearly, this is a metaphysical rather than an existential argument.

A more sophisticated argument was advanced by **Rousseau**, who focused on the role of human nature in developing his ethical system. He viewed human nature as composed of authentic wants and needs, which although driven by self-love, is not inconsistent with wider feelings of sympathy and compassion. Natural man is basically good rather evil, and his desires are a response to objects of desire, rather than something inherent in human nature. Human nature can, therefore provide a basis for a moral system. Institutions, particularly those involving law making and law enforcing, arise from a "social contract" designed to overcome the disorders arising from social inequality. The regrettable reality, he acknowledged, is that institutions have been used by powerful individuals as instruments of despotism and inequality. So, in order to discover how we should conduct our lives, Rousseau argued that we need to understand our shared human nature. He claimed that correct action—the response to the ethical question "What ought I do?"—should be based on a "true conscience", which he believed was embodied in the expression of the "general will" arising from "deliberative assemblies". Unlike institutions, the general will is never corrupted. Needless to say, this argument is a supply-side metaphysical construct, which poses a potential and very real danger, which was realised later in the case of Revolutionary France, the USSR, and Nazi Germany.

In Britain during the eighteenth century, a number of leading philosophers emphasised an empirical approach to understanding both reality and ethics. **David Hume** (1711–1776), for example, rejected the rationalist ethics of his predecessors both in England (Locke) and the continent (Spinoza, Rousseau, etc.). He argued, with considerable psychological insight, that ethical rules to guide our actions cannot be the outcome of reason, as men are driven not by reason but by "passions". It is the passions arising from the prospect of pleasure or pain that determine the actions of mankind. As is well known, Hume wrote: "Reason is, and ought only to be, the slave of passions, and can never pretend to any other office than to serve and obey them". Moral rules, therefore, are determined by man's desires and needs, both of which Hume regarded as given and unchanging. Similarly, Hume's contemporary and friend, **Adam Smith** (1723–1790), the worldly philosopher and founder of British deductive economics, viewed moral rules as arising from the passionate nature of men.

The upheaval ushered in by the Industrial Revolution appears to have had consequences for the way philosophers saw themselves and their world. On the European continent the empiricism of the previous century was cast aside, and philosophers in Germany employed grand metaphysical systems in an attempt to make sense of these social earthquakes—a phenomenon similar to the impact that the collapse of the USSR had on Russian intellectuals after 1989. New technologies were not only transforming economies, but were responsible for shaking up strategic ideologies and world views. This was the era of the great German philosophers Kant, Hegel, Schopenhauer, Nietzsche, and Marx. In contrast, the cautious and pragmatic British—such as Bentham and J.S. Mill— clung onto the certainties of their commonsensical empirical approach, for fear they might fall into the abyss.

Immanuel Kant (1724–1804) believed in the power of rational thought to explain and reform his world. In the field of ethics, Kant argued that, as nature was both impersonal and non-moral, any system of ethics had to be based on reason rather than human nature. Morals must be independent of how the world works. It is the reasoned "will" rather than "human inclinations" that should determine the way men act. Men should act out of a sense of duty—duty for duty's sake— rather than in response to their inclinations. Duty is willed (the "moral imperative"), whereas inclinations are given. Only "good will" is good, because we can choose our duty, but not our inclinations. Only by obeying the "categorical imperative" ("you ought to do such and such") are men freed from the slavery of their own inclinations. Clearly this is a dangerous line of reasoning as it is susceptible to distortion by antistrategic ideologists. It is easy to see, for example, why some Nazi war criminals attempted to justify their actions in terms of Kantian duty.

Georg Hegel (1770–1831) viewed philosophy as an historical discipline; by which he meant the history of metaphysical ideas, not the history of reality. He treated human nature not as a given, as did his contemporary British empirical philosophers, but as the outcome of societal structure, which is subject to change. Like Rousseau, Hegel believed desires are elicited by the objects that men have presented to them by their society. As society changes over time—by passing through a number of stages in response to the Hegelian dialectic of thesis, antithesis, and synthesis—these objects of desire, as well as the resulting ethics, also change. The core characteristic of human life for Hegel is not human nature but human freedom, which is the outcome of reason. Each extension of freedom is generated by an extension of reason. History for Hegel involves an inevitable progress of freedom and reason to increasingly higher forms, finally culminating in the Prussian state and Hegel's own metaphysical philosophy. Both the Prussian state and Hegel's ideas are seen as the incarnation of the Absolute! Hegel believed that the whole of human history reflected the evolution of the Absolute Idea in a process of self-estrangement that finally achieves reconciliation with itself. Historical progress depends, therefore, on progress in thought. This is just metaphysical fantasy.

While the so-called Young Hegelians, together with Marx, struggled unsuccessfully to make sense of Hegel's bizarre metaphysical ideas, more grounded German thinkers, such as Schopenhauer and Nietzsche, rejected them outright. Both of these influential thinkers despised Hegel and viewed academic metaphysical philosophers as pampered time-wasters. **Arthur Schopenhauer** (1788–1860) is the most pessimistic, but also one of the most insightful, of philosophers. He viewed the Universe as totally meaningless, and the individual as valueless and burdened with a nature embodying the blind strivings of the "Will" (characterised by self-interest, malice, and base sexual desire) against which human reason is impotent. Man is essentially Will, unalterable Will; and all societies and epochs are equally plagued with evil. The arts and music are mankind's only consolation. For Schopenhauer, moral philosophy is based on error—the error of presuming that ethics can alter human conduct.

Friedrich Nietzsche (1844–1900) is the most brilliant and heroic figure in the history of moral philosophy. He was a relentless seeker after truth; a pursuit that cost him his sanity, because he refused to shield himself from the vivisector's sword of self-knowledge. Rather than employ the usual form of self-defence—"existential schizophrenia", which enables us to divorce what we do in order to survive from what we believe we ought to do—Nietzsche exposed himself to the sustained and relentless attack of self-knowledge. And was destroyed in the process. As he said prophetically in *Thus Spake Zarathustra*:

> With my tears go into your loneliness,
> my brother. I love him who wants to create
> over and beyond himself and thus perishes.

Nietzsche's task as a freelance thinker (he retired as the youngest Classical Professor at the University of Basel when he was only 35 years old) was to explore the historical and psychological causes of the moral vacuum of his day—that era following the "death of God"; to expose the falseness of the new "slave" morality; to revalue all values; and to introduce a new way forward in life, in the form of the "overman". To achieve this, Nietzsche developed a supply-side theory of morality based on the relative abilities and capacities of groups of individuals in society. For the elite—those strong individuals who, like himself, were of high intellect and self-assertiveness—there needed to be a "higher" morality that would train and prepare them for the "heights"; but for those of less ability requiring conventional support, a "healthy herd morality" would be required. Despite his brilliance, Nietzsche was more successful as a critic than as a creator of a new way of life. The overman is little more than a hollow construct, which may have been developed more meaningfully had Nietzsche survived mentally beyond the age of 45 years (he lived on for a further decade as a haunted ruin of his former brilliant self). While Nietzsche never developed a general theory of life, his work shimmers with fascinating insights into human experience, and he is the supreme example of the risk-taking seeker after truth.

In contrast to philosophers on the European continent, those in Britain took the safer, more pragmatic path of "utilitarianism", which not only influenced intellectual debate, but also became the basis of classical demand theory and policy evaluation. **Jeremy Bentham** (1748–1832), the father of British utilitarianism, was mainly concerned with jurisprudence and, in particular, with what new laws ought to be introduced into Parliament, and what old laws should be revised or replaced. To achieve this he needed a method to evaluate the impact of these laws. The principle he adopted as self-evident was that "it is the greatest happiness of the greatest number that is the measure of right and wrong"; and his measure of happiness was the excess of pleasure over pain. This became the central principle of utilitarianism.

John Stuart Mill (1806–1873) took up the theory of utilitarianism where Bentham left off. While he agreed that human desires could be measured with the "happiness principle", Mill thought that pleasure had to be evaluated qualitatively as well as quantitatively. To do this he distinguished between "higher" and "lower" pleasures, and claimed that the higher pleasures were of greater benefit to mankind. Needless to say, Mill's approach is highly subjective, and reflects his place in the British class structure. When pressed on this issue, Mill had to admit that his concept of utility as a measure of the right way to proceed could only be used as a guide. The pleasure principle has also been criticised as a narrow definition of human desires, and as providing support for people, groups, and societies that derive pleasure from destroying the lives of others (as in the Nazi holocaust).

The other important development in nineteenth century British ethics was the contribution of the great originators of evolutionary theory, Spencer and Darwin. **Herbert Spencer's** (1820–1903) work on evolution, which preceded Darwin's by eight years, tended to be more metaphysical, and Darwin's more empirical. Both, however, are supply-side theories. Spencer's view of ethics, which he viewed as "logically certain", was teleological, and focused on "the ultimate development of the ideal man". Progress in this matter "is not an accident but a certainty" (*Social Statics* [1851]). In other words, "moral truth", together with "physiological truth", are outcomes of an inevitable and irreversible "process of adaptation".

Charles Darwin (1808–1882), on the other hand, is interested in explaining moral standards in the present rather than the future. In *Descent of Man* (1871), Darwin argues that "moral sense" was not consciously developed or acquired, but had evolved through natural selection (in *Descent* called "social selection") in order to provide for the "general good or welfare of the community, rather than the general happiness". This concept, like natural selection itself, owed much to the political economy of his day (Thomas Malthus and David Riccardo). What Darwin did not understand was that ethics, like all human institutions, depends on the requirements of the strategic *logos* (hence is demand rather than supply induced), and can be reversed if the dynamic strategy of the *logos* is reversed and, therefore, cannot be evolutionary. Ethics is not the outcome of supply-side evolutionary processes, either metaphysical or existential.

In **the modern era**, many philosophers have embraced the metaphysical approach to ethics. And many of these have attempted to elevate their personal morality to an absolute level, and to insist that it is relevant to all humanity in their own and even earlier eras. The cast of offenders in this matter is too large to survey here, but it stretches from Brentano, Scheler, and Moore at the beginning of the twentieth century to Sartre, Foucault and Levinas in the middle and later decades of that century. Writers like **Franz Brentano** (1838–1917), **Max Scheler** (1874–1928) and **G.E. Moore** (1873–1958) believed that the type of actions we should perform are those that will generate more good in the world than any possible alternative action. What states are "good"?; those that are "intrinsically good", a property we cannot analyse or define, but which we cannot fail to recognise when we see it! Virtue, then, is self-evident.

Jean Paul Sartre (1905–1980) and **Michel Foucault** (1926–1984) were concerned with the problem individuals experience in facing up to the ethical ideal of existence. Their solution was personal transformation through courageous, honest, self-mastery. This personal transformation is an ethical response to their era, and is also the basis of social transformation. **Albert Camus** (1913–1960) distinguished his philosophy by focusing on the individual struggling heroically in an absurd world to provide life with *relative* meaning. His ethical principles of honesty, courage, and persistence emerge from this struggle, which also has societal implications through solidarity and communication with others. Finally, **Emmanuel Levinas** (1906–1995) defines the ethical in relation to the "other", even though the "other" remains wholly alien and unassimilable.

To round out this philosophical sketch, we need to consider the ethics of the **Green environmental movement** in the twenty-first century. This is more of a social movement than a school of ideas. In many respects it has replaced traditional religion for members of a younger generation of educated, middleclass trendies. Green philosophy is based on a metaphysical embracing of "nature", and an antistrategic rejection of the strategic *logos* and its agents. In its most extreme form, Green philosophy is anti-humanistic. Essentially, Green ethics is based on the notion of what is best for "nature" or "the planet" rather than what is best for humanity. The central fallacy here is the mistaken view that nature (rather than the strategic *logos*, which they have failed to recognise let alone understand) is the ultimate reality. They also insist on elevating their personal and subjective values to an absolute level, and imposing them on the rest of humanity. This approach to ethics is the greatest risk to strategic values and success since totalitarian Marxism. Interestingly, some of the most radical Greens are former Marxists.

To sum up: Echoes of all these metaphysical theories can be heard in our own time. They provide the language of moral justification and rationalisation. They also provide a major source of confusion, owing to the imposition of metaphysical moral justification on a world driven by the strategic *logos*. Metaphysical ethics are employed in two main ways in our contemporary world. First, they provide support for life-affirming existential schizophrenia. Despite the fact that humans are prepared to do whatever it takes to survive and prosper by following pragmatic strategic rules of conduct, we pretend to ourselves that we are really following the principles of some form of metaphysical ethics—reason, religion, or environmentalism. Second, people employ ethical language to justify acting according to strategic rules of conduct: "It is the right thing to do", is a phrase heard endlessly by those, particularly in public life, pursuing their own selfish interests. And to ward off criticism, to attack truth tellers, or to undermine strategic competitors, the morally self-righteous accuse those they cannot out-think or out-argue of being: "sexist", "racist", homophobic", "ageist", and so on. End of debate!

STRATEGIC ETHICS

Simply stated, strategic ethics is the very new study of the rules of conduct required to facilitate the requirements of the strategic *logos*.

These rules of conduct are the habits of mind and action that have been found through experience to support the successful exploitation of the dominant dynamic strategy being pursued by any society at a particular place and time. The basic question underlying these rules of conduct is: What is best for the strategic *logos*? What the individual strategist—and we are all strategists in this technological era— needs to ask is: If I want to be successful in a materially progressive society, how should I conduct my life? When strategists refer to "good" action, or "the right thing", they mean what is "good" or "the right thing" for the *logos* and, therefore, good for all the participants in that society. This involves a repudiation of all those metaphysical theories of the past.

It is important to understand the difference between metaphysical ethics and strategic ethics. **Metaphysical ethics** were, and are, designed by and for the educated elite. Higher education, if not philosophical training, is required to understand the deductive arguments of metaphysical ethicists. In fact, a considerable program of highly specialised training is usually required to persuade an intelligent individual to ignore commonsense and embrace ideas that, to the untrained mind, appear nonsensical. **Strategic ethics** on the other hand, consist of commonsensical rules of conduct that are relevant not just to the educated elite, but to all strategists in any society. Rigid adherence to metaphysical rules of conduct would destroy the strategic *logos*, and lead to disorder, poverty, misery, and death.

Strategic rules of conduct are conventionally accepted habits of mind and action that are part of a child's upbringing and formal education that help to ensure the success of the strategic pursuit. These rules are largely the outcome of trial and error over many generations, and tend to be absorbed unconsciously by the latest generation. They are informal rules of behaviour passed from one generation to the next. The great benefit of these conventions is that each generation is spared the time and cost of having to rethink their appropriate relationship to the *logos*. This is one of the many instances where mankind attempts to economise in the use of the most scarce resource in the Universe—intelligence (see my book *The Selfcreating Mind*

[2006]). As we shall see, strategic virtues—such as justice, fairness, incorruptibility, and fidelity—are not good in themselves. They derive their virtue from being "good" for the strategic *logos* and, as a result, "good" for society and all its members. This is so because they help to maximise strategic success; to maximise the probability of survival and prosperity.

Conventional strategic rules are absorbed despite the confusion generated by metaphysical philosophers, who pontificate about ungrounded virtues, such as truth, love, altruism, charity, goodness, and so on. This is possible because we instinctively know what is in our best interest, and because we are able to compartmentalise metaphysical values on the one hand, and strategic values on the other through the survival mechanism of "existential schizophrenia". So it is possible to be ruthless, brutal, unempathetic, deceitful, greedy and grasping in our daily activities, but think of ourselves as truthful, empathetic, generous, kindly, and altruistic. Because of existential schizophrenia we are able to remain relatively sane in an absurd and ruthless world. And we are able to adopt the ethical vocabulary and concepts of metaphysical philosophy while living our lives according to strategic rules of conduct. Only when existential schizophrenia breaks down in a minority of individuals do they experience life crises.

The Source of Strategic Ethics

The only basis for an objective set of practical rules of conduct is the strategic *logos*, because this is the final arbiter; the ultimate reality. All other ethical concepts are metaphysical, as they rely on either some concept of the Absolute or Divine, or a set of personal ethical concepts that some philosopher has attempted to universalise and make absolute. For the strategic *logos* to be successful, strategic agents need to think and act in a supportive way. They need to develop attitudes and habits that assist in the acquiring of skills required to successfully pursue the dominant dynamic strategy, together with various supporting activities and institutions. There a number of levels of society at which this operates: at the levels of the individual, family, community, and government.

The individual

Individual strategists are required to act in a disciplined, sober, reliable, modest, relatively honest, relatively empathetic way in order to cooperate with other strategists in response to strategic demand generated by the *logos*. When large numbers of individuals fail to act in this predictable way, chaos rather than order rules, and their society fails to succeed, or, if formerly successful, it stagnates and collapses. This usually occurs following sustained internal or external crises. The role of the individual strategist is the same, irrespective of the type of prevailing *logos*.

The family

While the role of the family, like all other social institutions, varies according to the dynamic strategy being pursued, it is important that it is sensitive to the requirements of the *logos*. Its primary function is to provide recreation—literally re-creation—for the individual strategists it contains, and for procreation and initial education of the next generation of strategists, in order to ensure the continuity of the *logos*. The relative importance of these two prime functions will differ significantly between, say, the family-multiplication strategy (which requires a relatively large family unit averaging about 10 people) and the technological strategy (which requires a relatively small family unit, averaging about 2.5 people). The difference is due to the changing requirements of the *logos* for human inputs into the dynamic process of life. Whether we like it or not, life is about the *logos*, not about people.

Of particular importance in a study of ethics is the initial care and education of children provided by the family. It is the family that provides implicit and explicit advice about how to conduct oneself in society. Much of this training is "absorbed with mother's milk". Adult family members provide role models for the children to follow, as well as giving more formal instruction and advice. It is in functional families that children learn to conduct themselves honestly, openly, fairly, tolerantly, studiously, respectfully, considerately; as well as defensively, competitively, doggedly, persistently, and effectively.

In dysfunctional families, the values imparted to children are often counterproductive for the society and its underlying *logos*.

In advanced twenty-first century societies, the role of the family is changing. With the falling strategic demand of the technological *logos* for population, family sizes have been falling to uneconomic sizes; to the point where increasing numbers of young people are considering living alone and outsourcing the realisation of their emotional and physical needs. At the same time, the increasing participation of women in well-paid employment is loosening the economic ties formerly holding families together. Increasingly, families are breaking up and former family members are creating new hybrid families or even living independently. This has challenged both the re-creational and the balanced educational roles of the family. Instead of absorbing strategic values from both father and mother, children are increasingly exposed to only one parent, to a range of less-interested step parents, or to low-paid professional carers. It would be surprising in these circumstances if the children affected are being exposed to a balanced range of strategic rules of conduct. This could be a challenge for the *logos* in the future.

Community organisations

Community organisations develop in response to the requirements of the prevailing strategic *logos*; and these requirements depend on the type of *logos* concerned, and the manner of its development. Over the course of human history, as shown in Table 4.1, these organisations have included the following:

- Kinship hunting and gathering teams, and kinship and tribal raiding parties, operating under the family-multiplication strategy;
- Military (armed forces, engineering and logistical teams) and imperial administrative systems under the conquest strategy;
- Commercial systems (trading and financial organisations; shipping, finance and insurance firms) and state naval and foreign service organisations operating under the commerce strategy; and
- Industrial (factories and multinational organisations) and commercial (finance and insurance firms) organisations, and state bureaucracy operating under the technological strategy.

Table 4.1 Strategic Organizations—the Past 100,000 years

Dynamic Strategy (*Logos* type)	Major Strategic Organisations	Support Organisations
1. Family multiplication (Hunting *logos*)	• Kinship hunting & gathering teams • Kinship & tribal raiding parties	• Initiation & hunting rituals • Toolmaking groups • Trading groups • Witch-doctors

2. Conquest (Military *logos*)	• Military system
	  – armed forces
	  – engineering division
	  – logistical division
	• Imperial administration
	  – central organisation
	  – local governors
		• Training organisations
		  – military skills
		  – engineering techniques
		  – leadership and
		    administrative skills
		• Arms factories
		• Military technology
		• Prophets & oracles

3. Commerce (Mercantile *logos*)	• Commercial system
	  – trading networks
	  – financial organisations
	  – shipping firms
	  – insurance firms
	• State navy
	• State foreign service
		• Training organisations
		  – business & commercial
		    skills
		  – navigation
		  – naval skills
		• Ship-building organisations
		• Transport technology
		• Religious & scientific
		  guidance

4. Technological (Enterprise *logos*)	• Industrial system
	  – factory organisation
	  – multinational corporation
	• Commercial system
	  – finance firms
	  – insurance firms
	• State bureaucracy
		• Training organisations
		  –scientific technological
		    skills
		  – commerce skills
		  – higher education
		• Research & development
		  organisations
		• Economic forecasting

Source: Snooks, *Ephemeral Civilization* (1997: 59).

All these organisations and systems require disciplined, sober, cooperative, dignified, studious, well-mannered, well-dressed conduct. To build on the formative training provided by the family, these different strategic societies need to generate a wide range of skills through support organisations (see Table 4.1). For example:

• The "hunting" *logos* (pursuing the family-multiplication strategy) establishes social groups to provide initiation and hunting rituals, tool-making skills, trading skills, as well as the specialised arts of the witch-doctor.

- The "military" *logos* (pursuing the conquest strategy) develops training organisations to provide military, engineering, administrative, and leadership skills, together with techniques needed in arms factories, military machines, and the specialised skills required by prophets and oracles.

- The "mercantile" *logos* (pursuing the commerce strategy) creates training organisations to pass on skills required in business, commercial, navigational and naval activities.

- And the "enterprise" *logos* (pursuing the technological strategy) requires formal, sophisticated education and training in the fields of science, technology, commerce, research and development.

This brief outline shows that the disciplined, sober, cooperative conduct required by the strategic *logos* varies in emphasis according to the dynamic strategy being pursued. In the hunting *logos* the emphasis is on conduct required for procreation and migration to new territories, and it is transmitted through small, decentralised family and tribal groups. For the military *logos*, the required conduct relates to expansion through ruthless and brutal military activity and territorial control, which is transmitted through centralised state-controlled, large-scale organisations. In the case of the mercantile *logos*, emphasis is on exploitative commercial conduct undertaken privately with commerce-controlled state support. And for the enterprise *logos*, the emphasis is on private enterprise undertaken with state contributions to infrastructure, defence, and national strategic direction.

In other strategic organisations—including the judiciary, the church, and the media—the standards of conduct are clearly enunciated and demanding, but often honoured in the breach rather than the observance. **The judiciary** is meant to apply the virtues of fairness and justice in a "universal" and consistent way. As a study of history shows, the concept of "universality" is interpreted by all societies as applying only to the strategists in society. For example, in ancient Athens (commerce society) this meant free male citizens, who were a minority of the population that also included females, slaves, and workers of foreign origin; in Rome (conquest society) it involved an even smaller proportion of the population who constituted the warrior elite; in medieval Europe (conquest society) it included only male nobles; in Venice (commerce society) it encompassed a wider group of male merchants and financiers; in early industrial Britain (early industrial technological society) it included a larger group (but still a minority) of propertied males; and in Western societies today (late industrial technological society) it embraces all competent citizens, both male and female (and everything in between). So, justice has always been selectively applied, along strategic lines. **Justice has never been regarded as a "right" for all people, only a "right" for those who have played an active and powerful role in the strategic** *logos***.** If there was a crippling crisis in our technological society—possibly as a result of the imposition of a global climate-mitigation command economy—which could not be adequately resolved, the conquest strategy would re-emerge (as the only alternative strategy available) and "universal" justice would be dismantled.

In the provision of justice, consistency has always been a problem, reflecting the individual nature of the process and the role of corruption in society. Corruption is inversely related to the effectiveness of the rule of law; and the rule of law is a reflection of the type and effectiveness of the prevailing *logos* and the strategic institutions it generates (see Table 4.2). The degree of corruption is highest in societies where the prevailing *logos* concentrates power in the hands of a small proportion of the population—namely the conquest and early commerce societies—and lowest where power is more evenly distributed—namely in democratic, technological societies. And the degree of corruption is also highest in dysfunctional societies of any *logos* type. Yet, while corruption is minimised in functional, technological societies, it still exists. Also in advanced Western societies, the judiciary can act in idiosyncratic and nonstrategic ways. While the judiciary is properly independent of government in modern democracies, there is no way to ensure that it operates strategically if it is a power unto itself. How can the judiciary operate strategically? Possibly by making judges responsive to strategists through elections.

Table 4.2 Strategic Institutions—the past 100,000 years

Dynamic Strategy (*Logos* type)	Political System	Ruling Elite	Economic System	Constitutional and Legal System	Commodity Exchange	Factor Exchange	Property Rights	Risk Control	Social Intercourse
Family multiplication (Hunting *logos*)	Hunting band Tribal kingdom . Head of family Tribal chief	Hunter/warriors	Subsistence Barter	Tribal rights and privileges Family rights and privileges	Rules of barter	Nil	Traditional rights of land use Protection by tribal force	Kinship support Gift-giving Invoking of spirits	Taboos Tribal & family customs & codes of behaviour
Conquest (Military *logos*)	Kingdom Empire . Monarchy Dictatorship Oligarchy	Warrior elite Land-owning aristocracy	Centralised systems: Feudal/manorial Totalitarian	Divine right of kingship King's court Lords' courts	State marketing system Barter	Labour: coercive labour systems Capital: plunder Land: state control and distribution	Right of conquest Elite rights Protection by armed forces	Religious support Benevolence of elite Regional diversification	Codes of elite conduct Religious codes and laws
Commerce (Mercantile *logos*)	City-state Nation-state Empire . Merchant princes Councils elected by merchant elite	Merchant elite Upper middle class	State-controlled market systems	Limited constitution Courts for middle classes	Private monopoly marketing system Guilds Codes of merchant conduct	Regulated markets: Labour: master & servant regulations Capital: usury laws Land: ownership restrictions	Extensive rights for middle class over real & financial capital Protection of law—restricted	Charity Insurance on mercantile operations Limited state assistance	Criminal & commercial laws Religious codes & laws
Technological (Enterprise *logos*)	Nation-state Mega-state . Parliamentary democracy Universal franchise	Business/labour interests Consumer class	Free market system Various degrees of state intervention	People's constitution Universal court system	Free markets State regulation: tariff protection prices surveillance consumer protection	Free markets State regulation: wages policy workers compensation immigration central banking money markets	Universal rights over all forms of property Protection of law—universal	Widespread insurance against loss, damage, etc. of all types of property, life, contingencies Extensive state compensation Welfare Economic regulation	Criminal & civil laws Arbitration & small claims regulations Family laws Secular codes of conduct

Source: Snooks, *Ephemeral Civilization* (1997: 56-7).

The role of **the church** has changed considerably since the Industrial Revolution began in Britain about 1780. Prior to this great technological paradigm shift in Western Europe, the Christian church provided the strategic ideology for the commerce *logos* and, before the fifteenth century, for the conquest *logos*. This proved challenging for the church. While it claimed to uphold a system of morality granted by God through His Son Jesus—consisting of faith, hope, and charity—and to safe-guard the souls of its flock, the church was also called upon to provide access to a strategic guardian who would ensure their society's material success. Members of the same aristocratic families provided sons who went into both the strategic "business" (conquest or commerce) and into the church (to ensure God's support of the family business). Needless to say, church morality was usually subordinated to strategic ethics, with the result that many churchmen lived dissolute lives just like their brothers in the family strategic business. While the church's two distinct functions were resolved in favour of their society's strategic activities—the only reason the state and wealthy strategists supported it financially on a generous scale—there were times when leading churchmen made the mistake of upholding God's law rather than that of the king or prince. In such cases the "meddlesome priests" were summarily removed—for example, Henry II had Thomas Becket murdered in 1170 for choosing God over king

Since the Industrial Revolution, the role of the church has been transformed. "God is dead" precisely because the modern technological *logos* has no need of the old Christian strategic guardian or His strategic ideology. The new strategic ideology is a belief in the effectiveness of science—the ideology of "scientism"—in supporting the industrial technological strategy. Accordingly, the church has been relegated to a minor role in society, more akin to the early nonstrategic community created by Jesus of Nazareth. It would appear to be a matter of "in my beginning is my end". Christianity now caters for those who are unable to come to grips with the real strategic meaning of life; those who use it as a way of resolving the problem of reconciling what they actually do and what they believe they ought to do (owing to an ineffectual existential schizophrenia mechanism); and those who have failed strategically in life. Yet, even in these less conflicted circumstances, a disturbingly large proportion of churchmen (and, no doubt, churchwomen) fail to live up to the church's ethical, or even decent secular, standards.

Finally, **the media** plays an important role in a democratic society; namely that of strategic communication. Major media outlets—newspapers, television, and radio—help to provide a flow of information between strategic leaders and strategists. And with "talk-back" radio and, more recently, social media, this information flow works both ways. This is an essential function in a democratic society, by which strategists can make their interests and requirements known to strategic leaders—essential if leaders are to facilitate these requirements—and by which leaders can explain their strategic initiatives and directives to society's strategists. Of course, in undemocratic societies, the media is employed as an organ of state propaganda; and social media is tightly controlled, as in China today.

But if this strategic communication is to work effectively, the media, both traditional and "social", needs to adhere consistently to established and workable rules of conduct. The usual rules of conduct include: accuracy, fairness, balance, transparency, disinterestedness, and the priority of public interest. While these standards are generally respected in democratic countries, there are regular instances of misconduct, owing to the political bias of members of media organisations—arising from the intervention of self-interested media owners or from the political culture of journalists in a media organisation—and a desire to become players in the political game as well as observers and reporters. It should be recognised that truth is rarely the objective of the media, and is usually an early casualty in the pursuit of influence and profits.

Social media is a new and disturbing agent in human communication. There are, as yet, few rules of conduct and even these seem to be over looked in a depressing flood of anonymous, irrational, irresponsible, and vindictive rant. This form of expression demonstrates the irrationality and darkness of human nature when operating in unrestrained environments. Never before has it been so easy for social and behavioural scientists to observe aspects of human nature formerly hidden from public view. This medium has considerable potential for strategic communication, and is being used increasingly by strategic leaders, but so far it has been largely misused in an orgy of narcissistic self-indulgence.

The government

The reason for the emergence and maintenance of government is to provide strategic leadership. Basically, strategic leadership involves facilitating the objectives of society's dynamic strategists, who are responding to the requirements of the *logos*. This is achieved by coordinating the efforts of the strategists, directly through government directives and incentives, and indirectly through cultural institutions such as religion, ideology, and the arts. In particular, the state provides basic infrastructure that is beyond the financial resources of individuals and corporations; it negotiates political and economic deals with other societies; it protects the dynamic strategy (and, hence, the strategic *logos*) at home and abroad; it encourages the resurgence of old unexhausted strategies, or the emergence of new strategies if the former have been exhausted, during recessions and depressions; and it provides basic facilities for the education, training, and research required to nourish the prevailing dynamic strategy. It also helps to establish the rules of strategic conduct.

This is a proactive rather than a passive role, and it is provided by representatives of the strategists for the benefit of the strategists. It is a role that changes with the nature of the strategic *logos* and the consequent strategy being pursued (see Table 4.2). Under the hunting *logos* (family-multiplication strategy), strategic leadership is provided by family heads and tribal leaders; under the military *logos* (conquest strategy), leadership is provided by warrior kings, dictators, or republican oligarchs; under the mercantile *logos* (commerce strategy), leadership is provided by merchant princes or ruling councils elected by the merchant elite; and under the enterprise *logos* (technological strategy), leadership is provided by democratically elected parliaments. The origin and maintenance of government, therefore, is strategic in nature, not the outcome of a social contract as theorised about by Hobbes and Rousseau.

To undertake a successful strategic pursuit, with a flourishing *logos*, strategic leaders listen carefully to what strategists in their society say they need to meet their goals, and these leaders respond objectively to what they hear. That is the ideal. Unfortunately, the modern world has lost sight of the type of leadership that underpinned the emergence of great civilizations in the past. Instead of seeing themselves as facilitators of their society's longrun dynamic strategy, and supporters of its driving strategists, contemporary governments have focused upon intervening in this process in a piecemeal and short-run manner in response to vocal minorities that are seen as electoral threats. The outcome is the disruption of longrun strategic interests in favour of short-run trendy ideas and ideologies. As a consequence, the greatest challenge facing the modern world is not the antistrategic attacks in advanced societies by fundamentalists from the Middle East, but rather the antistrategic climate-mitigationists from advanced Western societies. If the radical mitigationists have their way, and a global command economy is established (the only way radical mitigation measures can be effective), the transition from exhausting industrial technological paradigm to forthcoming Solar Revolution will stall and lead to a major long-term economic, social, and political crisis. To avoid this, Western governments will need to rediscover the lost art of strategic leadership.

What are the virtues of strategic leadership; how are they distorted; and how can they be recovered? The virtues for a strategic leader are:

- A determination to serve the interests of his society (which is an expression of the *logos*) even if doing so does not maximise his material interests. Hopefully, doing the "right" strategic thing should not minimise his interests, otherwise potentially effective leaders will not want the job.

- The strategic vision to be able to understand that his responsibility is to the strategists, both as producers and consumers, and to achieve a balance between their interests. The strategists are agents of the *logos*.

- The strength of mind and will to resist pressure from minority groups pushing ideologically-driven antistrategic interests.

- The integrity necessary to avoid corruption, which undermines the strategic interests of society and disrupts the *logos*.

- The determination to act, and see that the entire administration acts, in a fair and just way; not because fairness and justice have intrinsic value—are good in themselves—but because it is "good" for the strategic pursuit; "good" for the survival and prosperity of the entire society and of its individual members.

These strategic leadership virtues are always liable to distortion owing to a failure of strategic vision, strategic resolve, and personal integrity. Leaders are subject to all the deficiencies and flaws of human nature. In particular the loss of strategic vision is increasingly likely in the modern world, owing to a growing distance opening up between the strategists on the one hand and political leaders on the other. In earlier eras, political leaders were closely linked to their society's dynamic strategy. Leaders of conquest societies (such as Rome) were usually successful warriors, or, at least, came from military families; leaders of commerce societies (such as Venice) were usually highly successful and wealthy merchants; and leaders of early technological societies (nineteenth century Britain) were usually from successful and wealthy industrial families. In these earlier societies, strategic leaders were representatives of the strategic elite, who ruled their society in the economic interests of their strategic class.

In modern society, political leaders are usually trained in law or orthodox finance/economics, and have virtually no practical experience of their society's technological strategy. They do not come from the main strategic families in society, nor do they develop any understanding of strategic dynamics from their university training. They are preoccupied with static rather than dynamic concepts of society; such as balancing budgets, targeting inflation, and intervening in society to actually disrupt the dynamic strategic process. In a modern pluralistic society, it is necessary to train future political leaders in the strategic sources of their society's dynamics to make up for the deficiencies in their non-strategic background and their old-fashioned conventional training. This will not be an easy matter, as educational institutions are also stuck in the past, and have failed to provide society with a real understanding of itself.

A Working Model of Societal Ethics — Political Leadership Struggles

Political leadership struggles in Australia during the first half of the 2010s, provide deep insight into the real role played by ethical rules of conduct in modern society. This is because of the very transparent nature of political leadership struggles in a democratic society, which clearly show how humans respond in a competitive environment where the potential rewards are high. Similar struggles take place in other parts of society, but there are few observers as the media doesn't have the same access to players in the game of life, and even these observers are silenced by overly protective defamation laws. Australia has attracted international attention in this respect because it has experienced five changes of Prime Minister in just five years, with three of these changes resulting from coups within the ruling party (two in the Labour government and one, so far, in the Liberal-National government). I focus here on the last coup, which took place suddenly on 14th September 2015, less than two years after a resounding electoral victory by the now deposed Liberal Prime Minister.

A particularly intriguing feature of the 2015 coup is that it occurred less than a week before a by-election, which would have been the first real test of electorate attitudes for a struggling Prime Minister. I do not intend to analyse the reasons for the coup, apart from noting that it was driven by the personal ambitions of the Challenger who, six years earlier, had been replaced as opposition leader of the Liberal Party by the now deposed Prime Minister. My interest in this political struggle is in the distance between the *stated* and *actual* ethical values of the various participants, which were clearly exposed by a salivating media.

A good place to begin is the reporting of the stated ethical values of the young Candidate attempting to win the by-election for the ruling political party. The Candidate was a distinguished serving officer in the Australian army, who clearly embraces the values of service taught at military college and tested on the battlefield. Here is an extract from a speech reported in the media that he made on winning the by-election:

I go to Canberra as someone with much to learn. I don't understand every political process or issue and I don't intend to. But, I'll be guided by the values that have been tested in the defence of our nation and that I believe are essential to effective leadership— *honour, integrity, compassion, humility, and service.* I'll make mistakes like any new member of Parliament, but *I will always strive to do **the right thing***.(My emphasis)

Such sentiments are highly commendable, and would provide an excellent platform for conduct in the political arena, provided they are combined with a vision of strategic leadership. From time to time we hear similar, if less earnest, expressions of moral virtue from our politicians, although usually to justify questionable actions undertaken rather than as an ethical framework prior to taking up office. In particular, the electorate is constantly told by political leaders following a questionable action that it was "the right thing to do". This hackneyed response to criticism of their actions and policies is employed as a substitute for rational argument. When politicians cannot justify themselves on objective grounds—which is much of the time—they resort to taking the high moral ground and asserting that their course of action was "the right thing to do".

The question we need to ask is: How well did the ethical values of the political profession hold up during the 2015 struggle for the Prime-Ministership?

- It will come as no surprise that the first casualty of politics, as in all other areas of human activity, is **truth**. We are told that leadership bids have nothing to do with personal ambition or retribution; that old leaders are only deposed in the best interests of the Party and the country; and that all the coup plotters actually respect, if not love, the Old Leader, and feel deep compassion for him.

- In any leadership struggle, **loyalty** is redefined. When the numbers appear to be going against the Old Leader, most of those professing to support him begin to reconsider their positions. In 2015 the Old Leader's deputy—dubbed the "eternal deputy" by the media, as she had served under three different leaders in the past—promised her support to the Challenger (who she had abandoned at the change of leadership some six years earlier) in order to retain the deputy-leadership and her current portfolio (Minister for Foreign Affairs). Actually, as recently disclosed (December 2015), this deal was done some seven months before the coup, when the Challenger was testing the numbers for an attack. One of the duties of the Deputy Leader is to watch the back of the Prime Minister and to give advanced warning of any moves against him. Other cabinet members also did secret deals with the Challenger to either retain their old jobs or to gain more prestigious ones. It was said of one of these deserters, whose seat in Parliament was endangered, that he is "always on the winning side of every leadership spill". Amusingly, as could be seen through the tv camera, not all MPs who accompanied the Old Leader into the Party room prior to the secret leadership ballot, returned with him!

There were, to their credit, cabinet ministers who openly supported the Old Leader, and who walked with him both to and from the Party room ballot. But even these supporters refused to go voluntarily to the back bench to accompany their Old Leader. Instead, they fought to retain their old jobs, most without success, with one cynically explaining his actions in the Senate (or upper house) with the slogan: "the king is dead, long live the king"! One can only imagine what the Anglo-Saxon warrior who became a lonely "wanderer" when his lord was lost in battle, would have thought. (But, then, this Old English poem was a romanticised story, not reality.) So much, then, for the virtue of loyalty in politics and, by extension, in the rest of society. Curiously, one of the short-comings of which the Old Leader was subsequently accused, was an excess of loyalty shown doggedly to his friends and advisors in Parliament. This was not something the New Leader could be accused of, as he relegated his faithful "best friend in Parliament" to the backbench to make way for his new supporters.

- **Honesty,** we are told constantly, is a much valued virtue among politicians. Yet, the New Leader and the Deputy-Leader seem to have been economical and selective in their use of this virtue. Consistently, the Challenger denied categorically that he was interested in challenging for the leadership of his party, and, even if he were, he rated his chances of being successful as "near to zero". These denials were repeatedly made despite the fact that close associates have said that he had long held the ambition of being Prime Minister (a recent biography written before the coup was titled *Born to Rule*), and despite the recent (December 2015) revelation that he had actively been planning a coup with close colleagues, including the Deputy Leader, for more than seven months before he struck suddenly and without warning. Similarly, the Deputy Leader denied knowing anything about the forthcoming coup until she was approached by a number of senior colleagues on the weekend before it happened. We now learn that she knew of the plot some seven months before the coup took place, and was even aware that one of her chief staff members would be attending a meeting of conspirators the week before the coup. What happened to the virtue of honesty?

- **Honour** is also a virtue honoured more in the breach than in the observance. How honourable is it to barter support for the Leader in exchange for relatively well-paid and prestigious jobs? Would they not argue, in calmer times, that principle is more important than material well-being? Yet clearly the reverse was true when the chips were down. All the chief plotters in the coup, who symbolically accompanied the Challenger on his walk to the Party room showdown, received positions in the new ministry, even if one of their number was under investigation for an earlier moral and legal indiscretion for which he was later removed. And, as mentioned earlier, of the Old Leader's supporters, none went voluntarily with him to the backbench. The latter made it clear that jobs were more important than principle or friendship. Where is the honour here?

- **Compassion** is something only felt, if genuinely felt at all, after the dark deeds have been done. The Challenger, once he held the reins of power, told us that he felt considerable empathy for the loser, and praised all the good work he had done for the Party and the country over the previous six years. In public interviews, the Challenger expressed the belief that he possesses the virtues of empathy, respect, and humility. In his own words: "Losing the prime-ministership is tougher than losing the leadership of the opposition. I am very empathetic for him". Needless to say, the Challenger's professed empathy was not greater than his desire to get to the top, nor enough to prevent him from publicly destroying another person's career and life. Empathy was never in danger of turning into compassion, which may have required greater consideration of the consequences of political assassination. Quite clearly, empathy, which is not the same as compassion, is a feeling that has no impact on the way we conduct ourselves in the competitive environment of life. Self-interest will always trump empathy.

How does the claim that the Challenger felt great empathy square with his other claim in the media that the coup was "not personal, just business"? The New Leader was quick to assure the public that he was not motivated by feelings of hatred and vengeance over his own loss of leadership of the Party in opposition six year earlier. To the contrary, the coup was undertaken in the best interests of the Party and the country. His advice to the Old Leader was to get on with life and not let hatred consume him. Clearly these comments do not arise from empathy, let alone compassion.

- **Service** is clearly a subjective notion. What most politicians are referring to when they talk about "service", is not service to the society but service to themselves. The Challenger was quick to assure the public that the Old Leader should not get too upset about being forcibly removed from high office, because no one (except the new incumbent?) owns the prime-ministership, as the position is only taken "to serve others". Politicians are not being singled out here for special criticism. Remember, this political review is intended as a working model for the wider society. It shows openly what usually remains hidden. All humans are self-serving, to one degree or another.

- **Real political ethics** came under a very searching spotlight during the 2015 Australian leadership coup and its aftermath. Most players claimed to be motivated by ethical concerns, yet their actions clearly demonstrated that this was just not true (our first casualty). In the commentary that followed, it was interesting to hear the frank views of a former deputy leader of the ruling party. This frankness was only possible because he had retired a decade earlier and was no longer part of the competitive game of politics. He claimed, with an air of authenticity, that the Party offered rewards not for loyalty, but for being on the winning side. He further said that what the Party regarded as "right" was political success, and what it regarded as "wrong" was political failure. Needless to say, these are core strategic values, not "politically correct" metaphysical values. It brings us back full circle to the interpretation of virtue by the early Greeks.

To sum up: What, then, is the moral of this tale? Quite transparently, all the players in this political drama were pursing strategic desire—to maximise the probability of survival and prosperity—and were operating according to *strategic rules of conduct* rather than *metaphysical ethics*. This, however, is not to condemn them, as it is exactly what one should expect from strategic leaders in a successful dynamic society. The only critical observation I would make is that while they predictably conducted themselves according to the strategic rules of conduct, they pretended to be following a "higher" set of ethical principles. This practice is also normal for humanity that has difficulty facing the self-centredness of their daily actions. As we have seen, this is an outcome of an existential duality in our nature, which can only be resolved through the exercise of "existential schizophrenia" (the psychic mechanism behind hypocrisy). It is to deceive ourselves as much as to deceive others.

A PREVIEW OF "SUPRALOGOSIAN" ETHICS

Having sorted out the differences between metaphysical and strategic ethics, how are we to live our lives? As this matter is discussed in detail in the final chapter, only a preview is provided here, in order to place the conventional approach to ethics in a wider context. As the dynamic-strategy theoretical framework shows, the possible responses to life, which are driven by strategic *logos*, include: participating in it without reservation (as strategists); attempting to undermine it (as antistrategists); attempting to isolate oneself from it (as nonstrategists); or, wrestling it (as "supralogosians" — "individuals who reach beyond the *logos*"). In each case, the ethics adopted are a response to the *logos,* either positively or negatively. **The *logos* is the measure of all things.**

For those who find life to be absurd, meaningless, degrading, and mindless, but who don't wish to undermine it, or to put their heads in the sand, there is another way. It involves recognising the existence and role of the strategic *logos* in originating, sustaining, and transforming life, facing it squarely, and wrestling it in order to experience an honest and truthful way of life. This is the path of the supralogosian—the individual who aims to live beyond the limits of a world defined by the strategic *logos*; to acclimatise, like the lone alpine conifer, to the bracing heights.

The most important issue in life for the *logos*-wrestler is the search for truth. This involves a life-long attempt to discover the meaning of life in both a general and individual sense. It means following the search wherever it might lead despite all the risks involved. The other **supralogosian virtues**, which are essential to this journey, are loyalty, honesty, courage, and moderation. It is essential to realise that these virtues are aspirational and difficult to follow, owing to the fact that human nature has been developed as a strategic, not a moral, instrument. The central issue for the supralogosian individual is the struggle rather than the achievement.

Ultimate Reality

Chapter Five
Evil

Since the beginning of civilization, the philosophical issue that has most exercised the minds of thinkers and ordinary people alike has been how to lead a good life. The question of evil has attracted less attention. While evil in a metaphysical sense has always been recognised and discussed in a theological context, evil in an existential sense is a modern preoccupation. While this chapter deals briefly with metaphysical evil—often called "the broad concept of evil"—its main focus is on existential evil as it has been discussed in premodern and modern times. As will become clear, the modern discussion of existential evil—often called "the narrow concept of evil"—is detailed, fragmented, and contentious. The reason for this is that contemporary thinkers have failed to develop a comprehensive and integrated theory of evil. In redressing the balance, this chapter presents a holistic theory of both evil and good.

PREMODERN DISCUSSION OF EVIL

While most premodern thinkers viewed evil in metaphysical terms, some, such as the early Greeks and Chinese Taoists, thought of it in more secular and existential terms. A brief outline follows.

The Ancient Greeks

Good and evil, as shown in the last chapter, were viewed by the early Greeks in terms of the impact that an individual's actions had on society. A good person was "brave and capable" and had a positive and favourable influence on the Greek city-state; whereas an evil person was "cowardly and incapable" and had a negative and unfavourable strategic influence. Gradually this strategic approach to good and evil was transformed into metaphysical terms. The Thracian philosopher

Democritus (c.460–370 BC), remembered primarily for his theory of atoms, contributed to this development, which reached its pinnacle in the work of Plato (c.428–347).

While the Form of the Good is the transcendent principle of all goodness in **Plato's** metaphysical theory of Forms, he fails to examine the problem of evil in a similar way. Men commit evil (*kakos*) acts because they wilfully fail to develop their spirit and reason sufficiently to overcome their sensual desires. The main reason for the dominance of desire over reason is, according to Socrates and Plato, human ignorance. They believed that no one who knows better will deliberately commit evil acts—"virtue is wisdom". It was in order to compensate for the ignorance of the majority in society that Plato saw a role in the *Republic* for the guardians under the wise rule of the philosopher-king, who had achieved control over self. Similarly, **Aristotle** argued that virtue was the outcome of a disciplined nurturing of reason and wisdom. In other words, according to the Socratic school of thought, good and evil were the outcome of human qualities. But, as will be demonstrated, this supply-side theory is unable to account for changes over time in the interpretations of good and evil.

Europe in the Middle-Ages

While early Christian thinkers were influenced by classical Greek philosophers—particularly Plato and Aristotle—they rejected the notion that individuals alone were responsible for good and evil. **Augustine of Hippo** (354–430) argued that owing to "original sin", human nature was transformed, so that all mankind from the time of the Fall was condemned to live in sin, owing to the "privation of that which is good" (known as "concupiscence", or tendency toward evil). Accordingly, humans are totally depraved, lack the ability to do good, and are unable to respond to the will of god without divine grace. As written in Ephesians (2: 8&9) in the King James Bible: "For by grace are ye saved through faith; and not of yourselves: it is the gift of God: not of works, lest any man should boast". Original sin was the outcome of the seduction of Adam and Eve by the Devil into disobeying a direct order from God not to eat of the tree of knowledge.

For turning away from God, Adam and Eve's former perfection was lost and their sinful nature was passed onto all succeeding generations of mankind. Could this be a parable also about the thinker who defies the *logos* in search of the truth?

This Augustine concept of original sin has been responded to in different ways by different Christian sects at different times in history. Although Western Christianity, after much heated debate, generally accepted this doctrine, different factions within the church emphasised or omitted different aspects of it. **Anselm of Canterbury** (1033–1109) separated original sin from Augustinian concupiscence by defining it as "privation of the righteousness that every man ought to possess"; **Thomas Aquinas** (1225–1274) argued that the supernatural powers possessed by Adam and Eve before the Fall were lost, but their natural powers of will, passion, and reason were retained so that mankind could respond fully to God's call; following Aquinas, the **Roman Church** insisted that while man's nature was weakened and inclined to evil owing to the Fall, he does not personally bear the guilt of Adam and Eve; the protestants **Martin Luther** (1483–1546) and **John Calvin** (1509–1564) reaffirmed the Augustinian concept of man's inherent evil and inability to do good except through the grace of God and redemption by Christ; and the **Eastern Orthodox Church** accepted that human nature is sinful but rejected Augustine's concept of original sin and hereditary guilt.

Overall, the Christian church views good and evil in an entirely metaphysical light. Good is the monopoly of God, and is something the human race can never attain on its own. Evil is something that owes its origin to Satan, who is the leader of the rebellious fallen angles, and has characterised the nature of man ever since the Fall when Adam and Eve succumbed to the Devil's seductions. Mankind's only hope for salvation from sin and evil is by redemption through the sacrifice of Jesus Christ, which is the outcome of the grace of God, and not of any independent action by human individuals. As suggested in the earlier chapter on ethics, this medieval view of good and evil is very different to that of the ancient Greeks, because it was a response to a different dynamic strategy and to a different strategic *logos*.

Eastern Religions

In the matter of evil, eastern religions can be divided into two main groups: those that interpret the world in terms of absolute good and evil; and those that view evil as an outcome of human free will. Zoroastrianism and Hinduism can be included in the first category, and Islam and Buddhism in the second.

Zoroastrianism had its origins in the vision received by Zarathustra (or Zoroaster in Greek) from the Persian god Ahura Mazda, who directed the prophet to receive and preach the revealed truth. This probably occurred in the early seventh century BC. As Zarathustra lived during a time of economic and social chaos in Persia, he unsurprisingly associated order with Truth and chaos with the Lie. In his search for the truth, Zarathustra abandoned the pantheon of Iranian strategic guardians and elevated the chief amongst them, Ahura Mazda, to the supreme position of the One God of the cosmos, who at the end of time would triumph over evil and chaos personified by the Lie. To Zarathustra, the world of the senses was merely a stage on which the great metaphysical battle between good (Truth) and evil (Lie) could take place. These absolute characteristics that rule the world are embodied by the divine beings Ahura Mazda (good/Truth) and Ahriman (evil/Lie). On the last day of this world, Ahura Mazda will finally triumph over Ahriman and his evil followers, leaving the Wise Lord in complete command of his creation. Evil in Zarathustra's world, therefore, is absolute, but will finally be vanquished.

Hinduism, which is based on a large number of ancient texts (the Vedas, the Upanishads, the Epics, and the Puranas), possesses a variety of responses to the problem of evil. The main ones are outlined here. The Puranas and the Vedas view existence as a constant struggle between order and chaos, whereby some of the gods attempt to maintain divine order in the face of an onslaught from demons, determined to create chaos. In this divine struggle, some gods (particularly Vishnu) represent good and the demons represent evil. Other gods, such as the creator god Brahma, are responsible for creating evil as well as good, owing to the need to provide dynamic tension in the Universe. As the divinities are present in each human being, the eternal struggle between good and evil is acted out also at the individual level.

Hinduism also tells a story about the fall of mankind from an original life of virtue. It would seem that most religions find it difficult to believe that a divine creation could have come into existence accompanied by the stain of evil. The Hindu "fall" occurred when demons destroyed the Golden Age of peace, causing men to act in evil ways. Evil arises when dharma, which is the natural force of virtue that permeates the Universe, is rejected. Those individuals who violate dharma accrue negative karma that will cause evil to visit them in the future. Owing to the Hindu belief in rebirth, unhappy events experienced in this life may be the result of evil acts in a previous life.

Buddhism claims that good and evil are innate and can be found in every person. Evil is said to have three roots—greed, hatred, and delusion—which are characteristics of everyman. These three roots, which are generated by desire or mental dysfunction, bring suffering (Dukkha) to afflicted individuals, and to others with whom they have contact. Dukkha can be removed by overcoming delusion or ignorance and by controlling basic desire. Good in Buddhism, therefore, is a negative quality involving three "wholesome" roots of non-greed, non-hatred, and non-delusion. This negation of evil can be achieved through mental cultivation (right effort, mindfulness, and concentration), the exercise of ethical conduct (right speech, action, and livelihood), and wisdom (right understanding and intention). In other words, goodness and happiness can be achieved through the control, if not the elimination, of desire by the use of reason. Budda (Prince Gautama Siddhartha, c.563–c.483 BC), therefore, had much in common with Plato: both were antistrategists, because to eliminate desire is to destroy the driving force in life.

Islam has no role for original sin—as Allah forgave Adam and Eve—or absolute evil. God is the source of all good in the world. Mankind is naturally inclined to do good, because this potential was part of God's creation; a potential that can be fulfilled because of the availability of God's love and mercy. God has also made it possible for individuals to come closer to him—this is the meaning of life—by instituting the test of choosing between good and evil thoughts and deeds. Every good act allows a person to rise through the stations of closeness to God, whereas every evil act causes a person to move further from God. In contrast to Christianity, good works are pleasing to God. Where then does this leave extreme Islamic terrorists?

What are the origins of evil in Islam? While people are naturally inclined to do good, there are two forces constantly at work in the world that lead people into evil activity. One is Satan (or Shaytan) and the other is human desire. Satan's power is limited to that of seducer, and he can be resisted by seeking refuge in God. There is no epic struggle between God and Satan in Islam, as there is in Zoroastrianism. The choice between good and evil is a matter of choice for each individual, who has been granted free will by God. In the final analysis, good and evil arise from human nature, even if influenced by God and Satan. But this is so only because God has created the world in this way.

Ancient Chinese Philosophy

Chinese conception of good and evil is relativist rather than absolute. The two main schools of thought are Confusion and Taoist. In the **Confusion school**, mainly as a result of Mencius (c.371–c.289 BC), good and evil are seen as responses of human nature to its natural and social environments. Mencius argued that man's original nature is good, but that if he is constantly subjected to negative influences in society, evil will emerge. In order for good to triumph over evil, the individual needs to cultivate positive aspects in his life. The role of education is to bring out the innate goodness of human nature. But there were opposing views. Other Confusion scholars argue that Mencius was mistaken and that human nature is innately evil (Hsu Tzu, c.298–238 BC), or that human nature is not yet good, but can be trained to be so (Tung Chung-Shu, c.179–c.104 BC). A more recent Confusionist, Xun Zi (1130–1200), like Hsu Tzu, also argued that human nature is driven by self-interest and greed; and they both believed that the role of education was to transform human nature rather than to cultivate it.

In **Taoism**, it is believed that everything has its own "course of nature", or Tao, and that those who follow their Tao will become good and those who reject their Tao will become evil. This view implies that human nature is basically good, and only becomes evil when an individual deliberately goes against his true calling. But, as we have come to expect, there is no consensus in Chinese philosophy. Su Shih (1036–1101), for example, argued that as far as the principle of yin-yang is concerned, man's original nature is neither good nor evil; it is only by "putting our nature into practice" that either good or evil emerges. The Way, or Tao, is determined by the alternation of yin (negative) and yang (positive), which provides the basis for the dynamics of life. So it is with good and evil—the existence of one implies the existence of the other; nothing is absolute. Whatever the original nature of man—innately good or evil—it is possible through dedicated self-cultivation and enlightened education to ensure that good triumphs over evil. And following the Way leads to ultimate truth, which, to the Taoist, is the Supreme Being.

MODERN DISCUSSIONS OF EVIL

While evil is still discussed by religious thinkers in metaphysical terms, most modern scholars see evil as a secular and existential issue. High profile genocides in the twentieth and twenty-first centuries have focussed the attention of philosophers on the issue of evil in the world, even though our species has committed mass slaughter of peoples ever since we eliminated the Neanderthals in Europe and the Middle East some 40,000 years ago (See my book *Dead God Rising*, 2010, ch. 2). Mass slaughter in the pre-modern world caused little comment, because it was associated with the conquest strategy pursued to survive and prosper. But by the turn of the twentieth century the conquest strategy had been displaced by the technological strategy, which made it theoretically possible for viable modern societies to survive and prosper without resorting to conquest and its heavy and systematic loss of life. Conquest and genocide in the technological era have been undertaken only by irrational (because it is not a sustainable economic option) antistrategic societies as the outcome of major disorienting crises. It is eye-opening to review the worst of these campaigns of carnage.

Owing to excessive competition in the twentieth century between technological societies in Europe, fuelled by paranoid leadership in Germany, a highly destructive and destabilising war (1914–1918) broke out in Europe. The effects of that war, together with the punitive reparations imposed by the victors on Germany, led to a crippling economic crisis in that country, which in turn allowed antistrategists led by Adolf Hitler to hijack German society and to pursue an irrational conquest strategy. As conquest is not a sustainable strategy in the technological era, the "thousand-year" Third Reich lasted a mere 12 years. But during those 12 years (particularly between 1942 and 1945), the Nazi regime murdered about six million Jews, together with as many as five million Romani (Gypsy), "incurably sick" Germans, Communists, homosexuals, Poles, and Soviet prisoners of war.

While Nazi genocide caused the most outrage during the twentieth century, other major genocides were committed by other antistrategic European countries that also emerged owing to war-induced crisis. Stalin, who in the early 1920s ruthlessly rose to control the antistrategic USSR, was responsible for the deaths of between 20 and 50 million people, through forced collectivisation (late 1920s), deliberate famines (1932–1934), brutal labour camps, the "Great Terror" of 1937–1938, and other political executions. Also in the early twentieth century (between 1915 and 1923), Turkey turned against its non-Muslim minorities, killing between 800,000 and 1,500,000 Armenians, 275,000 to 750,000 Assyrians, and 200,000 to 1,000,000 Greeks.

Later in the twentieth century, communist-inspired genocide returned to the world in a series of dysfunctional antistrategic societies, with Pol Pot murdering one to three million Cambodians between 1975 and 1979 (a gruesome reality disputed by radicals like Noam Chomsky); with Mengistu Haile Mariam responsible for the "Red Terror" in Ethiopia, killing 30,000 to 500,000 people; and with Mao Zedong, in a war against Chinese peasants between 1958 and 1962, responsible for the deaths of between 45 and 60 million people—the greatest mass slaughter in history.

Needless to say, this is not a complete catalogue of world genocide over the past century, but even so it includes the deaths of around 124 million people at the hands of murderous antistrategic dictators. There are many more cases of smaller but still significant episodes arising from the barbarous, callus, and uncaring treatment of minorities, particularly in Africa by both colonial and indigenous regimes. This extends right up to the moment of writing this chapter, with many thousands of people in Iraq and Syria being butchered by Islamic extremists (ISIL) and even by the murderous government of Syria. Western attacks against these extremists have also caused significant casualties, although not as deliberate acts of genocide. But my point has been made clearly enough. Even in our modern technological era, massive murderous acts against humanity have been, and continue to be, perpetrated. This surely needs to be described for what it is: **evil on a massive and continuing scale**. This, then, is the background against which modern philosophers have discussed the issue of evil in the world.

Modern Origins

The first Western philosopher to develop a purely secular theory of evil was **Immanuel Kant** (1724–1804), who argued that humans have the propensity (the will) for both good and evil, and that we are free to decide which path we will take. Good and evil are not the outcome of divine or other supernatural forces. His explanation of evil, although secular, is as usual a supply-side theory. Kant's theory of evil focuses on man's intent and ability to pursue either self-interest or moral law. The outcome of an individual's actions is irrelevant as to whether he is evil or good. A person deliberately pursing self-interest who thereby performs good works has, according to Kant, an evil will. Only a person who does good works because they are morally right, displays a good will. Kant recognises three stages in the process of evil corruption: the first concerns a person with a "weak" will, who wants to do good works, but fails owing to psychic frailty; the second concerns a person with an "impure" will, who does good works partly because they are morally right and partly out of self-interest; and the third and final stage concerns a person with a "perverse" will, who persistently elevates self-interest and self-love over moral law—this person, according to Kant, is thoroughly evil. Kant's personal view is that the third stage is the one most characteristic of humanity; that humans are, by nature, radically evil, in that we subordinate moral law to self-interest.

There are a number of major problems with Kant's theory of evil. First, there is the philosophical problem of what is, and how we are to know, "the moral law" in a theory that is meant to be secular. As Kant discounts the divine origins of moral law, he is left with the issue of elevating his person ethics to an absolute standard. Second, and of more interest to this book, Kant's theory of evil is antistrategic, antilogosian, and, hence, anti-life. As my entire empirical research program and the resulting realist general dynamic theory demonstrates, the driving force in life is strategic desire, which inextricably embodies self-interest. Moral codes are adapted by successful societies to accommodate the central role played by strategic desire in life. Only philosophers seem unaware of this critical issue. Any attempt to suppress strategic desire—as in Plato's *Republic*—would be doomed to failure. Ironically, those who have attempted to do so have been regarded as evil by strategic societies. In common with earlier metaphysical moral theories, Kant's is diametrically opposed to reality; a reality in which desires drive and ideas either facilitate or complicate.

Response to Genocide

Kant's theory of evil, of course, predates the regular and massive genocide events of the technological era, but he influenced modern theories that did address this monstrous exercise in evil. The first significant philosophical response to genocide in the twentieth century was made by **Hanna Arendt** (1906–1975) with the publication of *Origins of Totalitarianism* (1951) and *Eichmann in Jerusalem* (1963). These works make an important contribution to the analysis of evil in the modern world, even if her analysis of totalitarianism can be disputed. Totalitarianism was in reality, the outcome of the collapse of strategic societies (Germany and Russia) at critical stages of their economic transitions owing to the impact of the First World War (see my book *Ephemeral Civilization*, 1997), rather than to forces underlying the rise of antisemitism, racism, imperialism, and "mass man".

In *Origins of Totalitarianism*, Arendt argues that evil took on a "radical" new form in Nazi and Stalinist society. While she employs the term "radical evil", as did Kant, Arendt employs it in a different way. Rather than referring to the elevation of self-interest over moral law as in Kant's theory, Arendt sees radical evil as the outcome not of self-interest, but of the fanatical desire for total control over the lives of other people. This dehumanising process, she argued, was the essence of totalitarianism.

Yet, in reality, totalitarianism was all about maximising the self-interest of the antistrategists. In order for the antistrategists to successfully hijack a crisis-ridden strategic society and to expropriate the surpluses of that society, they needed to overwhelm and control the strategists and to substitute a bureaucratic, rule-based economic system for the former market-based system. The antistrategists were rent-seekers who needed to control the former strategic profit-seekers. This was not control for the sake of control, but control to create and maintain an antistrategic society that would meet the self-interest of the antistrategists. Both antistrategic and strategic societies are driven by the universal motive of strategic desire. It is the high degree of centralised intervention required to make antistrategic societies work in the short-run (there is no way they can survive in the longrun as they have no directional strategic compass), that leads to human abuse and genocide.

In *Eichmann in Jerusalem*, Arendt turns her attention to the role of individual participants in the totalitarian system. Eichmann, who had played a prominent role in organising the deportation and transportation of German and European Jews to Nazi extermination camps, was captured by Israeli operatives (Mossad) in Buenos Aires, Argentina in May 1960. He was placed on trial in Jerusalem in 1961. Arendt was present at Eichmann's trial as a special reporter for the *New Yorker*. Her report surprised and shocked many of her readers. She concluded, after observing the former Nazi defend himself, that "desk murderers" like Eichmann were not psychotic, but "terrifyingly normal", and what they did was the outcome of "sheer thoughtlessness", which they attempted to justify by appealing to the very German ethical principle of "devotion to duty" (from Kant to Martin Heidegger, [1889–1976]—with whom Arendt, as a student, had an affair). Eichmann and many other Nazi bureaucrats represented what Arendt called "the banality of evil"; a condition beyond ordinary wrong-doing motivated by self-interest. It was an outcome of individuals accepting the duty of their role as a functionary in a brutal totalitarian system of murderous control.

How can Arendt's ideas be evaluated in the context of my dynamic-strategy theory? She has undoubtedly provided an interesting analysis of the way people, who might otherwise lead normal lives as "good" dutiful citizens, get drawn into the machinery of the antistrategic state by pursuing normal self-interest. Self-interest is not evil in itself (as Kant would have us believe), only when it is pursued blindly within an antistrategic society. The mistake people like Eichmann make is to view the antistrategic state in the technological age as the normal state. In the non-technological age, a conquest society could be regarded as normal—it was normal for its era—but in the technological age it is definitely abnormal and its values must be regarded as deviant and perverted. Certainly other technological societies saw Nazi Germany in this way. It would have required people like Eichmann to view Nazi values in a very self-contained and unhistorical light to regard Nazi Germany as a normal society in the mid-twentieth century. Nazi propaganda, of course, did not attempt to portray German society as normal for its time, but super-normal, and as part of a tradition that glorified its warrior/conquest past rather than its technological present. Nazi propaganda presented German values as different to those of other societies of the time; they were higher, harder values that were required to save Germany and the world from the "evil" weaker values of inferior races that were undermining the resolve of mankind to achieve its glorious destiny. Such an argument would never appeal to balanced, intelligent, and imaginative people, which is why they were the first to be eliminated by the Nazis. But it worked for the rest. **Evil flourishes where desire dominates reason in antistrategic societies.**

If it is impossible to pursue the normal strategic objective of self-interest in an antistrategic society without participating in evil, what options are available to individuals caught up in this process? There are four broad possibilities. The first is to do what thousands of heroic Germans—intellectuals and activists—did when the Nazis came to power, and that was to speak and act out against the antistrategic regime. Most of these principled people were captured, tortured, sent to concentration camps, and brutally executed. While this resistance is high commendable, it is not an option for the entire population as it subverts the objective of life, which is to survive and prosper. The second is to do what the large majority of German people did, and that is just to go along with the antistrategic state, participate in the material and patriotic returns from conquest (up to 1942) and suffer the reverses. The third is to do what a minority of especially ambitious and greedy Germans did, and that is to actively participate in the machinery of repression and control. Some of these committed Nazis were tried for war crimes following Hitler's defeat. The fourth is to do what some religious and other ideological groups did, and that is to create their own nonstrategic communities as a buffer against an oppressive antistrategic state. The latter is particularly interesting, because it is exactly what small nonaligned communities within those societies dominated by repressive regimes have always done. An example is the nonstrategic community established by Jesus of Nazareth in Palestine when it was under the repressive control of Imperial Rome. Clearly people like Eichmann took the third of these options, in a context where there were other options available. Individuals in category three deliberately chose the path of evil.

During the later twentieth and the early twenty-first centuries, an increasing number of philosophers have given attention to the issue of evil in the modern world. This work is detailed, fragmented and contentious. This is the legacy of a failure to develop a general theory about society and the way its moral values are determined. There is no contemporary consensus over whether evil is the outcome of evil character (imbedded in human nature) or of evil action (the product of the circumstances and frequency of bad works); whether evil is a distinct category of wrong-doing, or just the worst kind of wrong-doing; whether or not evil requires the existence of harm; whether or not evil action requires evil motivation (shades of Kant) and intent to do harm; whether or not evil-doers are sane and can be held responsible for their evil actions; whether or not evil-doers can be absolved because of abusive or neglectful early lives. In other words, contemporary analysis of evil has become part of the usual academic game of unrealistic and unhelpful disputation.

A NEW THEORY OF EVIL

The central problem in the history of ideas concerning the origin and nature of evil is the failure to provide a credible theory. While it is a simple matter to give a graphic account of man's inhumanity, thinkers down through the ages have found it difficult to define evil let alone explain how it might arise. We have seen that pre-modern thinkers have looked to supernatural forces to explain what appears to be inexplicable, and even modern thinkers who adopt a secular approach have difficulty accounting for the moral laws used as a standard for evaluating the seriousness of wrong-doing. My argument is that the origin and nature of what we call "evil" can only be satisfactorily explained by employing a realist general dynamic theory of life.

The Dimensions of Evil

The dynamic-strategy theory tells us that in reality there is no universal or absolute standard of evil. The regular and systematic slaughter of large numbers of people that today appears to shock people living in technological societies was, for most of human history, considered to be normal and morally acceptable. It is sobering to realise that the era of conquest has accounted for over 96 percent of the history of civilization, which began in the Middle East some 5,500 years ago. In the great conquest societies of the ancient and medieval worlds, slaughtering large numbers of people was considered to be "just business", because it was the most effective way of generating economic growth in those times. If a society wanted to increase its wealth, population, and power significantly higher than could be achieved through the practice of agriculture—as all societies did—then conquest was the strategy they needed to ruthlessly pursue. The only alternative strategy was commerce, and it was available only to those societies in protected regions dominating trading routes; whenever commerce societies came into conflict with conquest societies, they were swept away. The conquest strategy required a society to conduct continuous warfare against its neighbours to gain new lands, slaves, loot, and wives. In turn, this required large-scale human slaughter on an annual basis. Such a society regarded the qualities needed to be successful in the brutal dynamic strategy of conquest—strength, courage, and ruthlessness in battle—as the qualities of a "good", not an evil person.

Only technological societies, which no longer need to pursue conquest in order to survive and prosper, regard large-scale human slaughter as morally unacceptable. Conquest in the technological era is just not as economical in achieving survival and prosperity as is industrial innovation; otherwise our attitude would be no different from the ancients. Interestingly, we do not regard as evil the brutal military actions that we undertake in order to defend ourselves from would-be conquerors (as in the First and Second World Wars), or even to proactively defend our technological strategy (as in Vietnam in the 1960s and 1970s, or in the Middle East from the 1990s to the present). Or, at least, not until these actions fail in cost-benefit terms, or impose unacceptably on our civil liberties (conscription). Life is all about survival and prosperity, not metaphysical ethics.

One further historical example (and there are many more) will help to make my point; and that is the vexed issue of slavery. While modern technological societies regard slavery as inhuman, for the vast majority (over 96 percent) of the existence of human civilization it was regarded as a normal part of life (as late as the 1860s in the southern states of America) and completely consistent with human and even Christian moral values. Why? Because slavery was an essential component of the conquest strategy, and a significant component of plantation economies even in the early technological era. Pre-modern conquest societies were only able to grow rapidly by forcibly acquiring land, labour, and capital from surrounding societies. As people initially had to be forced into the expanding conquest system of an aggressively ambitious neighbour, they became part of a coercive, rather than a voluntary, labour system; but even then there were regular ways in which acclimatised slaves could gain their freedom and join the ranks of the strategists. Even pre-modern Western commerce societies—such as ancient Greece, Venice (as late as the fifteenth century), Britain (which engaged in the Atlantic slave trade, and did not abolish slavery in the Empire until 1833), and most other European nations—embraced slavery, because they also employed military action to acquire colonies needed to expand their trading empires and to acquire slaves in the process. Until very recently, therefore, the world has condoned a large-scale system of slavery, which was considered not only economically necessary, but morally acceptable.

Yet slavery is regarded by modern technological society as morally bad—indeed evil. Whether we like it or not, the only reason for this attitude is that in a technological society, slavery is not required to generate sustained economic growth. The American Civil War was relentlessly pursued at great cost by the Northern industrial states, not to free black slaves, but to impose the Northern dynamic strategy (a mega internal market) on the Southern States (see my book *Ephemeral Civilization*, 1998: ch.11). The story about going to war to free the slaves is convenient propaganda for the current leader of the free world. As the US still had large numbers of plantation and domestic slaves (some 4 million, or 12.6 percent of the total population, in 1860) a mere 150 years ago, they are not about to abandon this moral myth for the truth (which is why North American academics attempted to ignore my analysis of this issue in *Ephemeral Civilization*). Here we have "existential schizophrenia" on a national scale.

This historical account of conquest and slavery has interesting implications for the future. If the technological strategy was ever derailed in the future, the world could revert to conquest as the only viable dynamic strategy available. If this did come to pass, the large-scale slaughter and the enslavement of people could re-emerge. This is already happening in the Middle East, where societal chaos has seen the menacing emergence of the caliphate of Islamic State. It is essential that we do not unintentionally create the conditions for chaos by intervening massively in the dynamics of the strategic *logos*. My point in raising this scenario yet again, is that so-called moral values are not evolving as many rather curiously believe (how do they account for continuing conquest, genocide, and slavery?), but are a response to the requirements of the *logos*. What this means for the way concepts like good and evil are regarded by societies rather than metaphysical thinkers, is that they are relative—relative to the nature of the prevailing strategic *logos*, and to the dynamic strategy it is pursuing. In no sense are human moral values and ethics evolving. They are Janus like—capable of changing abruptly both backwards and forwards.

Strategic Definition of Evil

The only way the concept of evil can be scientifically defined is in terms of the values and ethics of specific strategic societies and, hence, their strategic *logoi*. Absolute "moral laws" cannot be defined scientifically, as divine or supernatural forces cannot be empirically verified. Strategic societies have always regarded the plans and actions of antistrategic individuals, groups, or societies as evil, because they are directed at undermining or overthrowing the existing strategic *logos* as well as seriously harming its citizens. For example, Egyptian society described the antistrategic pharaoh Akhenaten (c.1352–1336 BC), who discarded the old strategic guardians in favour of the single sun god Aten, as a criminal (i.e. evil); Rome described those following the antistrategic early Christian ideology as "atheists" (disbelievers in the pagan strategic guardians); President George W. Bush labelled the antistrategic societies of Iran, Iraq, and North Korea as the "axis of evil"; Australian Prime Minister Tony Abbott habitually referred to the terrorist Islamic State as the "death cult" (to be antistrategic is to be anti-life); and more recently (December 2015), President Obama, echoing his former Australian colleague, called ISIL the "cult of death"; and the current Australian Prime Minister Malcolm Turnbull went further, calling Islamic terrorism in Paris (November 2015) "the work of the Devil". Evil, therefore, has always been defined by strategic societies as those ideas and actions that seriously threaten and undermine the *logos*, the giver of life.

The Dynamic-Strategy Theory of Evil

Evil, according to the dynamic-strategy theory, is not embodied in human nature, nor is it the outcome of demonic metaphysical forces, but rather it is a predictable response to strategic circumstances that generate what I call "strategic frustration". Strategic frustration operates at both the individual and societal levels, and it is the outcome of leadership failure (at the organisational and societal levels), invasions, major wars, and major natural calamities (real or imagined).

Strategic frustration

The concept of "strategic frustration" first emerged from my analysis of strategic leadership and its failure in the modern world, in my book *The Global Crisis Makers* (2000). Strategic frustration refers to the psychological response of individuals, groups, and societies to persistent barriers raised against their participation in the strategic pursuit. In essence, it is the outcome of the denial of the powerful force of strategic desire. It is the opposite of strategic satisfaction, which is the balanced state of mind achieved in individuals and groups when they are able to participate freely and fully in the strategic pursuit.

Failure of modern strategic leadership

When I coined this term (in the initial form, "frustration of the strategists") in 2000, I saw it as a modern phenomenon, occurring at the societal level, where a significant gap can emerge under critical circumstances between the strategic expectations of individuals throughout society on the one hand, and the ability of leaders to meet these expectations on the other. It is primarily the outcome of the failure of modern strategic leadership, owing to the fact that modern leaders have increasingly failed to understand their role as representatives of the strategists in facilitating their strategic desire. Also it became clear that strategic frustration could arise in a less systematic way in the modern world from major crises such as the First World War. The classic case was Nazi Germany, an antistrategic regime that owed its political success in the early 1930s to the strategic frustration experienced by the German people subjected to intense economic insecurity owing to the economic and strategic difficulties experienced in the 1920s and early 1930s as a result of crippling war reparations. In a similar way (as discussed in more detail later in the chapter), the rise of the antistrategic Islamic State in Iraq and Syria, was the outcome of strategic frustration created by a series of Western invasions from the 1990s to the present time.

The psychology of strategic frustration

As my work on the dynamic-strategy project developed further, I realised that the concept of "strategic frustration" would need to take a more central role in my general theory of life and the strategic *logos*, both at the societal and individual levels. The next step in the development of this concept occurred during the writing of my book *The Selfcreating Mind* (2006), where my interest was in explaining human nature and the nature of human mental disorders. This led to the development of a strategic psychology in which psychic disorders are seen as the outcome of malfunctioning mechanisms of human nature—namely a loss of strategic integration owing to the mind-body duality—and in which neurotic disorders are seen as an outcome of strategic frustration. This frustration leads to distressing mood disorders, which are strategy-challenging rather than strategy-terminating as in the case of psychotic disorders. This discovery meant that strategic frustration was the source of "individual neurosis" as well as "societal neurosis" (as discovered earlier).

In normal individuals, mood swings involving hypomania (mild mania) and mild depression play an important role in advancing the strategic pursuit. Feelings of elation arising from successful strategic participation provide the emotional incentive to continue with past strategies, whereas depressed feelings arising from unsuccessful participation provide the emotional incentive to abandon past strategies and circumstances and to seek out new, more profitable ones. These emotions can only be regarded as disorders if they become extremely intense and persistent to the point where they bear little relationship to their strategic genesis.

Mood disorders, therefore, arise from strategic frustration, which can be caused by external and internal factors. The external source of strategic frustration in a normal society is the failure of strategic leadership or the imposition of oppressive controls by political, business, union, or other organisational groups. In the face of these difficulties, some individuals are unable to respond appropriately owing to quirks of personality and the nature of their life experiences. There are always a number of options open to the frustrated individual. They can fight, submit, withdraw to the periphery of an organisation or society, or resign and start anew. Some individuals are unable to make the appropriate choice that would ease their strategic frustration and, as a result, they suffer intense depression. For whatever reason, they are unable to respond to this emotional mechanism that normally provides an incentive to improve their participation in the strategic pursuit.

Some people also suffer strategic frustration because their innate drives do not match the particular dynamic strategy being pursued by their society. A heightened sexual drive, for example, is essential to the family-multiplication strategy (procreation and migration), but not to the mature phase of the technological strategy, which does not require territorial expansion fuelled by population increases to achieve economic growth. Instead of being a pillar of society, one may instead be branded a sexual deviant. Or again, a heightened aggressive drive is essential for the conquest strategy and for war to defend other strategies, but not for the technological strategy during peacetime, when the warrior/hero type is likely to be regarded as a dangerous thug. These strategic misfits will always exist in human society, because human nature has been fashioned by strategic selection (in response to the *logos*) so that it has the flexibility to respond to the demands of *any* dynamic strategy. In these examples, the strategically frustrated individual, unable to understand why he or she is so far out of tune with their society, will lash out at others (and be regarded as a psychopath or terrorist), retreat into deep depression, or internalise these instincts and suffer from feelings of guilt and even masochism. It is the price we pay for our strategic success as a species in an unpredictable world.

Strategic frustration in the pre-modern world

The next step in the development of the strategic frustration concept was made in *Dead God Rising* (2010). In this book it became clear that strategic frustration was not just a modern phenomenon, but had existed throughout history and had emerged from more wide-ranging causes. While the failure of strategic leadership was not as systematic as in the modern world, it did occur from time to time. In the ancient world, for example, Akhenaten (1352–1336 BC) of Egypt, and Caligula (37–41) and Nero (54–68) of Rome lost sight of their strategic responsibilities as leaders; while in early modern Europe Charles I (1625–1649) of England refused to provide strategic leadership for the economically dominant commercial interests; and both Louis XVI (1754–1793) of France and Nicholas II of Russia failed to provide the necessary economic and social reforms at critical stages in their countries' transition to technological societies. The result of this failure of strategic leadership was rebellion and war. Needless to say, there are other examples in world history of the failure of strategic leadership, but my point has been made

It also became clear in my later work, that strategic frustration was a common occurrence in regions of the pre-modern world subject to regular invasions. The most notable case was (and still is!) the Mediterranean lands of Palestine and Syria, which occupied the borderlands between the ancient superpowers of Egypt and Mesopotamia; and later Greece and Rome. As these borderlands straddled very rich trade routes, they were highly attractive to the superpowers. From the sixth century BC to the first century AD, Palestine and Syria suffered the age-old frustration of long periods of superpower domination punctuated by short periods of self-rule while the superpowers were otherwise distracted. Owing to this external oppression, Palestinian societies were unable to generate their own pattern of strategic development as did Egypt, Mesopotamia (in various guises), Greece, or Rome. Throughout the long periods of colonial domination, Palestinians never lost their intense desire for political independence, which was needed to pursue their own dynamic strategies of conquest and commerce. But their successes were tantalisingly brief, and generated much sustained strategic frustration, which in turn produced both individual and societal neurosis.

The responses to strategic frustration in Palestine were three-fold: strategic, antistrategic, and nonstrategic. The **strategic response** was—as is always the case—the most common one. Most people in the occupied territories attempted to accommodate themselves to the ruling colonial power. Ordinary people attempted to go about their usual economic and social activities, while ambitious families and individuals attempted to progress through the colonial hierarchy. Many found success, even if modest, and were able to overcome any initial strategic frustration. Some Palestinians, however, were not prepared to cooperate with the colonial power and became freedom fighters, or terrorists, depending on one's perspective. While these terrorists, usually young hot-heads advised by more experienced social leaders, were in a minority, they made their presence felt. This sporadic terrorism was the **antistrategic response**. Their only chance of success depended upon their rebellion coinciding with the declining fortunes of the colonial superpower. The revolt of the Hasmons in Judea is a rare example in this region of good rebellious timing. It occurred in 167 BC and was directed against the increasingly oppressive Seleucid empire (a post-Alexander Greek dynasty), which decided to convert the Temple of Jerusalem into a Hellenistic cult centre based on the worship of the Greek god Zeus. Following a guerrilla war, Juda Maccabees—son of the rebellious priest Mattahias—retook Jerusalem, cleansed the Temple, and rededicated it to the Jewish god YHWH. The internationally besieged and weakened Seleucids were finally driven out of Judea in 141 BC and, for the first time since 586 BC, an independent Judahite kingdom was established under the Hasmonean dynasty. This dynasty adopted the conquest strategy to expand steadily, until about 100 BC it included all the lands of Palestine. But this independence did not last for long; in 63 BC, just 78 years after Judah had secured its independence, the Romans under Pompey reduced Palestine to its former colonial status. This short period of independence merely heightened the agony of strategic frustration, which led to a further series of unsuccessful revolts against an empire that had no intention of releasing its control.

The third response to colonial rule in the ancient world was passive resistance—a **nonstrategic response**. After four millennia of strategic failure and strategic frustration, the indigenous people of Palestine were extremely receptive to charismatic sages, teachers, healers, messiahs, and apocalyptic seers, who could offer a peaceful solution to the destructive psychological effects generated by this harsh reality. Strategic frustration induced deep depression in many people, who, as a result, experienced a loss of psychic energy, purpose, and direction in life. The existing religion of Judaism, which was professed by the educated elite that achieved accommodation with the imperialists, provided little consolation for the majority of Palestinians. It merely offered the promise of restitution at the end of time, which seemed no closer under the Romans than under the Egyptians, Assyrians, Babylonians, or Persians. What the people of Palestine badly wanted was psychic relief in the here and now, not in some distant and uncertain future. And this is what the nonstrategic community of Jesus of Nazareth offered—a nonstrategic society whereby its members could lead meaningful lives separated from the stark strategic reality of Roman colonialism. It was all about how to live a better life here and now, not a messianic message about life in the hereafter. Jesus's message was: live a simple, unencumbered life; be cautious but courageous; give when asked and ask when in need; treat all people, irrespective of gender or class, equally; respond without aggression to the aggression of others; and don't be consumed by anxiety or ill-feeling (see *Dead God Rising*, 2010: 144-52). These early teachings of Jesus were later distorted by Paul of Tarsus in order to create a messianic religion known as Christianity, which ultimately became the conquest ideology of the late Roman Empire. This is one of the great ironies of history: how a nonstrategic ideology induced by Roman imperialism could, some three centuries later, be transformed into the strategic ideology of Roman conquest (and, later, the conquest ideology of medieval European kingdoms).

Terrorism in the twenty-first century
Modern terrorism follows an ancient pattern driven by a universal dynamic—strategic frustration. Islamic terrorists are antistrategists who have emerged from societies unable to achieve strategic success.

Between the conquests of Alexander the Great (333–323 BC) and the twentieth century, the Middle East was invaded and occupied by the Seleucids (301–70 BC), the Romans (40 BC–600 AD), the Parthians (70 BC–230 AD), the Persians (230–360), the Arabs (650–1071), the Seljuks (from 1071), and the Ottomans (1600–1918), The attraction of this region in the pre-modern era was the rich riverine lands of Mesopotamia and the major overland routes of commerce between East and West. In the modern era this region attracted the close attention of Western superpowers because of its vast deposits of oil that were critical to the success of the technological strategy. While the First World War imposed a huge cost on the allies, a major benefit for Britain and France was the control they gained over Middle Eastern oil supplies by defeating Turkey and driving out the influence of Germany from this region. Following the war, Britain, which had controlled Egypt since 1882, gained further control over Palestine, Transjordan, and Iraq; while France exerted control over Lebanon and Syria. Both land grabs were sanctioned by the League of Nations as Mandates in 1920.

A region that had experienced more than two millennia of conquest and imperial occupation from the time of the first incursions from the West (Alexander) can be expected to be suffering an extreme case of strategic frustration together with individual and societal neurosis. Most indigenous people managed to accommodate themselves to this strategic reality, but a growing number of ethnic and religious groups resumed agitating for superpower withdrawal and local control. Because of changing strategic objectives (arising from a mature industrial technological *logos*), Britain and France began slowly withdrawing from the Middle East in the middle years of the twentieth century. Britain withdrew from Iraq in 1932 after imposing the Hashemite (Sunni) monarchy; from Transjordan between 1941 and 1946; from Palestine in 1948 leaving unresolved the tension between Israelis and Arab Palestinians; and from Egypt in 1956. Similarly, France withdrew from Lebanon and Syria in 1946, leaving republics in place.

Predictably, the somewhat arbitrary political arrangements left behind by Britain and France did not survive for long. Only a very brief sketch of subsequent difficulties will be provided. The Israeli state in Palestine has been a source of continual conflict, with both dispossessed Palestinians and other sympathetic Arab states. Not surprisingly a number of militant groups have emerged, the most prominent being Hamas. Iraq has become a hotbed of militant activity since the British left in 1932, initially with unrest from Assyrian, Yazidi and Shia groups; then a series of coups between 1936 and 1941; a number of protests of increasing severity from 1945 to 1948, culminating in a military overthrow of the monarchy and the establishment of a republic in 1958; then in 1963 the Baath Party under Ahmed Hassan al-Bakr (as Prime Minister) seized control, and in 1979 Saddam Hussein forcibly assumed power from al-Bakr, taking both roles of Prime Minister and President; in 2003 the Americans and their allies invaded Iraq and occupied the country until 2011, when they installed a Shia-dominated government; and since then Sunni militants have renewed an insurgency, which from 2013 developed into a civil war and led to the declaration of the Islamic State and the conquest and annexation of large parts of Iraq and, more recently, Syria.

After France's withdrawal in 1946, the Republic of Lebanon faced growing sectarian tension, which developed into a destructive civil war from 1975 to 1990 between Christians and the joint forces of the PLO, Muslim militias, and left-wing Druze. And this conflict was complicated by incursions from both Israel and Syria. Similarly, the Syrian Republic left in the wake of France experienced a series of coups between 1949 and 1970 when Hafez al-Assad seized power and proclaimed himself President, a post he held ruthlessly until his death in 2000, when his son Bashar al-Assad succeeded him. Early promise of a more liberal regime was quickly extinguished as Bashar brutally supressed political and popular opposition, which led in 2011 to the outbreak of civil war with the army defending the regime against many rebel groups including, most recently (2014 to date), Islamic State. Currently (2015), many Western powers (USA, Britain, France, and Australia) are engaged in destructive bombing raids against ISIL in Syria, while Syria's old ally Russia is complicating these problems by attacking anti-ISIL forces in that country. The end result is chaos.

The patent inability of indigenous peoples to construct a viable and sustained strategic *logos* in any of these Middle Eastern countries has generated social, political and economic chaos, which in turn has led to strategic frustration of such an intensity that there seems to be no end to violence and bloodshed. In Syria, for example, people of normal strategic inclination have finally given up on making any reasonable life for themselves, and are deserting their country in huge numbers in the hope they can find refuge in Europe, which has played a major role in their misery. But the size of the mass migration, which is placing pressure on European resources, together with terrorist attacks in the European metropolis, will probably overwhelm any feelings of compassion and guilt felt there. Already, right-wing parties in France and Germany, which want to stem the inflow, are growing in popularity. In Syria, only those who seek solutions in violence and destruction appear perversely happy to remain, and to use these devastated countries as a base for fighting back at Western countries they hold responsible for the chaos in their region. These militant groups are using Islam as an ideology for their antistrategic activities, which involve conquest, rape, and slaughter on a large scale.

Ironically, it was (as I show in *Dead God Rising*, 2010: ch. 5) strategic frustration that motivated the prophet Muhammed to develop Islam (about 610 AD) as *a strategic ideology of conquest* in order to unite the Arabs in a prosperous society. Muhammed had for many years been concerned by what he saw as a crisis in Arab society in the early seventh century. It seemed to be impossible to create a stable and prosperous life-system in Arabia, because Arab tribes fought fiercely with each other in a "murderous cycle of vendetta and counter vendetta". The strategic chaos of the seventh century in the Middle East appears very similar to that existing there today: "tribes" locked in a "murderous cycle" looking to conquest in the name of Islam to resolve the intractable problem of endless strategic frustration. But, there is one difference. In the technological era of today, conquest is considered to be evil, whereas in the pre-modern world it was considered normal. Consequently, peace-loving Muslims today are forced to deny the conquest origins of Islam.

A new feature of Islamic terrorism is its emergence in Western societies, which have provided a haven and a new start in the strategic pursuit for displaced Muslims from the Middle East. While the vast majority of Muslim immigrants welcome the chance to live normal strategic lives, a small proportion of young males (and a much smaller group of female accomplices) have turned their backs on these new strategic opportunities and have become antistrategists intent on attacking their host countries. These disaffected individuals, many born in their host countries, feel they are unable to meet the requirements for strategic success owing to the costly high standards of training and education required by technological societies. Clearly they lack the necessary discipline, perseverance, and capacity for the hard, dedicated work required for success. They are suffering a form of self-imposed strategic frustration arising out of self-indulgence. It is easier to believe the extremist Islamic ideology telling them it is not their fault, but rather the fault of the "Crusader" societies. They are encouraged by extremist ideologues not to strive to reach the heights of strategic success, but to pull down these heights and to get their just rewards in the afterlife as martyrs.

Is there a solution? There is, but only a long-term one. It involves destroying the committed terrorists—the unturnable antistrategists—and eliminating strategic frustration by assisting in the establishment of strategic societies in the Middle East that satisfy the strategic desire of the vast proportion of its peoples. This will be an extremely difficult task; but only by creating a viable strategic *logos* in each of the Middle Eastern societies, will order, progress, and security be achieved and the future of the peoples of this region secured. Time is of the essence, because by the middle of the twenty-first century, oil—the black life-blood of the Middle East—will have disappeared into the sands.

WHAT IS EVIL?

We are finally in a position to answer this elusive question. Evil is one of three broad responses to the dynamic outcome that I have called "strategic frustration". These responses, which arise from different psychological propensities of human nature, include: the normal, or strategic, response; the "good", or nonstrategic, response; and the evil, or antistrategic response. In other words, good and evil are *abnormal* responses to the frustrations of life. These values are not innate to human nature, nor are they embodied in the strategic *logos*; rather they are the outcome of an interaction between the strategic *logos* and our complex human nature. **Good and evil occupy the interactive space between ourselves and our life-system.** Yet, as these values arise out of deliberate human choice in stressful strategic circumstances, we are responsible for the evil we do. These three responses are as follows:

- **The normal, or strategic response,** arises from a proactive, competitive, competent, and balanced personality in the face of strategic frustration. This is an outcome of the psychological propensity of the large majority of people, even in difficult circumstances. It is the response that drives the strategic *logos*. These people are neither good nor evil, they are just "strategically normal". Good and evil are not innate to human nature. There is no gene selected (by the strategic *logos* over the very longrun) for good or evil, because both these qualities will endanger the *logos*. This is so, because evil is the outcome of antistrategic activity, which undermines strategic society; and because good dilutes strategic desire, which drives strategic society. Both good and evil must be treated carefully.

- **The good, or nonstrategic, response** arises from a cooperative, passive, and nonaggressive personality in the face of strategic frustration. This personality type involves only a small proportion of the total population, which is important, because it tends to undermine strategic desire, the driving force of the *logos*. It has been responsible for the emergence of nonstrategic communities— such as those of Jesus of Nazareth or Buddha—trying to protect themselves, together with their friends and relatives, from a harsh strategic environment. These communities are "good" in the sense that they are self-supporting, self-healing cooperatives. While they are small refuges in a brutal world, these communities are effective (for the distressed individuals they nourish and protect), but if they were ever to become the rule rather than the exception, the strategic *logos* would collapse and human life would be plunged into chaos and misery. **Goodness is only good in small doses.**

• **The evil, or antistrategic, response** arises from an aggressively violent and unbalanced personality that exhibits a tendency toward paranoid and psychopathological disorders. And this strategic activity flourishes with support from larger numbers of people who appear more balanced, but who (like Eichmann) are willing to treat the antistrategic regime as normal, despite its abnormal and distorted ideology and practice. This is the response that most endangers the *logos*, because it is antistrategic in nature, and, when unchecked, it leads to the deaths of large numbers of people. It is a response that knows no internally directed limits; it can only be contained by the *logos* during periods of strategic success, and once set loose by strategic frustration it can only be controlled by total destruction. **Evil is the thought and action that deliberately and energetically attempts to destroy the strategic *logos*.** Evil is anti-*logos*—anti-life.

Good and evil, therefore, have the same incubating source—strategic frustration. These qualities are not part of human nature, not part of the strategic *logos*, not part of any supposed supernatural world. They are brought into being by major crises leading to malfunctions of the strategic *logos* and to the sustained disruption of strategic success. This is why it is dangerous to court disorder and essential to work to achieve an orderly strategic *logos*.

Ultimate Reality

Chapter Six

Truth

Truth has been a central subject in religious, philosophical, political, and popular discussion since civilized societies first emerged. Many individuals, organisation, and societies have claimed to have discovered the truth about existence, and many more have professed their truthfulness. And certain key institutions, such as religious organisations, universities, the justice system, and the media, claim to be based on the truth. Most of these claims are more than a little exaggerated. As Shakespeare's Hamlet may have said about truth: "it is a custom more honour'd in the breach than the observance". The truth is that truth is not central to the dynamics of human society.

Two key aspects of truth are explored in this chapter: seeking the truth about life; and telling the truth about motivations, actions, events, and situations. It is shown that these two aspects of truth are interrelated and have the same origins or causes. Essentially, people prefer fantasy to truth, because truth undermines the desire to survive and prosper and, hence, endangers both the individual and the strategic *logos*. Truth is the ultimate vivisector.

WHAT IS TRUTH?

A statement faithfully reflecting known facts about the real world meets the usual definition of truth. This concept, however, has various shades of meaning. The remainder of this chapter is concerned with the following five characteristics of truth and it's opposite, untruth.

- **Existential truth** is the term I have employed to embody the usual definition of truth: correct statements about the real world.

- **Ultimate reality or truth** refers to the system of reality—the strategic *logos*—that underlies the dynamics of human society.

This universal life-system is the highest form of knowledge and explanation about life; the system that makes sense of all other less holistic relationships and interactions. It should be realised, however, that there is no single strategic *logos*; there are as many *logoi* as there are workable human and non-human societies. Nevertheless, the set of identifiable interacting relationships in each individual *logos*, operates according to the same dynamic mechanism, and the same laws of life/history. Conceptually, this is similar to dynamic systems operating in the physical world. For example, while each solar system in the Universe is distinct, each shares the same dynamic mechanism and the same laws of physics.

- **Utilitarian truths or facts.** We need to note that there is one limited form of "truth" that should be distinguished from our holistic concept of truth. In order for human society—particularly urban society—to flourish, the *logos* generates a strategic demand for empirical knowledge required to facilitate the progress of the current dynamic strategy. This is usually associated with the requirements of technology in all four types of dynamic strategy, but particularly the technological strategy of the modern era. These are the utilitarian facts or "truths".

- **Myths** are those statements (or more accurately "stories") that rationalise the way we live our lives. These myths, which are tenuously called "truths" by society, are imaginative constructs driven by the need of strategists to avoid facing the potentially damaging real truth about their lives. These are stories about our origins, our motivations and objectives, our strategic guardians, and our future. This is the way we are able to exist in a world of unbearable greed and brutality.

- **Lies**, as we are all aware, are deliberately incorrect statements told, not out of some perverse will to deceive, but to improve our prospects in the competitive race to survive and prosper. There is no gene, as such, to lie; just plentiful opportunities to improve our material prospects if we do.

TRUTH IN PHILOSOPHY

Before examining the dynamic-strategy theory of truth, a brief outline of the history of this subject in philosophy is required to provide context. This is not meant to be a scholarly piece (there are no footnotes), just a background sketch.

Truth is an important topic in philosophy, being one of the most central and most discussed. Accordingly, the intelligent reader would expect to learn something significant about the subject. Let me say from the outset that such a reader of philosophy is going to be severely disappointed. Philosophers are concerned not with revealing the truth about reality, but rather with exploring the metaphysical nature of truth—what truth statements are, and what makes them true, or false. We are told that: "explaining the nature of truth becomes an application of some metaphysical system, and truth inherits significant metaphysical presuppositions along the way" (*Stanford Encyclopedia of Philosophy*). In other words, philosophy deals with metaphysical claims about what might conceivably exist (ontology) rather than what actually does exist (science, both natural and social). And philosophers employ the metaphysical methodology of deductive reasoning rather than the realist methodology of inductive reasoning; metaphysical thinking rather than strategic thinking (see my book *The Selfcreating Mind*, 2006). **Philosophers are concerned with theories about truth, rather than with truthful theories.**

While there are a large number of contemporary theories about truth, most are based on two contrasting theories which, in one form or another, can be traced back to the ancient Greeks. These theories are known as the "correspondence theory" based upon a philosophy of realism, and a "coherence theory" derived from a philosophy of idealism. A recent (2009) survey of some 1,972 philosophers from 99 leading university departments in the USA, UK, Europe, Canada, and Australia, found that 51 percent supported correspondence theory, 25 percent favoured deflationary theory, 7 percent gave the nod to epistemic theory, and 18 percent were recorded as "other" (*philpapers*, 2013). Realism (82 percent of respondents), therefore, seems to trump idealism (merely 4 percent) in the world of contemporary philosophy. Curiously, "deflationary" or "minimalist" theory, which claims the allegiance of a quarter of these philosophers, argues that the term "truth" does not denote a real property of either propositions or sentences; and it is not employed in everyday speech. Hence the use of the term "is true" in a sentence is redundant and should be abandoned. These, so called, "theorists" wish to "deflate the artificial importance of the word 'truth'"; which is hardly a profound insight.

Correspondence Theory

The origins of modern correspondence theory can be traced back to Aristotle, who adopted a more realistic approach to philosophy than his teacher Plato. What do philosophers mean by realism? The essential claim of realism is that the world exists objectively and independently of the way we think about, and describe, it. Further, realists claim that every "truth-bearer" (proposition or sentence) can be deemed true or false. Realists accepting the correspondence theory claim that a proposition is true if it "corresponds" to known facts about the world. In the group of theories that fall into this category—theories held by Aristotle, Aquinas, Avicenna, Kant, Moore, and Russell, to name but a few—the truth-bearers are said to be propositions, sentences, or even beliefs. These truth-bearers are usually required to represent facts (although some contemporary philosophers have attempted to build correspondence theories without facts!); to be "meaningful" and, hence, say something about the world; to be true or false; and to provide "truth conditions", which tell us how we are to know what is true.

It is somewhat strange that philosophers regard the correspondence theory as a "theory", when it merely postulates that truth should reflect reality. It is even more astounding that the "deflationists", who appear to be no more than text editors, actually regard themselves as theorists. In the sciences, this simple assertion is rightly taken as given—otherwise science is without foundation—and scientific theories hypothesise complex relationships between real-world variables, which can be tested using real-world facts. This difference of approach contrasts the deductive metaphysical methodology of philosophy with the essentially inductive method of science. When science tries taking short-cuts by starting with an assertion and then testing it against real-world facts—the so-called "hypothetico-deductive" method—it runs the risk of distorting reality and making the mistake of employing a metaphysical methodology. In the world of science, ideas arrived at metaphysically often survive in the face of evidence to the contrary, and are usually only replaced by other metaphysical ideas. Darwin's theory of natural selection is a case in point (see my book *The Collapse of Darwinism*, 2003).

Coherence Theory

The coherence theory of truth is an outcome of idealism, which holds that reality (at least as we know it) is immaterial as it is merely a construct of the mind. This theory is often traced back at least to Plato, who argued that truth is an abstraction. While Plato claimed that ideas are real—hence is not an idealist in the modern sense of that term—his theory of Forms is all about *ideal* Forms, which are universals that exist independently of any particular instance. Plato's Form of the Good, which is the ultimate Form that determines all other Forms, is consistent with modern coherence theory.

Modern coherence theory—which was influenced by Spinoza, Leibniz, Hegel, and F.H. Bradley—was developed by Harold Joachim (1868–1938), who claimed that truth is the "whole complete truth". What he meant by this is that that individual beliefs or judgements are true only to the extent they are part of a complete system of beliefs or judgements; and that individual systems are only true to the extent they are part of a single "whole complete truth". This is a holistic concept that seems to echo Plato's theory of Forms in which the highest Form of the Good determines the truth of all other Forms. In the coherence theory, therefore, truth is a matter of how beliefs are related to each other rather than to the outside world. Needless to say, such a theory requires some metaphysics to suggest how truth can be derived from ideas rather than the real world. Only idealists, who are in a very small minority in the ranks of contemporary philosophers, are able to accept this type of thinking.

While a realist thinker does not find this approach meaningful—both Moore and Russell reacted against this idealism in their philosophy—it has some interest: but only when the process of logic is reversed. The methodology of working from the single "whole complete truth" to the validation of lower-order judgements or beliefs is unconvincing. Yet, if we start from the grass-roots level of existential facts in order to draw up historical patterns of experience (timescapes), which are then explained by developing an inductive general dynamic theory, it is possible to arrive at a realist system (the strategic *logos*) that does indeed validate the component parts (the laws of life and history). But, of course, this is a realist not an idealist "whole complete truth": what I call "ultimate truth" or "ultimate reality".

EVALUATING PHILOSOPHY'S APPROACH TO TRUTH

At the beginning of this background sketch, it was suggested that those general readers hoping to discover the truth about life by consulting the philosophical literature would be disappointed. Philosophy, as it turns out, has little to tell us about reality, and even less about ultimate truth/reality. The response from philosophers to this criticism is always: "it was never our intention to tell you about reality, only about the type and status of questions one might ask about reality—if it exists".

This is a rather weak response, given the considerable intellectual effort devoted to philosophical discourse over the past couple of millennia, and the high claims made by philosophers for the importance of their subject. Philosophers sell themselves vigorously—owing to their fear they will be found out—as the discipline of wisdom; the discipline of Socrates, Plato, Aristotle, Kant, Descartes, Hume, Mill, etc. Who could argue against that? In fact, a counter argument can be made, to the effect that much of the intellectual content—certainly the most productive and useful—has been stripped away from the discipline of philosophy over the millennia since the time of Plato and Aristotle, and has been relocated to newly established disciplines, such as physics, biology, chemistry, economics, politics, and sociology. All that is left today is a metaphysical rump! Their proclaimed intellectual heroes would not even recognise the philosophy discipline today as the discipline of wisdom of yesterday. As there is no strategic demand for philosophical ideas today—owing to a rate of return approaching zero—these metaphysicians have to hope that the unsuspecting taxpayer will not see through their grand self-justifications.

The critical test for any intellectual discipline, as far as the host society is concerned, is whether it can provide a meaningful account of the real world. The philosophers of truth—and of most other subjects—fail this test. While philosophers may claim that they ask and evaluate the type of questions that those in the natural and social sciences need to ask about reality, even this desperate argument fails to stand scrutiny. Scientists do not find the type of questions debated by philosophers about the nature or existence of reality to be at all useful in their work. Science would be undertaken just as effectively even in the total absence of philosophical discussion, because it is a response not to abstract metaphysical ideas but to strategic demand generated by the *logos*.

The only superficially persuasive argument for tax-payers to fund the discipline of philosophy in universities (it cannot survive in the real world) is that it provides training in critical and logical thought. But the counter arguments are even more persuasive. The first is that other academic disciplines also provide training in logical thought, while at the same time providing an analysis of reality critical to the success of modern technological societies. Only in pre-modern societies were metaphysical ideas, both in the related disciplines of philosophy and theology, able to provide helpful mystical ideologies. Secondly, while philosophy certainly can provide training in deductive thinking, it is unable to provide training in inductive or strategic thinking, as can the natural and social sciences. It is strategic thinking that is critical to the success of the strategic *logos*.

There is, however, an even more fundamental flaw in philosophy's claim to provide intellectual insight into the nature of truth. How is it possible for philosophers to discuss meaningfully the nature of truth if they don't know what the truth actually is; and, worse, are not interested in finding out? How often have we heard philosophers say or imply that empirical work is not worthy of serious scholars.

Instead of relating to the complexity of the real world, they relate only to the simplicity of each other's ideas. Ideas rather than reality are the touchstone of philosophy. They build their castles in the air.

This is also true of other areas of philosophical work. Take the laws of history—another issue of interest in this book—for example. Philosophers feel able to speculate about whether laws "govern" the universe or not—they adopt either a Humean or non-Humean stance—without any practical understanding of what laws are. Further, when talking of laws, philosophers concern themselves only with those pertaining to nature, not history. They express either "learned" scepticism or outright disbelief in the laws of history, without even bothering to investigate how history could possibly generate systematic patterns in the absence of laws. Is this possible in the physical world? Of course not. Needless to say, philosophers offer no explanation of these patterns of the past, presumably because they have more important issues to think about. The orderly structure of the world is taken as given.

Surely it is essential to understand the existential character and functions of issues before it is possible to philosophise about them. Otherwise the philosophical analysis will lack meaningful content; it will be a hollow straw man. T.S. Elliot could have had philosophers in mind when he wrote these lines:

> We are the hollow men
>
> We are the stuffed men
>
> Leaning together
>
> Headpiece filled with straw. Alas!
>
> Our dried voices, when
>
> We whisper together
>
> Are quiet and meaningless
>
> As wind in dried grass
>
> Or rat's feet over broken glass
>
> In our dry cellar
>
> Shape without form, shade without colour,
>
> Paralysed force, gesture without motion;

A STRATEGIC APPROACH TO TRUTH

Owing to the failure of philosophy to tell us anything meaningful about the reality of truth, we need to find a new way. A way that is realist rather than metaphysical, employing an inductive rather than a deductive methodology. This is the "strategic thinking" method I used to explore the "laws of history" in my 1998 book of the same name. The laws of history explain the truth about reality.

The central problem in establishing the laws of history is the difficulty experienced in recognizing them. Not because the regularities from which they can be derived do not exist, but because social scientists throughout the ages have persisted in looking in the wrong places. The metaphysical historicists have looked into their own imaginations, the positive historicists and new institutionalists have not looked beyond historical events and structures, and the antihistoricists have preferred not to look at all. The answer to the question 'If history has laws how would we recognize them?' is that we must look at the **mechanisms or processes** underlying the regularities of the everyday world. It is from these regularities that the laws of history can be derived. To do this we must look to a new form of historicism—"existential historicism".

The Old Historicism

The ancient Greeks were correct. It *is* very difficult to study a world in flux and to derive laws of history. Far easier is it to examine a world in equilibrium, particularly in the social sciences. But the type of issue that can be examined using equilibrium analysis is severely limited and certainly excludes the centrally important matter of societal dynamics. There has been a twofold response by historicists to this difficulty. The metaphysical historicists from Plato to Marx focused upon ideal sociopolitical forms that constituted in their minds either the beginning or the end of history. Dynamics in this framework is the supposed movement towards or away from these ideal states, which is regarded as either progress or regress. As discussed in my book *Laws of History* (1998), the socalled 'laws' governing such movement have no empirical validity.

The positive historicists—Comte, Mill, Buckle, the historical economists, and Rostow—attempted to overcome the problem of examining a world in flux by focusing upon historical outcomes. These outcomes are either the trends in key variables that are apparent over time, or are the stages through which, it is claimed, societies have passed. In both cases the general conditions of economic progress are associated with these outcomes. Either the actual *trends* in variables such as population or national wealth are regarded as historical laws which can be naively extrapolated into the future, or the conditions required to achieve certain stages of progress are given a law-like authority and are extrapolated onto other countries that have yet to achieve a certain stage in the nominated progression. In both cases predictions about the future are precariously based upon historical patterns that cannot be regarded as universally applicable. This is the old historicist fallacy.

Existential Historicism

How can we recognize the laws of societal dynamics? Certainly not by philosophizing about the essence of things (metaphysical historicism) or by attempting to generalize the historical patterns of events, or institutions (positive historicism). We will only recognize the laws of history and discover the strategic *logos* (the ultimate reality) by exploring the **dynamic historical mechanisms** in the real economy that are responsible for the apparent regularities in human existence. This is the essence of the new "existential historicism". As shown in *Dynamic Society* (1996) and *Ark of the Sun* (2015), there is a high degree of consistency in the way human society changes, just as there is a high degree of consistency in the way the physical world changes. If it were not so it would be impossible to plan for the future and, accordingly, human civilization would not have emerged. We need to model the deeper forces underlying these superficial patterns.

What is the method of existential historicism? Basically it is a quaternary system of analysis which involves the discovery of historical patterns (or timescapes), the construction of a general dynamic model, the derivation of specific historical mechanisms, and the construction of an associated model of institutional change.

Essentially, this quaternary system is a set of **inductive steps** (if not rules) that goes a long way to resolving the "problem of induction". These inductive steps emerged as I wrote a series of books between 1974 and 1997. We need to consider each of these four levels of analysis.

Timescapes

Timescapes provide pictures of the dynamic outcomes of human society throughout time both in quantitative and qualitative terms. The quantitative pictures, which are the "truth-bearers", show the numerical relationships between important economic variables such as real GDP, population, and prices. And this showing is the beginning of understanding. These timescapes, as demonstrated in *Dynamic Society* and *Ark of the Sun*, reveal considerable historical regularity. First, despite the major impact of exogenous forces, these statistical pictures show surprisingly regular wave-like fluctuations (rather than cycles) in the behaviour of all societies. These include the "great waves" of *about* 300 years and the "long waves" of *about* 40 to 60 years that were experienced in the ancient, medieval, and modern eras alike. While these great and long waves appear to possess some regularity, we should focus not on the precision of their length (the historicist fallacy) but on the mechanisms that generate growth of a fluctuating nature. This matter is discussed in greater depth in *Longrun dynamics* (1998). Secondly, these wave-like fluctuations are experienced in the New World as well as the Old World. Thirdly, these wave-like fluctuations have taken place in a dynamic structure of technological paradigm shifts that I have called the "great steps of human progress". The importance of these timescapes is that they describe the **strategic pathways** taken by various societies over time, *pathways that cannot be deduced logically*. In addition, the qualitative pictures reveal patterns of institutional and organizational change of an economic, political, and social kind. These qualitative pictures, developed in my book *Ephemeral Civilization* (1997), show quite clearly that institutional change is not an evolutionary process, as it reverses on itself in response to the circular strategic sequence of conquest▶commerce▶conquest.

What is the significance of these timescapes? The first and essential point is that they are not an end in themselves, as they were for the positive historicists (with the notable exception of J.S. Mill) and the institutionalists, but merely a beginning. Timescapes are our starting point not our goal. The patterns of our timescapes are only partial regularities in human experience. They are the regularities of outcome. Universal regularities are to be found only in the dynamic processes that underlie these surface patterns. It is from the dynamic *processes*, therefore, that the laws of history can be derived. It is because these dynamic processes have not been previously identified that we are told that history has no laws—that history is just part of a cosmic lottery. What is the probability of that outcome in a game of chance? The second point is that timescapes suggest causal relationships that need to be tested empirically before we can construct our general dynamic model.

The general dynamic model

The general dynamic model is the second stage of our analysis. This model is constructed inductively using the historical method, which involves an examination of our timescapes (particularly of a quantitative nature) showing dynamic relationships together with other historical data concerning the nature of society. The general model is capable of explaining how and why a society emerges, grows, stagnates, declines and, sometimes, collapses. It is a model concerned with the way human decision-makers attempt to achieve their objectives in a variety of economic environments, why and how these ways are eventually exhausted, and why a previously successful society falters. It is a model that possesses universal validity as it can be used to explain the dynamics of human society throughout space and time once the specific fundamental conditions are known. It is a model that can even be used to explain the vicissitudes of life over the past 4 billion years. This model was first developed to study human society in *Dynamic Society* (1996), extended to all life in *The Collapse of Darwinism* (2003), applied to the study of the human mind in *The Selfcreating Mind* (2006), used to explain religion and scientism in *Dead God Rising* (2010), employed to explore the future in *The Coming Eclipse* (2010), and generalised in *Ark of the Sun* (2015).

While this general dynamic model can explain growth and decline in general terms it needs to be informed by specific historical conditions in order to suggest specific mechanisms that can explain the dynamics of individual historical eras. There are three fundamental conditions that must be explored. We need to know whether we are dealing with an 'open' or a 'closed' society. This is a question about the degree of external competition. We need to know the degree to which global resources are fully employed, given the prevailing technological paradigm. And we need to know the nature of that technological paradigm.

The historical mechanisms

The dynamic mechanism operating in any historical era, therefore, can be understood through an application of our general model to the prevailing historical conditions. This is the third stage of our analysis. As shown in *Dynamic Society* and *Ark of the Sun*, this generates three distinct dynamic mechanisms that span the entire history of mankind. They are the "great dispersion" of the palaeolithic era, the "great wheel of civilization" of the neolithic era, and the "great linear waves" of the industrial era. These mechanisms are related to each other within a dynamic technological structure called the "great steps of human progress". While each of the three great dynamic mechanisms is specific to its own technological era, it is universally applicable in that era. And because the great-steps concept transcends historical eras, it is universally applicable across all time. Also, it would be possible for an earlier dynamic mechanism to reappear if a conscious attempt were made to change one of the prevailing fundamental historical conditions. If, for example, we were able to change one of these conditions for the modern era, namely to eliminate all competition through a climate-mitigation command economy, the future might see the re-emergence of the great wheel of war and conquest. Prediction of the future, therefore, depends on the ability to correctly establish the changing fundamental conditions of human society.

The model of institutional change

This extended dynamic-strategy model can also be used to explain institutional change. This is the fourth stage of our analysis. As shown in *Ephemeral Civilization*, institutional change can be explained as a response to the unfolding and replacement of dominant dynamic strategies by the *logos*. An unfolding dynamic strategy generates a dynamic demand—consisting of strategic demand and tactical demand—for a range of inputs including facilitating institutions and organizations. The central mechanism by which strategic and tactical demand are converted into institutional change is the competitive struggle between various groups in society for control over the dominant dynamic strategy. This is called the "strategic struggle". The groups include the "old strategists" and "new strategists" (profit-seekers), the "antistrategists" (rent-seekers), and the "nonstrategists" (dependants and non-participants). Institutional change is an outcome of a secondary dynamic mechanism.

To sum up: It will now be clear what response should be made to Karl Popper's myopic view of induction and the rules of induction. His vision of induction was as limited as that of the positive historicists, who he attacked with relish. Popper maintained until the end of his long life that:

> Sensible rules of inference do not exist. The best rule I can extract from my reading of the inductivist literature would be something like this: 'The future is likely to be not so very different from the past'. This, of course, is a rule which everybody accepts in practice; and something like it we must accept also in theory if we are realists . . . The rule is, however, so vague that it is hardly interesting. And in spite of its vagueness, the rule assumes too much, and certainly much more than we (and thus any deductive rule) should assume *prior* to all theory formation; for it assumes a *theory of time*. (*Unended Quest*, 1992:147)

Popper is justified in attacking crude historicism (extrapolation of the past into the future), but he is wrong on a number of key matters. First, while there will never be any mechanical rules of induction equivalent to the rules of deduction, my general 'steps of induction'—the existential quaternary system—are clear, precise, and do not make strong assumptions of the type assumed by Popper.

Induction is not only possible, it is essential if we are to understand the dynamic process of human society. Second, Popper is mistaken in his assertion that deduction (in conjunction with falsification) is superior to induction, because Popperian non-empirical hypotheses (often guesses) are invariably unable to embrace the complexity of the world or its underlying dynamic processes. How often are we told by scientists that their latest discovery was "completely unexpected"? Third, contrary to Popper's assertion, my existential historicism does not assume the future "is likely to be not so very different from the past", because its predictions are based not on historical trends, but on the predictable operation of the dynamic-strategy model. My general dynamic theory is able to predict *structural change*, which neither the crude historical method nor the hypothetico-deductive method championed by Popper can possibly achieve.

Take for example the topical issue of climate mitigation. Owing to the deficiencies of the deductive method, natural scientists and economists are unable to employ it to predict what the costs and benefits of a full-on climate-mitigation program versus "business as usual" might be. Hence, despite their ridicule of induction (questioning whether it even exists), they have actually quietly abandoned the deductive method and adopted the *crude* historical method so as to extrapolate recent historical trends into the distant future (next 100 to 200 years) without even considering the problem of structural change. What structural change you ask? The coming of the Solar Revolution from the middle decades of the twenty-first century. This revolution will not be based on the second-best wind and solar panel technologies currently being promoted, but on radical new direct means of accessing the sun's energy—see my books *The Coming Eclipse* (2010) and *Ark of the Sun* (2015). In relative terms, this new economic revolution will be at least as significant in its global impact as was the Industrial Revolution; and in absolute terms its impact will be infinitely greater. The inductively derived dynamic-strategy theory demonstrates not the poverty of historicism, as Popper would like to claim, but the poverty of deductivism, which is the method of philosophical metaphysics.

Deriving the Laws of History and Discovering the Strategic *Logos*

The laws of history can be derived using the quaternary system of analysis. But to do so we must focus not on the timescapes, either quantitative or institutional, but on the general model, the dynamic mechanisms, and the model of institutional change. Timescapes merely show the pattern of outcomes from the more fundamental dynamic process. The fatal mistake made in the past by the old historicists (and institutionalists) and, today, the climate mitigationists, is to view these patterns as laws in themselves that could be universalized and extrapolated into the future. With the notable exception of J.S. Mill, it did not occur to philosophers that dynamic mechanisms might underlie these outcomes. And even Mill was unable to uncover these mechanisms.

Just as there are three sources for the laws of history, so there are three categories of laws, each operating at a different level in human society. Those laws derived from the general model are the primary laws of history and have been called the **laws of societal dynamics**. They are the laws that govern the behaviour of individuals as they pursue their objectives of survival and prosperity by investing in one of the four main dynamic strategies; and the way societies respond to these strategies. These primary laws are derived and presented in *The Laws of History* (1998) and *Ark of the Sun* (2015). The secondary laws are called the **laws of historical change** and they are derived from the dynamic mechanisms underlying the historical development in each of the three epochs of human history. As these mechanisms were reconstructed by applying the general model to the quantitative timescapes, the secondary laws can be thought of as being derived from the primary laws. Finally, the tertiary laws, or the **laws of institutional change**, are derived from the dynamic-strategy model employed in *Ephemeral Civilization* to explain institutional change. As this model was constructed from both the general model and the dynamic mechanisms, the tertiary laws can be thought of as being derived jointly from the primary and secondary laws of history.

The existential quaternary method has been even more fruitful than I thought when I derived the laws of both history (in 1998) and the laws of life (in 2003). When I was researching my first book on truth, entitled *The Death of Zarathustra: notes on truth for the risk-taker* (published in 2011 but completed in 2004), I realised that my dynamic-strategy theory and the derived laws of history pointed to something even more exciting and revolutionary, namely the outlines of a hidden universal life-system, which I called the strategic *logos* (see chapter 3). The strategic *logos* is a discovery that could only be made using the existential historical method. It is not an entity that could be meaningfully discovered or explored using the deductive method of philosophy. The strategic *logos* is an existential, not a metaphysical, entity. And from this ultimate reality, historical patterns and laws derive their true meaning.

To sum up: It is one thing to establish a procedure to derive laws of history, and quite another to claim that the resulting law-like propositions have any validity. The tests that laws must pass are threefold. They need to be applied successfully to cases other than those from which they were derived; they need to give rise to other propositions that can be tested successfully against known facts; and they need to prove successful in predicting future changes in human society. Failure to pass these tests is the only basis on which these law-like statements can be abandoned. It is not enough to express an untested belief either that an individual proposition is not true or that there can never be any laws of history, as is common in philosophy. Laws and their refutation are a matter of science not of metaphysics.

The dynamic-strategy models of both fundamental and institutional change developed by using the historical method in *Dynamic Society* and *Ephemeral Civilization* were based upon representative samples of societies in the past, rather than upon every society the world has ever known. Hence the laws derived here from those models will need to be tested against the rest. If any one of these law-like propositions can be refuted, and if it cannot be supported indirectly through an association with other confirmed laws, then it must be abandoned. It is anticipated that these laws will be useful in future formal studies of the rise and fall—or rise and rise—of human societies.

These laws can also be used to construct other models to explain aspects of dynamic processes not surveyed in *Dynamic Society* or *Ephemeral Civilization*. Having completed these foundational works,

I expressed the opinion that: "In this way it should be possible to develop a new set of detailed dynamic models in economics. These models will differ from those currently employed in economics by being based on real historical processes rather than on the intuition of deductivists". Following up on this claim, I researched and published three books in the field of realist economics using these laws: namely *Longrun Dynamics* (1998), developing a theory about the longrun dynamics of advanced strategic societies; *Global Transition* (1999), developing a general theory about economic development in the Third World; and *The Global Crisis Makers* (2000), developing an analysis of strategic economic policy.

Prediction is a major reason for the development of laws. To do so, it is essential that the law-like statements in my book *Laws of History* be neither trivial nor so general that the resulting prediction is totally meaningless. When these laws were propounded (1998) I anticipated they would be able to say something useful about the big issues facing human society in the future. This has proven to be the case, not only in predicting both the Solar Revolution and the implications of climate change and climate mitigation (in *The Coming Eclipse*, 2010), but also the resolution of the "clash of civilizations" as well as issues about humanity's deep future (in *Ark of the Sun,* 2015). This constitutes a serious challenge to the scepticism of philosophers about the existence of laws of history; and it demolishes the inflated claims of philosophers to understand reality or the meaning of life.

TRUTH-TELLING

While truth-seeking is the main focus of this chapter, some consideration should be given to closely related issue of truth-telling. It is an issue that has been explored in greater detail in my book *The Death of Zarathustra: notes on truth for the risk-taker* (2011). As argued earlier, **truth-seeking** is the outcome of a sustained curiosity about the nature of reality, and a passion for discovering the meaning of life. **Truth-telling** requires the virtue of courage to present this reality to others, in a strategic environment in which truth is feared rather than welcomed. Courage is required because the vast majority of people in society do not wish to face the greedy, brutal reality of their daily lives. Rather, they wish to maintain the delusion provided by "existential schizophrenia", their innate psychological survival mechanism. Exposure to the truth is disturbing to the strategist and dangerous to the truth-teller, owing to the high degree of probability of retaliatory action against him: ask any "whistle-blower".

While society has no interest in unrestrained truth-telling—which is why there is no truth gene—there is an agreed role for constrained truth-telling. Indeed, there are institutions in modern technological societies that claim, contentiously, to have truth as their foundation stone. These institutions include the State, the legal system, the media, and science. Their claims are very recent, and are an outcome of the particular type of dynamic strategy—technological change—pursued by modern advanced societies. In the pre-modern era, institutions such as the State and the legal system were operated to maintain the wealth and power of the small elites that controlled conquest and commerce societies. These institutions were instruments of sectional power, not of universal truth, justice, and fairness. And institutions such as science and journalism didn't even exist. Only with the industrial technological paradigm shift, which in the space of a century or so transformed all members of economically advanced societies into voting strategists, did institutions like the State, the judiciary, and the media begin making claims about operating on the basis of truth, justice, and fairness. And only since technological change became central to the dynamic process of survival and prosperity—since the occurrence of the Industrial Revolution in Britain from 1780 to 1830—has science emerged as an organised activity devoted to truthfully exploring and explaining reality. In contrast, Third World countries are still mired in the past and, at best, pay only lip-service to these ideals. But even in advanced technological societies, truth-telling is subordinated to individual and societal self-interest. As most of these institutions have been discussed in the earlier chapter on ethics, I will restrict my comments here to the State and to science.

The State

The primary role of the State is to provide strategic leadership. This is a role that regularly conflicts with the supposed virtue of truth-telling at the various levels of individual politician, political party, and government. In the ethics chapter, a case study detailing the 2015 Australian leadership coup, demonstrated quite clearly that individual politicians value self-advancement more highly than truth-telling. Even the casual observer of politics will know that this is only the tip of the ice-berg when it comes to the blatant untruths that politicians tell in an attempt to cover up indiscretions of various kinds. They are famous for denying accusations of behaviour unbecoming a public figure until the evidence is overwhelming. Similarly, political parties are less concerned with telling the truth about their objectives and policies than with winning elections and gaining political power. Political parties regularly abandon the policies that enabled them to win government, once they are comfortably in office. This occurs so regularly that currently the electorate finds it difficult to trust party-political leaders.

We are all aware of the economical way politicians and their political parties have with the truth, but few of us fully understand the really big lies that governments tell; largely because few understand the nature of strategic leadership. Successful strategic leaders are those who intuitively understand the requirements of the underlying dynamic life-system, and who attempt to facilitate the objectives of its leading strategists, while achieving and maintaining an acceptable distribution of strategic income and wealth. These leaders understand that it is necessary to take hard and ruthless action abroad to protect the dynamic strategy their society is pursuing. They also understand that the citizens of their country are highly deluded about their own ethical standards. As history shows, humans are driven by strategic desire, which requires tough measures to be undertaken by their leaders in the world; yet, they do not want to take personal responsibility for these measures. This is an example at the national level of the psychological mechanism of "existential schizophrenia". Strategic leaders, therefore, have little option but to tell the truth to their international rivals, while telling lies to their own people.

The classic modern example of this leadership tactic is the rationalisation surrounding the invasion of Iraq by the USA and its allies in March 2003. The real reason for this invasion, as I argue in

The Death of Zarathustra, was about ensuring the supply of a critical strategic resource. It was an object lesson to Middle-Eastern oil-producing countries of what would happen to them if they continued to threaten to limit oil supplies—a critical strategic resource for the West—as they had done during the mid-1970s, causing stagflation and economic uncertainty. This lesson was not lost on other Middle-Eastern leaders, who, since the ruination of Iraqi society, have been careful not to artificially reduce oil supplies. But, sensing that the real reason for invasion would be unpalatable to the self-deluded chattering classes in the West—intellectuals, media, and self-promoting "do-gooders"—the leaders of the invasion force told their peoples that this military action was a righteous war to prevent an evil dictator (and Saddam Hussein certainly was evil by any standard) deploying "weapons of mass destruction" (WMD). Many in the West believed, or wanted to believe, this propaganda, and were "shocked" to discover that no signs of WMD could be found by objective observers after the invasion had been successfully accomplished. Yet most of these people refuse to see either the connection between their continued prosperity and this form of ruthless strategic leadership, or their own self-delusion and double standards. The immediate costs of this war in terms of both resources and lives were high: there are several studies of Iraqi deaths ranging from official US estimates of 60,000 to the disputed Lancet estimate of 650,000 (amounting to 2.5 percent of the population), each of which reflects different attitudes to the truth. The ongoing costs to Iraq arising from this societal instability, together with the rise of Islamic State, are even more serious. But this only makes the cynical object lesson directed at the Middle-Eastern oil producers by the Bush regime even more effective.

There is nothing new about this type of government duplicity, or general hypocritical complicity by the public. It is the outcome of "existential schizophrenia" that has characterised the history of human society, particularly during its commerce and technological phases, when we find it convenient to ignore the real forces underpinning our prosperous life-style. Another modern example is the Vietnam War involving the USA (1962 to 1973), although at this stage of the Cold War, securing strategic territory was more important than securing strategic resources. During the Vietnam War, the citizens of the US and its allies (Australia, NZ, Philippines, Thailand, and Taiwan) were told that this was a conflict about defending a small "democratic" state (South Vietnam), rather than a war to contain communist China. The cost of this war in defence of the dynamic strategy of the USA was, as usual, large in terms of both economic resources and lives (in the vicinity of 3 million people, mainly Vietnamese, but also Cambodian, Laotian, American, Australian, and other allied military personnel). This was a much more costly war than the later war in Iraq.

In the pre-modern period, the nature of government duplicity varied according to the dynamic strategy being pursued. Conquest societies, which were typical of this era, did not attempt to disguise the reason they invaded other countries; everyone knew and applauded the fact that it was done to increase per capita income and wealth to a level not possible from the practice of agriculture alone. Indeed, so as to involve the entire populace in the reality of conquest, strategic leaders either staged elaborate war games (such as were played out at the Coliseum in Rome) or sacrificed thousands of captured warriors in elaborate public religious ceremonies (as performed in Tenochtitlan in the Aztec Empire). But in commerce societies, where greater psychological distance could be achieved between daily life and brutal strategic reality (gossiping and haggling in the market place rather than watching blood sports), self-delusion concerning human motivation could be maintained. This was further enhanced by the development of philosophy, characterised by unworldly idealism. It is not surprising, therefore, that the strategic leaders of the ancient commerce society of Athens anticipated the approach taken by President George W. Bush to strategic defence by some 2,400 years. As I discuss in detail in my book *The Death of Zarathustra* (2011: 29-43), Thucydides (in *History of the Peloponnesian Wars*) examines the cynical way that Athenian leaders handled the invasion of the neutral colony of Melos. He recounts how the Athenian leaders were brutally honest with the Melians, informing them that unless they capitulated, Athens would invade their island and destroy their society. They admitted to their victims that Melos provided no military threat, and that the objective was to expand the Athenian commerce empire.

Despite this frankness, the Melians took the courageous but suicidal decision to reject Athenian demands; with the predictable result that Athens invaded Melos, killed all the males of military age, and sold all the women and children into slavery (something that even President Bush didn't attempt!). But, having told the truth to the Melians, the Athenian leadership told lies to their own self-deluded people by representing the invasion as necessary to the defence of Athens from the aggression of Sparta; despite the fact that the Spartans had no intention of using Melos as a base in their hostilities with Athens. Leadership duplicity goes hand in hand with the complicity of a self-deluded public in order to achieve strategic success.

Science

This is one of the few organised activities in modern advanced societies that takes truth-telling seriously. Why? Because the technological strategy of the *logos* demands an accurate description and analysis of physical reality. And this demand is effective because utilitarian truth—a restricted and "useful" form of truth—is essential to the successful operation of the *logos* pursuing the dynamic strategy of technological change. When scientists fail to tell the truth about strategically important aspects of reality, modern technological societies take this matter very seriously. Scientists found to have falsified their research, are publicly named, shamed, and dismissed from their research posts. The public may cheat and lie, but the intellectual priesthood is expected to be beyond reproach; but only because serious lapses are bad for business, not because it is "immoral".

Yet, even these serious sanctions are not sufficient to prevent a significant proportion of scientists and other intellectuals from employing untruthful means of satisfying their self-interest, especially when they lack the necessary ability, luck, or patience to succeed honestly. The extent of academic cheating in science has already been outlined (chapter 4). How do these highly educated and intelligent cheats live with themselves? In exactly the same way as everyone else—through the survival mechanism of "existential schizophrenia".

TRUTH AND ULTIMATE REALITY

What, then, does the dynamic-strategy theory tell us about truth and ultimate reality? So far we have seen that there is a scientific way of discovering not only the truth about the everyday world—existential truth—but also the truth about the underlying universal life-system, or strategic *logos*, which is the ultimate reality of life. Existential historicism is able to achieve what the deductive method of philosophers and many disciplines in the social sciences has never been able to achieve. The burning question is: why have intellectuals experienced so much trouble in arriving at the truth?

A critical problem for mankind—as discussed in chapter 2—is the need to balance the two material aspects of our human nature: the "unconscious organism" driven by strategic desire, and the "strategic cerebrum" dominated by reason. This complex dialogue between body and mind constitutes a problematic relationship that I've called "strategic dualism". As we have seen, it is very difficult for the rational mind to accept the reality of something as dominant in life and as morally embarrassing as strategic desire. It is, what I call, man's "existential dilemma".

The coping device of "existential schizophrenia (first proposed in my book *Ephemeral Civilization*, 1997 and developed fully in *Selfcreating Mind*, 2006) is a non-pathological condition that enables individuals to divide their thinking into two mutually exclusive compartments. In one compartment we deal with our actions, thoughts, and justifications that are necessary to survive and prosper, which reflect our irrational, selfish, and ruthless selves; and in the other, we deal with the way we like to see ourselves, as rational, compassionate, and altruistic. While the contents of these two compartments of the mind are incompatible, over hundreds of thousands of years we have become experts at keeping them apart, and in resolving the existential dilemma through sleight of hand. We are experts in deluding ourselves. Without the mechanism of existential schizophrenia, a large proportion of humanity would commit suicide out of disgust, or otherwise undermine strategic desire, which would critically damage the strategic *logos* and put an end to life as we know it. Truth endangers life.

Box 6.1   Truth or Fantasy?

Humans prefer fantasy to truth. They do so because they wish to find release from the horrors of life and their complicit involvement in these horrors. As people wish to be diverted from what they are, they value entertainment above realistic insight; which is why leading mass entertainers on the stage or in the sports arena are fabulously wealthy and thinkers are forced to work in universities. In the pre-modern world, diversionary activities—which were limited both by technology and the lack of significant leisure time enjoyed by the masses—took the form of war games (hunting, archery, sword play, jousting, wrestling, and boxing), blood sports (gladiatorial combat), religious festivals, and the consumption of strong drink and tobacco. Blood sports as diversion? Actually it is not hard to understand how our ancestors were able to find diversion in blood sports—able to enjoy the misfortune of others while they were, for the time being, safe in their auditorium seats—because those of us today who are addicted to blood-thirsty drama at the cinema or on television do exactly the same thing; vicariously participate in the misfortune of others. It is why, not very long ago, the middle classes in Victorian Britain used to attend public hangings and ogle unfortunate deformed people in side-shows. But in the modern world, the scope for diversion is almost infinite. As we know, it takes the form of escapist "novels" (actually there is nothing novel or new about them), cinema, television, other electronic media (computer games, mobile phones, social media, facebook, and internet surfing), and travel. While younger people appear addicted to the mindlessness of electronic media, older people find diversion in reading "real" books, watching films during the day in dark rooms, and travelling the world. Travel is a particularly fascinating form of diversion, as it involves rapid transport in hermetically sealed capsules through as many countries as possible in as short a time as is feasible. The usual rationalisation is that by doing so, one gets to know the world and to broaden one's mind. In fact, travellers going at the speed of light through Europe, Asia, or the Americas learn nothing more about the world or themselves than they could have by sitting in a dark room at home watching a colour travel movie. It is merely a way in which older people, who wish to consume most of their accumulated wealth before they die (as if that makes any difference once they are dead!), can divert themselves from the grossness of their existence and the certainty of their forthcoming deaths; rather than a way in which they can discover the truth about life. It also grants them bragging rights among their families, friends, and neighbours. Of course, I know, there is always the odd exception to such generalisations!

While existential schizophrenia supports life, it undermines the search for truth, and enables individuals to be untruthful in their dealings with each other. As we tell lies to ourselves, we have no trouble telling lies to others, particularly when we can gain materially from doing so. The overriding objective in life for individuals is to survive and prosper, not to be virtuous. Therefore, **the strategic *logos* has no need for truth-telling and, hence, there is no strategic demand for metaphysical virtue.** Existential schizophrenia is also a barrier to gaining access to the truth about life. People, even those who are highly educated, see the world through very subjective lenses. We like to see the world in a way that rationalises and justifies our desires and self-interest. We prefer a warm and comfortable fantasy to a bleak and uncomfortable reality. We prefer philosophies that support our metaphysical, racial, class, and gender prejudices, to those that are actually true, real, and discomforting. Most public and private arguments are all about issues contributing to material self-interest, but are thinly disguised by their authors taking the moral high ground; in claiming to be doing "the right thing". **All "moral" arguments in everyday life are really about material self-interest—nauseatingly so.** This is also the case with many intellectual arguments.

This conclusion about the role of truth in human society begs the question: If man has a vested interest, because of his dual nature, in avoiding the truth and in telling self-seeking lies, why do some people actively seek the truth and avoid telling lies? It should be made clear that we are talking about a very small proportion of any population, because if truth-seeking/telling ever reached significant levels, the strategic *logos* would be endangered and the survival of humanity would be undermined. The only reason a tiny proportion of overabundantly curious people seek out and tell the truth is that they possess an underactive existential schizophrenia mechanism. A handful of people are unable to hide their true selves from themselves. They are unable to completely deceive themselves; they are unable to look away at all times. This is, however, a relative issue, as no individual is completely free from self-deception. They only survive at all because their underactive existential schizophrenia mechanism still offers a minimum of protection.

Yet, some courageous individuals take huge risks by attempting to dismantle even this minimal protection. They find in truth-seeking the most extreme of extreme sports. One such individual was Friedrich Nietzsche (1844–1900), who deliberately refused to take any precautions, until the pressure of his truth-seeking was so intense, he retreated into madness (see my book *The Death of Zarathustra*, 2011). When existential schizophrenia completely malfunctions, individuals like Nietzsche must find other psychological means of blocking out the horror of existence. Others have employed even more bizarre psychological defence mechanisms, such as the German woman in her late 20s, who suddenly went blind and began developing multiple personalities (*PsyCh Journal*, 2015). After ten years, one of these personalities began to see again, and following this most of her personalities gradually resumed their sight for most (but not all) of the time. Could it be that the horror of life became so unbearable that blindness was a preferable option? Others have committed suicide when the strain of facing who they really are became too great to bear.

There is, however, an even smaller proportion of the population, who manage to tread a very fine line between facing the horror of reality and seeking the safety of delusion in order to discover the truth about themselves and their world. These individuals, driven by an intense curiosity, have an existential schizophrenia mechanism that operates effectively at a low level so that they can balance truth with delusion. These truth-seekers are the only ones who have any chance of understanding ultimate reality—the true meaning of life. Truth-seeking, therefore, is the outcome *not* of a general metaphysical "will to truth", but of an accidental combination of a hyper-active curiosity instinct and an underactive existential schizophrenia mechanism in a very small number of individuals.

Yet even among the effective truth-seekers, only an even smaller proportion has the required intellectual outlook, imagination, and tools of the scholars' trade to reach the ultimate reality of life. One requires an understanding of the dynamic materialist system underlying human society (economic skills); as well as the paths and patterns tracked by that system in the past (historical and biological skills); the nature of strategic agents (psychological and political skills); and a flair for strategic thinking. This combination of skills is not found in standard academic disciplines, and certainly not in philosophy. Accordingly, university thinkers (rhymes appropriately with blinkers), in order to protect their reputations, form an academic mafia to discriminate against the truth-seekers. This mafia is an exclusive group that promotes the second- and third-rate work of its members; boycotts the work of dangerous outsiders; steals ideas from outsiders, which it dilutes, removes the holistic framework, and presents in distorted form as their own work; and develops comforting myths about their importance, and about the "meaning" of their society. This mafia controls university departments, academic journals, publishers, and conferences. There is an international hierarchy in this academic mafia, which makes and destroys intellectual reputations, with the controlling bodies operating in the superpowers. In the English-speaking world before the Second World War, the centre of the intellectual mafia was England; since the war it has been the USA. Despite their claims to the contrary, these institutional intellectuals are the suppressors of truth—they are the truth-deniers.

Chapter Seven
Strategic Freedom

What is freedom? The conventional answers to this question emerge from discussions of the interrelated concepts of "free will" and "individual freedom". **Free will** is an elusive concept, which for thousands of years has occupied the attention of philosophers, largely using a theological framework in which God is both perfectly powerful and perfectly good. This inflexible framework resulted in convoluted arguments about the relationship between the omnipotence of God and the free will of His creatures who perversely depart from His goodness. These arguments are concerned with the free will not only of man, but also of God. Central to these arguments is the compatibility of God's will (the ultimate from of determinism) and the free will of mankind.

Modern secular philosophers have adopted and developed many of these earlier theological arguments by substituting the laws of nature and principles of biological evolution for a divine creator. In doing so they have grappled with the supposed contest between various perceived forms of determinism—physical, psychological, and biological—and the free will of man. This has resulted in individual philosophers taking three broad paths: denying that the world is deterministic; accepting that the world is deterministic, but maintaining that this is "compatible" with free will; or accepting the deterministic nature of the world and arguing that this is "incompatible" with free will.

Very little progress has been made in enlightening us about this issue. Why? Because philosophers have failed to develop a realist general dynamic theory of life to provide a context for this concept. They get bogged down in fruitless "mind experiments", which are no more than simple—if not simplistic—stories. The great search for wisdom begun by pre-Socratic Greek thinkers has ended up in story-telling and endless debates about the meaning of words.

My realist general dynamic theory—the dynamic-strategy theory—suggests that the key to free will is the flexibility expressed by our DNA, enabling us to respond effectively to a continuously changing strategic *logos*. Humans are driven by strategic desire to survive and prosper. This is genetically determined, as a result of "strategic selection" (not natural selection) in response to the requirements of the *logos*. If we wish to survive and prosper we have little choice but to follow the demands of our life-system. Yet, even here people can, and do, exercise free choice by opposing this driving force and committing suicide. Only a small minority, however, take this anti-life path. While we are driven to survive and prosper, we do exercise choice through the manner in which we achieve this basic urge. Life in general, and human society in particular, are populated by highly flexible strategic agents capable of responding to whatever demands are made of them by their particular strategic *logos*. **Herein lies the property of free will—namely the capacity to respond with varying degrees of freedom to the demands of the *logos*.** While free choice is possible here in the achievement of survival—means rather than ends—man's freedom is constrained by the need to meet the requirements of the *logos* communicated via strategic demand. Different forms of the *logos* result in different political structures, which provide different scope for free will. While it is possible to reject the demands of the *logos*, there are varying types of costs resulting from noncompliance, ranging from ostracism to imprisonment to death.

The concept of **individual freedom** is usually discussed within a political context. What form of political organisation, it is asked, will maximise individual freedom? There are, of course, various responses to this question, none of which takes into account the dominating presence of the strategic *logos*. There are two major issues here. First, it is the *logos* that determines the political organisation adopted by any society, not the ideas of political philosophers. As always, desires drive, while ideas merely facilitate. And second, there is no practical political system that can deliver true freedom, only what I will call "strategic freedom". Strategic freedom is the ability of individuals to fulfil their strategic desire to survive and prosper by exercising a degree of control over the dynamic strategy of their society. Only since the advent of the technological era, has the vast majority of any society's population been able to experience strategic freedom. And even in modern technological societies, true freedom—what I call "ultimate freedom"—is rarely achieved. As I show in the next chapter, ultimate freedom is only achieved by those willing to challenge the *logos* and **all** possible political systems that might be generated by it.

TYPES OF FREEDOM

Free will and freedom, therefore, are two very different but interrelated concepts. If we possess the capacity to make our own decisions and take responsibility for them, then we live in a world where free will is possible. But if we are denied the right to make our own decisions by the very nature of life, then the world is a deterministic system and free will doesn't exist. Even if free will exists, our ability to exercise it will vary according to the type of ecosociopolitical system in which we live. In totalitarian systems, the exercise of free will is tightly constrained, and its unfortunate citizens are limited in what they can think and express publicly, what type of education they have access to, what careers they can follow, and what goods and services they can consume. In totalitarian systems, strategic freedom is severely limited, whereas in free-market democracies strategic freedom is much wider and deeper. In free-market societies the individual has a greater say in the running of their lives and in the exercise of free will. Accordingly, the problem of strategic frustration that we encountered in earlier chapters is much reduced.

There are four different types of freedom in my dynamic-strategy theory: strategic freedom; self-destructive freedom; delusional freedom; and ultimate freedom. Each form of freedom has defined costs and benefits.

- **Strategic freedom** exists in the political and social space generated by the strategic *logos*. Each type of *logos* provides different scope for individual freedom, ranging from the most restrictive (military *logos*) through lesser restrictive (hunting *logos* and mercantile *logos*) to the least restrictive (enterprise *logos*). Strategic agents are free to exercise choices within the confines of any *logos* type according to the prevailing characteristic degrees of freedom. This means going with strategic desire and responding to the overall requirements of the life-system, but making a range of individual choices about how to achieve this. While the benefit of complying with this system is survival and prosperity, the cost is a relatively meaningless style of life. This approach is examined later in this chapter.

- **Self-destructive freedom** is the ability of the individual to exercise his free will by rejecting the demands of the strategic *logos*, by pursuing an antistrategic course aimed at overthrowing the prevailing strategic system, or by defying the imperatives of strategic desire and committing suicide. The benefits of both courses of action are freedom beyond that permitted by the *logos*, but the cost in both cases is death, either immediate or delayed.

- **Delusional freedom** is the outcome of the philosophical/ religious attempt to suppress desire, which is seen as the source of suffering (for example Buddhism or the philosophy of Arthur Schopenhauer). The aim of this approach is to achieve "liberation" from the tyranny of "base desires" and the cultivation of "desires for good". The existential problem here is that it is not possible to eliminate strategic desire, because life would not exist without it. Also there is a fundamental contradiction in this way of life, as its followers can only exist by demanding sustenance from those engaged in the strategic *logos*. The benefit of this course of action is presumably peace of mind, but the cost is mendicancy and intellectual inconsistency.

- **Ultimate freedom** is the outcome of recognising and understanding the strategic *logos*, and challenging its values ("wrestling the *logos*"), but not its existence. While the cost of this course of action will be a lower standard of living and possibly societal retribution, the benefit is the pursuit of a thoughtful and meaningful life. This approach is examined in the next chapter.

THE CONTRIBUTION OF POLITICAL PHILOSOPHY

Political philosophers have been concerned with theoretical explanations of existing systems and theoretical possibilities for ideal systems. These theories are not persuasive because they fail to recognise that real-world political systems are determined by the strategic *logos*, which is a dynamic entity totally unknown to them. While conventional political theories are unrealistic and inadequate for our task of analysing free will and freedom, I will deal briefly with the ideas of two influential political thinkers, Jean-Jacques Rousseau (1712–1778) and Georg Hegel (1770–1831), to illustrate how my political theory differs from the rest. This is meant only to be a background sketch for the development of the dynamic-strategy theory of freedom.

Rousseau famously states in *The Social Contract* (1762) that "man is born free, yet everywhere he is in chains". He meant by this evocative, but misleading, statement that humans in their natural state were free because they lived independently of any political system. But as soon as we formed political systems we lost our freedoms, because we were coerced into living according to the dictates of monarchs and dictators. Yet, it is possible, Rousseau argued, to create a political system in which individuals could once more experience freedom while enjoying the benefits of civilisation. This argument depends on a very unusual concept of "freedom" that he called the "general will", exercised through a "social contract". Essentially, Rousseau drew a distinction between the "will of all", which is the sum total of everything that the people wish to achieve; and the "general will", which is what is in the best interest of society as a whole. His idea of democracy was a society formed by a social contract in which all individuals would vote for the general will or common good. Hence, by subjecting themselves to the general will—however this might be determined—they could enjoy the benefits of civilisation without compromising their freedom. This could be achieved, he believed, by a universally elected aristocracy in a system where differences of wealth and class would be abolished—individuals give up their personal resources to the community—and where children would be educated to identify with, and vote for, the common good (or general will) rather than individual self-interest. From this elected aristocracy, a "legislator" would be chosen and he would determine the type of government he thought best for that society. As we saw earlier in this book, Rousseau was not the only thinker to theorise about a social contract; others included Thomas Hobbes and John Locke.

There are a number of major problems with this idea of freedom, together with the political system by which Rousseau thought it could be achieved. First, man is not "born free". There has never been a time when humans (or, indeed, any life forms) were free of the demands of the *logos* and its various organisational forms. Even in very simple paleolithic societies, the family, struggling to survive in a hostile world, has needed to interact with their particular and primitive *logos*. Rousseau correctly refers to the family as the most ancient of human societies, but he sees it as an artificially isolated entity. His family is unrealistically separated from the dynamic forces underlying the need to survive and prosper in a hostile world. In the real-world primitive hunting family, each member had his/her part to play in the struggle to survive, where the margin between life and death was very slender, and the average life-span (about 25 years from birth) was short. In these circumstances, freedom from the dictates of the *logos* was impossible. Only with the emergence of civilisation based on the Neolithic agricultural revolution, were surpluses created that enabled privileged members of society to address issues of life other than those of immediate survival. And even these privileged few could do so only while their society prospered. Freedom is a relative concept as it takes place within the confines of the strategic *logos*. Rousseau could not have been more wrong when he claimed that "man is born free".

The second problem with Rousseau's argument is that real freedom cannot be achieved if an individual is "forced" to subject himself to the "general will". One cannot be forced to be free in this manner. By responding to strategic desire in order to survive and prosper, our individual is actually complying with the dictates of the *logos*. True freedom, it is argued in the next chapter, requires us to struggle against, rather than submit to, the dictates of the *logos*. In Rousseau's language, this involves struggling against the "general will", not submitting meekly to it.

Third, Rousseau's requirement that class and inequality in wealth be abolished, to facilitate acquiescence with the general will, looks very much like communist totalitarianism. This perspective is reinforced by his further requirement that the younger generation be educated to identify with the general will rather than individual self-interest. In Russia, as is well known, this approach led to the forced substitution of a command economy for an emerging, but still fragile, free-market system. The outcome was the complete suppression of individual freedom in the short-term and, in the longer-term, the collapse of the USSR. Individual "strategic freedom" and economic viability go hand-in-hand in modern technological society. To suppress one is to suppress the other.

Fourth, Rousseau believes that the "social contract" is the outcome of deliberate human choice. A given group of individuals who, in their "natural state", are pursuing their own self-interest, decide as a group to surrender their individualism in order to enjoy the benefits of a centralised political society. In the process, they create a political organisation with a single will—the "general will". This rather quaint story about the transformation of the Many into the One reflects its eighteenth-century Enlightenment origins of the triumph of reason and hope over experience. What it fails to do is to provide a realistic explanation of how this large group of individuals comes to make such a momentous decision. In the twenty-first century, a more "scientific" approach has been taken to this issue by similarly side-stepping any explanatory mechanism and asserting that community cooperation is the outcome of the principle of self-organisation—an exercise in social physics. Complexity theory, however, is just as quaint as Rousseau's social contract theory.

While Rousseau's theory about freedom, which was a product of the eighteenth century Enlightenment, has a superficial plausibility, **Hegel's** theory, which was an outcome of nineteenth century German idealism, is both metaphysical and completely absurd. Hegel sees freedom, which is linked to reason, as the core characteristic of life. In his theory, history is seen as an inevitable progression of freedom to increasingly higher forms through a dialectical process of hypothesis, antithesis, synthesis. Historical progress is really progress in abstract thought—the Absolute Idea— whereby one epoch replaces another by thinking more thoroughly and more rationally; ending in the political organisation of the Prussian state and in the metaphysical thought of Hegel. Everyday reality is, in effect, an outcome of the mind of the Absolute Spirit or God. Ultimate reality for Hegel is the Absolute Spirit. The amazing thing is that many nineteenth-century intellectuals took Hegel seriously.

Now back to the real, real-world! The mechanism generating integrated societal systems, which has eluded early-modern and modern thinkers alike, is that embodied in the strategic *logos*. The types of political systems that have emerged in the past and the present—and will emerge in the future—have depended on the types of dynamic strategies that they have pursued. As I've shown elsewhere, the family-multiplication strategy requires a family-based organisation; the conquest strategy requires an authoritarian state; a commerce strategy requires a state organised for and by wealthy merchants; and the technological strategy requires more democratic organisations and institutions (see Tables 4.1 and 4.2). In other words, the appropriate political organisation at any time and in any place is a response to the requirements of the strategic *logos*, communicated through strategic demand (or logosian demand).

And nothing is set in concrete. As the *logos* is transformed, so are political (as well as economic and social) structures. If the dynamic strategy pursued by a transformed *logos* is reversed, then its political structures will also be reversed. This has been the case throughout history whenever the strategic sequence has been conquest►commerce►conquest. This was the normal circular strategic sequence in the pre-technological era, until it was broken by the unprecedented Industrial Revolution. But interestingly, this type of reversal occurred in the 1930s, when, owing to global crisis, countries such as Germany, Italy, and Japan switched their dynamic strategy from technological change to conquest, resulting in the transformation of democratic states into authoritarian states.

The limitations of political philosophy are the outcome of a failure to develop a realist general dynamic theory of human society. Only a realist theory of this type can provide an understanding of the way real political systems emerge and, therefore, how and why strategic freedom exists. Rather than do this, political philosophers employ rational thought to develop ideal systems that have the capacity to generate the freedoms they desire. It is hardly surprising, therefore, that conflicts emerge between the ideal and the real. By not coming to grips with the real dynamic forces transforming society, rigid ideal political structures can be imposed on any society, with costly, even disastrous, consequences. Recent examples include the imposition of Marxist inspired ideals on countries undergoing crises, such as Russia, China, North Korea, Vietnam, and Cuba. Real-world costs resulting from idealist political structures have been massive in terms of lost GDP, lost lives, and lost personal freedom. As we saw in an earlier chapter, Stalin and Mao were responsible for the deaths of up to 50 and 60 million people respectively. And the economic development—and hence the living standards—of Russia was delayed for three generations and of China by two generations. The economic and social cost involved is tragic; a tragedy that could have been avoided had a realist general dynamic theory encapsulating the strategic *logos* been available and embraced. But in a world where desires drive the actions of men and women, only those ideas that justify their materialist pursuit are ever likely to be adopted.

THE FLUCTUATING NATURE OF STRATEGIC FREEDOM

Strategic freedom is considered by most philosophers as the birthright of all humans. Rousseau introduced this idea in the late eighteenth century, just as European societies were attempting to break free from medieval constraints on the individual. This was a process of change driven by the emerging industrial technological paradigm shift—the Industrial Revolution. The transforming Western European *logos* required increasing individual decision-making flexibility and enterprise, and the radical redistribution of income provided individuals with the economic power to replace authoritarian political and social structures with more democratic ones. In the process, strategic freedom became more widespread. New *ideas* about freedom, however, only flourished in Western Europe in the following century, and then only because of the new requirements of the *logos*. Without this technological transformation, ideas about strategic freedom would have remained an unattainable curiosity. As always, desires drive and ideas merely facilitate.

Rousseau's assertion that freedom was man's birthright was completely novel in the eighteenth century. It was also completely wrong. Even in the "democratic" heyday of ancient Athens—the fifth and fourth centuries BC—only about 20 percent of the resident population of about 250 to 300 thousand people participated in government. These were the free adult male citizens. The remaining 80 percent—which included females, slaves, and foreign residents (Metics)—were unable to vote or make policy. And even this very limited form of direct democracy spanned a period (507–322 BC) of only 185 years, and was punctuated by significant disruptions. It was definitely not the outcome of an idea—of Greek political philosophy—but a response to the Athenian strategic *logos* of commerce, which required the direct participation of a relatively large number of free decision makers in mercantile activities. This was the era of the Athenian dynamic strategy of commerce, which succeeded the conquest strategy of the archaic era. When it was exhausted, it was replaced by a new era of conquest, which put an end to the experiment with democracy. So, in ancient Athenian history, strategic "freedom" was limited to the commerce era, and was non-existent in the conquest eras (except for a small warrior elite) that preceded and followed it.

The relationship between the transforming *logos* and strategic freedom can be broadly sketched throughout the past 2 million years (myrs). As discussed earlier, two interrelated dynamic processes dominate the history and future of human society. The first is the technological paradigm shifts—or fundamental economic revolutions—and the second is the set of dynamic strategies available to human society within each of the technological paradigms. There have been three technological paradigm shifts in the past 2 myrs: the paleolithic (hunting and gathering); the neolithic (agricultural); and the industrial (or modern). We are now rapidly approaching the fourth paradigm shift—the "Solar Revolution" —which my model predicts will begin during the middle decades of the twenty-first century. While these technological revolutions made it possible to employ different dynamic strategies, they had strong implications for individual freedom.

The essential point to grasp, contra Hegel, is that individual freedom has always been secondary to survival and prosperity. Whenever survival and prosperity could only be achieved by surrendering freedom, social groups had little hesitation in doing so. For example, when the Roman Empire began to implode during the fifth century AD, the great majority of Roman citizens were willing to surrender their Roman freedoms to regional war lords who could offer protection—and hence the prospect of survival—from the predatory Roman state, the marauding Roman army, and the threat of barbarian invasion. This new contract formed the basis of feudalism in western and southern Europe. While some individuals may have chosen death rather than change, the large majority, as always, chose survival over their former freedoms.

The first technological paradigm shift in human history—the Paleolithic (or hunting) Revolution—occurred in Africa about 2 myrs ago. It centred on the development of stone tools that enabled the transition from scavenging to hunting. The dominant dynamic strategy pursued—the only one available within the Paleolithic technological paradigm—was family-multiplication. This strategy combined procreation and migration within an extended family structure to extend their control over land resources required for hunting and gathering. It was the best way to maximise the probability of survival and a limited prosperity. The social structure required by the paleolithic *logos* enabled a range of limited strategic freedoms. This extended family group was usually male dominated, with older males exercising power and influence over relatives through their experience and knowledge of various initiation and religious rituals. Wisdom gained through experience was vital to the security of the group. While there was a well-defined power structure in the extended family, the need to act as a team when hunting or gathering provided scope for a degree of power sharing and, hence, some individual responsibility and freedom. The ability to influence decision-making informally also arose from the close personal relationships within the extended family. Certainly the degree of strategic freedom was greater in the Paleolithic than in the succeeding Neolithic era.

The second technological paradigm shift—the Neolithic (or agricultural) Revolution—occurred in the Fertile Crescent, stretching from Persia through the eastern end of the Mediterranean to Egypt, beginning about 11,000 years ago. It also occurred independently in the Mesoamerican region of the New World, about 8,000 years ago. This technological revolution was based on the development of cereals and the domestication of livestock, together the techniques and capital structures to do so on a large scale. The outcome was a steady growth of populations that formed urban settlements that in turn required the creation of complex social and political institutions and organisations. With time these political and social structures became highly hierarchical, with the emergence of states ruled by powerful kings, wealthy aristocrats, and influential priests. While small elites ruled over relatively large populations possessing limited freedom and responsibility, the degree of these qualities varied between different types of strategic systems.

The best predictor of the political system and degree of strategic freedom in the Neolithic era is the dynamic strategy that any society adopted and pursued. There were two possibilities in this era— the commerce strategy or the conquest strategy—the "choice" of which depended upon location, resource base, and competition. By employing one of these dynamic strategies, a successful society in the ancient world was able to increase its size, regional power, and living standards significantly above the levels dictated by agricultural productivity alone. Rome, which pursued a highly successful conquest strategy, had at its peak a population of at least 1 million in its metropolis and more than 50 million in its empire, at a time when agriculture alone could support a city of no more than 50,000 people at a considerably lower standard of living. Egypt, which pursued a highly successful commerce strategy for some three millennia, experienced an increase in population of between 1 and 5 million over this time at a relatively high standard of living. Both these societies exercised considerable power over their neighbours.

But this prosperity and power came at a cost to the ordinary citizen in terms of individual freedom, particularly in a conquest society. The conquest *logos* required a system of autocratic political and social structures, presided over by a relatively small but wealthy and powerful warrior and priestly elite. This elite, of course, was male dominated. While the ordinary citizens of the conquest society were moderately prosperous, they had no political power or influence. They had effectively traded former freedoms for survival and limited prosperity. Further, the conquest *logos* employed a coercive labour system, based on large numbers of domestic and industrial slaves. In Roman Italy between 30 and 40 percent of the population consisted of slaves; while in the rest of the empire that proportion was about 10 to 15 percent. And of these slaves, about half were owned by less than 2 percent of the Roman population. So both wealth and individual freedom in Rome were enjoyed by only a very small elite.

Those pre-modern societies fortunate enough to pursue the dynamic strategy of commerce—such as Egypt, Phoenicia, Carthage, Greece (800–550 BC), Venice, Britain (sixteenth-eighteenth centuries), and the Low Countries—were able to balance prosperity and economic and political expansion with a much wider experience of strategic freedom. The reason is that the strategic *logos* of commerce required the participation of a relatively larger proportion of the population in entrepreneurial activity than that of conquest. But this greater individual freedom could not be taken for granted. Commerce societies continuously looked extinction in the face in a world dominated by conquest societies. The vast wealth of commerce societies was always a great temptation to conquest neighbours. It was only a matter of time. Inevitably, the Phoenicians were swept aside by Alexander of Macedonia; Carthage was destroyed by Rome; Greece was also conquered by Rome; Egypt was finally absorbed into the Roman empire (after periods of conquest from Mesopotamia and Greece); Venice was conquered by Napoleon; and only the narrow Channel and luck prevented Spain invading commerce England. The outcome of these conquests was disastrous for the free citizens of former commerce societies; those who were not killed were dispossessed and sold into slavery, thereby forfeiting their former freedoms. Even in prosperous times, commerce societies possessed large numbers of slaves purchased with their trading wealth. In early fourth century BC Athens, there were twice as many slaves as free citizens (adult males). And slavery was an important institution in commerce societies even as late as the mid-nineteenth century. Freedom was a scarce and precarious commodity in the pre-modern world.

The third technological paradigm shift—the Industrial Revolution—was centred on Britain in the period 1780 to 1830; and since then has been spreading steadily around the world; at first in Western Europe and its overseas offshoots (North America, Australia, New Zealand, and parts of South America), later Japan, and now China, India, and Indonesia. Because the modern *logos* requires widespread decision-making and enterprise by its citizens, individual freedom has become universal in successful technological societies. This freedom developed gradually as the pioneer industrial societies introduced technological processes that required increasing strategic participation by their populations. This can be seen in the unfolding political franchise of populations in Western Europe and its overseas progeny during the nineteenth and early twentieth centuries. Strategic freedom went hand in hand with economic maturation. Yet, even today, democracy has not penetrated the global community very deeply. According to the UK *Economist*'s "Democracy Index" (based on five categories of electoral process and pluralism, civil liberties, government functioning, political participation, and political culture), for 2012, "full democracies" included only 11.3 percent of world population; "flawed democracies" accounting for a further 37.2 percent; and "authoritarian regimes" accounting for a relatively high 37.1 percent. It is essential to realise that global democracy will not improve significantly until all countries are transformed into successful technological societies. It is not something that can be induced by the West just telling or bribing non-technological political leaders to adopt democratic political and social structures. Even if they make a determined political effort, the old ways and elites will merely reassert themselves. Global democracy will happen, but it will take time. It is essential to take seriously the strategic maxim often stressed here: "desires drive and ideas merely facilitate", because wrong-headed intervention will only cause crisis and delay in this inevitable transition.

Today, for the first time in human history, there is no need for the average citizen to trade off strategic freedom for survival and prosperity. But this doesn't mean that strategic freedom is non-reversible. In the twentieth century, successful industrial societies going through the major crisis of global war and its aftermath were hijacked by antistrategic groups, which progressively removed individual freedoms. Examples include the Bolsheviks in Russia in 1917, the Fascists in Italy in the 1920s and 1930s, the Nazis in Germany in the 1930s, and militarists in Japan in the 1930s. In each case these antistrategists were able to exploit severe economic crisis—major attacks on the strategic *logos*—to subvert market mechanisms and political and social freedoms, and to impose centralised political, social, and economic control. In doing so, these antistrategists replaced technological dynamic strategies with command economies and conquest strategies. In the process, hard won strategic freedoms were lost, and were only regained at huge economic and human cost. This threat to strategic freedom is not just a thing of the recent past. Any successful attempt by powerful antistrategic groups to hijack the strategic agenda of the *logos* will endanger individual freedoms. We need, therefore, to resist the interventions of antistrategic groups.

THE LIMITATIONS OF STRATEGIC FREEDOM

To the rational mind, strategic desire is a reality that is difficult to accept and embrace. The realisation that life is dominated by a selfish struggle for existence and for material prosperity is repugnant to most thoughtful people. A common response is denial, which is made possible by the mechanism of existential schizophrenia that was explored in earlier chapters. As we have seen, a person may regard themselves as altruistic, honourable, and generous, but in reality they participate in daily activities that are self-serving, exploitative, and dishonourable. The daily revelations in the media about greed and corruption in political, business, and organised labour circles; cheating and corruption in sports teams and organisations; abuse and cover-up by members of church organisations; and falsification in scientific research are shrugged off as something that other people do. But the truth is that few resist the temptation to indulge in material and sensual excesses when the stakes are high enough and the probability of getting caught seems low. While these actions are considered to be the excesses of a few, they are in fact widespread, albeit hidden most of the time, even in ordered societies. In disordered societies they are the norm. The point is that these "excesses" arise from the basic urges and desires that underpin life. By indulging in these basic desires, the large majority of human beings are slaves to the dictates of the *logos*.

Is there an alternative to passively accepting the dominance of the *logos*? This is the most complex issue facing the rational mind. If life only exists because individuals respond to the dictates of the *logos*, how can there be an alternative? Herein lies the central paradox of life. Some seekers after truth believe that faith in God can lead to transcendence over the grossness of this world. But a great irony resides at the heart of this argument. As shown in my book *Dead God Rising*, God is a creature of the *logos* itself! From the earliest times, human societies, fearful that their life-system might fail like so many before them, have looked to strategic guardians for support and guidance. These early strategic guardians were eventually turned into gods, as the wealth of agricultural societies gave rise to powerful priestly classes. These gods lived and died with the societies that created them; only to be succeeded by new societies and new gods— "dead god rising". **It is deeply ironical, therefore, that people should turn to the guardians of the *logos* for transcendence over the dictates of the *logos*.** At the forefront of those turning to the "gods" to achieve transcendence near the end of their lives were the powerful and wealthy—kings, aristocrats, and conquistadors—who had spent their lives exploiting and killing the masses. Even the priestly classes spent their lives serving the *logos*, which they called God.

Others have approached the patent absurdity of life, which exists even in societies displaying strategic freedom, in ways that have changed their lives. One of the more interesting "schools" of philosophy was developed by the Cynics of ancient Greece and Rome. **Classical Cynicism**—as contrasted with the modern meaning of this word—is associated with two Athenians in the late fifth and early fourth centuries BC. Antisthenes (c.445–366 BC), close friend of Socrates (469–399), is widely considered the philosophical founder of Cynicism, while Diogenes of Sinope (c.410–320 BC) is seen as pioneering the practical life-style of the Cynic. The Cynic way of life—it was not really a school of ideas—attracted those who were disillusioned with the moral bankruptcy of conventional society. It flourished both in Greece and the later Roman Empire, finally disappearing with the collapse of Rome and the rise of the medieval Christian church in the fifth century AD. Cynicism was the most popular and influential form of Socratic philosophy in the ancient world, giving birth also to Stoicism, a more modest form of Cynicism developed by Zeno of Citium (c.336–c.265).

Classical Cynicism possessed a number of intriguing features, although the crude manner in which they were expressed alienated many. A sense of this can be seen reflected in the Greek word for Cynicism (*kunikos*), which means "dog-like". The central interest of the Cynics was in devising an ethical way of living in a sophisticated urban world; a way of living that enables the individual to experience a freedom and happiness that transcended Greek democratic freedom. Diogenes and the later Cynics insisted that a good and happy life could only be achieved by rejecting the prevailing conventions of society and replacing them with reason, nature, and virtue. This opposition to the claims of the state to dictate thought and behaviour—this violation of the rules of convention—is the central innovation of the Cynics. And they did so with a mocking and satirical sense of humour. The Cynics were unique in the ancient world in making freedom—particularly freedom of speech—the core of their philosophy of life.

Nature rather than civilization should, according to the Cynics, be the guide for the virtuous man, because social convention with its emphasis on wealth and worldly pleasures operate to constrain individual freedom. And the virtuous man should be self-sufficient rather than being dependent upon the dictates of society. By "nature", Diogenes meant the natural processes of the world, whereby life emerges, exists for a short time, and passes away. He viewed human society as deviating from the natural laws governing the process of life; he saw human society as artificial rather than natural (like other species); and he called for a return to the original path of life from which humanity had strayed. This could be done, he claimed, by achieving the necessary clarity of mind needed to eliminate confusion, and by disciplining the body to overcome desire through an exercise of the will. Diogenes argued that this return to nature could not be achieved through philosophical activity; indeed, he despised philosophers and constantly ridiculed his Athenian contemporary Plato.

By freedom, the Cynics meant the acquisition of individual liberty (*eleutheria*), self-sufficiency (*autarkeia*), and frankness or freedom of speech (*parrhesia*); particularly the latter. They believed it was essential to speak out fearlessly about the absurdities, contradictions, and naked self-interest of social conventions and of social leaders—to tell the truth to powerful authorities from a position of independence. And Diogenes was the exemplar of this central characteristic of Cynicism. There is a well-known story about Diogenes and Alexander the Great. According to his biographer (Diogenes Laertius in the third century BC), one day when Diogenes was sunning himself in the Craneion (a residential area on the lower slopes of Acrocorinth), Alexander stood over him and said: "Ask of me anything you desire"; to which Diogenes replied: "Stand out of my light!". Even if a myth, the point is clearly made—the free individual has no interest in flattering powerful political figures, or in receiving anything from them except being left alone. **Powerful individuals have nothing to offer the virtuous, self-sufficient thinker, who deliberately rejects recognition by others.**

Diogenes Laertius also records that when the great Cynic was asked what is "the most beautiful thing in the world", he replied "*parrhesia*", or free speech. And when asked "where do you come from?" Diogenes replied, "I am a citizen of the world" (*kosmopolites*), rather than a citizen of Athens, or even a Greek citizen. What Diogenes was saying, of course, is that he identified not with the coveted citizenship of Athens, but with all humanity.

Diogenes had a more complex and sophisticated conception of freedom than did European thinkers, such as Rousseau, some two thousand years later. Interestingly, Rousseau for a time played at being a Cynic, before dropping the pose completely and proposing a social system he thought would provide strategic freedom, rather than seeking freedom outside all social systems as Diogenes did. Diogenes, therefore, did not advocate freedom *within* the state, but freedom *from* the state and its artificial rules. Virtue, happiness, and freedom for Diogenes, depended not upon the socio-political structure of the state, but on the individual's internal resources.

But how convincing is Diogenes' viewpoint? Is nature a sound and effective substitute for social convention? And does it make more sense to identify with all of humanity rather than with the host society? Nature, it will be argued, is no less constricting and oppressive than human society. In fact, a major reason for the development of primitive society and, later, civilisation, was the desire to escape the savage and highly dangerous conditions under which all other species lived in nature. It was this escape that enabled the creation of a more secure and comfortable existence for mankind. To play at being part of nature in the centre of Athens, Rome, or any other classical city is not the same as struggling for survival in the natural world. In this, Diogenes and his followers were being somewhat precious. Also what the Cynics did not understand is that every other species living in nature does so in response to its own strategic *logos*, and is driven by the same life-force, strategic desire. In other words, every species, whether human or non-human, lives according to the dictates of their strategic *logos*. Individual humans, therefore, were no more free in their natural state than they were after they had developed complex social structures. All of life owes its origin and continued existence to the universal life-system I call the strategic *logos*. There is no escaping this fundamental law of existence. Also, the rules of any strategic society are not "arbitrary", as the Cynics claimed. It is the *logos* expressing itself through strategic demand generated by specific dynamic strategies that determine the nature of society's rules, or institutions. As we have seen, these rules, together with their implementing organisations, differ in a single society between the main dynamic strategies of family-multiplication, conquest, commerce, and technological change; but are very similar within any one of these dynamic strategies between different societies. Institutional rules in strategic societies are definitely not arbitrary. They are only arbitrary in antistrategic societies (such as the former USSR) as they arise from metaphysical philosophies, and the outcome is always the same—societal crisis and collapse.

Further, what does it mean to claim an allegiance not to a single state, but to the abstract concept of "humanity", as Diogenes did? As argued in chapter 2 (Box 2.1) "humanity" is merely the sum of all human individuals living and working in all the strategic *logoi* throughout the world. So "humanity" is no more free than the citizens of Athens; indeed much less so, as Athens was one of the few democracies existing in Diogenes' time. Anyway, one cannot exist within the abstract society of "humanity", only within a particular existential society at any one point in time. And, of course, their refusal to work, in favour of a mendicant lifestyle, did not grant the Cynics freedom from their society's *logos*, because they remained dependent upon the generosity of those who did participate positively in the economy. So, Diogenes was being disingenuous when he said he was not an Athenian (actually he was born and raised in Sinope), but a cosmopolitan. **The attitude of the ancient Cynics, therefore, was not a very serious response to the very real and serious problem of the "tyranny of the *logos*".**

While the Cynics displayed contempt for urban mankind, this did not lead them to withdraw from life and seek solitude. Rather they saw their role as enlightening people about their greed, corruption, lust, and depravity, and to show how everyone could change for the better by adopting a natural way of life. Essentially, Diogenes believed that human nature is capable of change and reform. What the Cynics failed to realise is that by rejecting the strategic *logos*—in Diogenes' case, the city-state of Athens—they were also rejecting life. This failure was an outcome of a deeper philosophical problem of not developing a realist theory of life; which meant that their interesting practical approach to the absurdities of life was superficial and, worse, antistrategic. They were distracted by playing the fool—even if their motives were deeply serious—and waging a daily war against a poverty-stricken and depraved world. **Diogenes' philosophy was basically a philosophy of revolt.** And like most other philosophers, they were concerned not with the way the world is but rather the way it ought to be; yet unlike most other philosophers, both past and present, they were prepared to live their philosophy by rejecting materialism in their own lives.

Even in the modern world, freedom has been thought of only within a social context. We have seen how Rousseau asserted that "man is born free, and everywhere he is in chains"; similarly **Jean-Paul Sartre** (1905–1980) asserted "man is condemned to be free". Sartre claimed that man, unlike animals that are required to do what they do ("being-in-itself"), is not programmed to be what we are ("being-for-itself"). Man can choose to live how he wishes, and to adopt whatever values he desires. But this freedom brings with it a cost in terms of "anguish, abandonment, and despair". Accordingly, humans pretend they are not free and shirk their duty as free agents; they end by being less than they could, or were destined to, be. On the other hand, he argues that even slaves are free to some degree as they can either accept their position in society, or rebel and face the consequences; a choice between life and death.

What Sartre and most other philosophers fail to understand is that choice is exercised within the restrictions and demands imposed by the strategic *logos*. Choice is made, and limited strategic freedoms are exercised, within a dynamic logosian structure. Sartre is correct when he says, in effect, that man is not programmed genetically to act in a predetermined way; but he is wrong to argue that we are free to do what we wish. We live within the confines of the *logos*. As a species, this is the only way we are able to survive and prosper. If we all rebelled against the tyranny of the *logos*, our society would stagnate and, eventually, collapse; and complex life would be extinguished along with is *logos*. **Man is but a slave to the *logos*.**

It will have become clear by now that Sartre's distinction between animals (being-in-itself) and humans (being-for-itself) is not valid.

Animal species, just like humans only survive by operating within their respective strategic *logos*. While they have more limited degrees of freedom, owing to lower levels of intelligence and less complex societies, they do make choices in their response to strategic demand. They do have varying, if limited, degrees of strategic freedom, and are not programmed automatons as Rene Descartes (1596–1650) asserted, and as Sartre appears to believe. This is a trap into which the Cynics did not fall. There is, in other words, nothing remarkable about human beings when it comes to strategic choice; it is all a matter of degree. While we are more highly evolved, our origins are just the same as other life forms. And as we all operate under the strategic *logos,* our "freedoms" are conditional. In the next chapter, we will consider whether it is possible and desirable to go beyond the dictates of the strategic *logos*.

Chapter Eight
Ultimate Freedom

Most thinkers pursuing individual freedom seek it within the framework of societal institutions and organisations. It is possible, they believe, to construct the ideal human society in which freedom and all the other virtues will flourish. Even the Cynics believed that, by rejecting contemporary conventions and returning to natural laws, it was possible to regain some sort of earlier, lost, sense of freedom and happiness. A more radical approach is taken here. Only when we reject the demands of the strategic *logos*—the "**tyranny of the logos**"—are we truly free. All societal institutions and organisations are merely instruments of the *logos*, and all those individuals who spend their lives within these boundaries are its slaves. Why? Because they uncritically respond to the dictates of the *logos*, communicated through strategic demand. Even the laws of nature, ardently sought by the Cynics, are determined by the strategic *logos*.

The path being blazed here is not an easy one to follow. To persistently challenge the demands of the *logos* has serious implications for survival and prosperity. This is one of the central paradoxes of life: to challenge its dictates, not to undermine its viability; to achieve a greater degree of freedom and happiness in life, not to seek oblivion. This challenge to the "tyranny of the *logos*" involves living in society, but maintaining a constant vigilance and a healthy scepticism of its corrupting influences; **being in the logos, but not of the logos**. It is a way of life that requires a constant critical attitude and truthfulness to living within this dynamic life-system. Only in this way can we achieve "ultimate freedom" in life.

THE DOWNSIDE OF STRATEGIC SUCCESS

Success in life is all about survival and prosperity. This involves constructing society in accord with the dictates of the *logos*, which generates a strategic demand for the type of human behaviour needed to achieve material objectives. A central mechanism by which this is achieved is "strategic imitation". Humans, just like individuals in all other species, make decisions based not on rational cost-benefit analysis, but on a combination of hope and strategic imitation. A relatively few energetic and enterprising individuals believe they know how to exploit existing opportunities to make their fortune. This belief is based not on rational calculation but on an emotionally based self-belief. Of this small group, only an even smaller minority succeed. And their success is due more to luck than special ability, as it is the market that sorts out winners from losers. This is something that society and, particularly the winners who are more than a little self-satisfied, fail to understand. The vast majority of the population, who are considerably less energetic, enterprising, able, and lucky, merely follow the successful few. This core mechanism I call "strategic imitation" (see my book *Dynamic Society*, 1996).

Strategic imitation is a powerful force. It is driven by greed and mindlessness: greed, because it involves a lust for material enhancement without vision; and mindlessness, because it leads to an unimaginative following after strategic leaders, which on occasion can lead to obscene and disastrous consequences. While Nazi Germany is the classic case, it may be displaced in the near future with the development of a global command-climate-mitigation economy. Strategic imitation, however, is a very effective mechanism for achieving strategic success. But there is a downside. It comes with a huge individual cost, even when successful for the society as a whole—the cost of being trapped in an unaesthetic collective journey through life. It consists of following the masses rather than striking out on one's own; of parroting the unchallenging and largely false views of the majority; of staying within the acceptable conventional boundaries; of blindly accepting the dictates of authority; of adopting a herd mentality and morality. There is no real freedom here.

There are many traps for individual integrity in strategic success. They are well known, but rarely avoided. They centre on an unseemly pursuit of material gain, at the expense of fundamentals that really matter, such as family, contemplation, openness to the beauty of the natural world, and creative involvement in the various arts and crafts. The unsavoury outcomes of strategic success are legion. They include exploiting others at work to maximise career prospects; self-promotion to improve one's position in any organisation; pursuing ephemeral recognition and fame at the expense of more fundamental and lasting values; mindlessly chasing after "famous" and influential people in politics, popular entertainment, sport, and other high-profile organisations; casting off old friends and partners for the thrill of the new; the mindless consumption of artificial goods (particularly electronic devices promoting narcissistic delusions) at the expense of a thoughtful life; and the abuse—physical, mental, or sexual—of those less powerful. These are the traps that the vast majority fall into by blindly following, rather than consciously challenging, the strategic *logos*.

Even in prosperous, law-abiding societies, there are individuals and groups that attempt to subvert the existing order for their own materialist ends. These are the antistrategists who consciously and deliberately exploit law-abiding strategists in their own society. For as long as these antistrategic groups are in a small contained minority, their impact on society and its *logos* is minimal. But when they break out of strategic containment—as in prohibitionist America in the 1930s or in a number of Middle Eastern societies today—they pose a risk to the *logos* which, in extreme cases, can lead to societal collapse. This domestic antistrategic attack can also spill over into neighbouring countries—once again evident in the Middle East—and lead also to their destruction. Of course, this antistrategic activity is not what I mean by "wrestling the *logos*". These antistrategic groups, these deviant dissidents usually called terrorists, are anti-life and pro-death. Freedom is not what they have in mind.

LIVING WITH STRATEGIC DESIRE—THE EXISTENTIAL SENSITIVITY CURVE

Living with strategic desire and following the laws of the *logos* is not always a morally comfortable pathway—at least for some. In order to survive and prosper, it is often necessary to do things that sensitive people find repugnant. This is particularly the case with a society pursuing the dynamic strategy of conquest, because it is very difficult to look the other way. In a conquest society, brutality is a way of life, with individuals required to kill or be killed on a regular basis to earn their daily bread. Societies like Rome did most of their killing and rape while on tour—although its citizens also enjoyed the murderous brutality of the Colosseum—while the Aztecs preferred to kill, and even to consume, their captives by the tens of thousands in bloody religious ceremonies at home so all its citizens could participate. While other dynamic strategies, such as commerce and technological change are less brutal—owing to different strategic demands rather than to different personal preferences—there are times when defence of these strategies requires, or is thought to require, brutal military activity, usually in someone else's backyard. The fundamental reality of existence is that human beings will do whatever it takes to survive and prosper.

Figure 8.1 Existential Sensitivity Curve

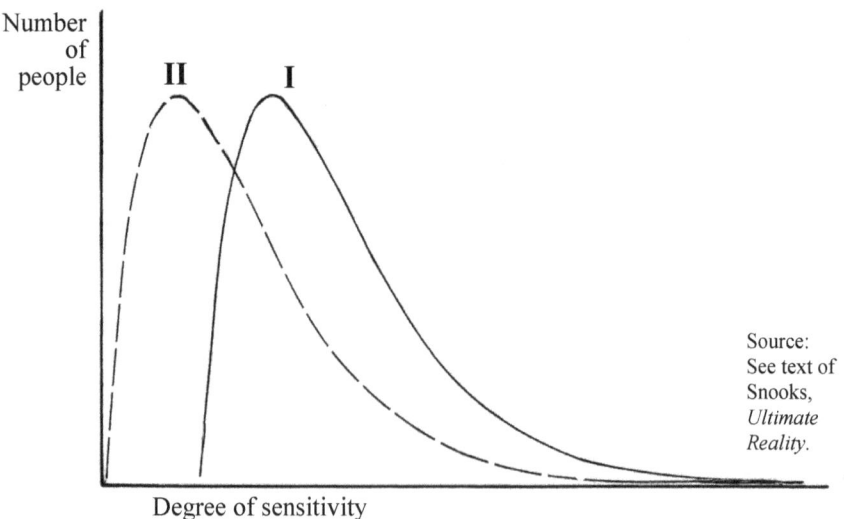

Source: See text of Snooks, *Ultimate Reality.*

Humans display a wide range of sensitivities to their personal involvement in the brutalities of existence. I have attempted to demonstrate this with the "existential sensitivity curve", which is a theoretical curve based upon the author's observation of the way societies have responded to the costs and benefits of war and conquest through the coping mechanism of "existential schizophrenia". As shown in Figure 8.1, this curve is highly positively skewed, with the bulk of the population of any society occupying the insensitive end. If this was not so, human society would not have been able to ruthlessly pursue the dynamic strategies need to survive and prosper; and, therefore, would not exist. Those people in the relatively insensitive majority are able to tolerate a considerable involvement, either directly or indirectly, in the brutality of their society's dynamic strategy, provided they are also able to reap the rewards of doing so. Indeed, "existential sensitivity" diminishes in proportion to the increase in material rewards arising from strategic brutality. In Figure 8.1, the curve shifts to the left from **I** to **II** as the material rewards for brutal strategic activity increases. Curiously we hear little about the trauma experienced by Roman soldiers returning home from a brutal conquest campaign, laden down with booty and the promises of grants of land in Italy from grateful generals and Roman politicians. In contrast, the modern soldier, who has little or no prospect of gaining materially from war, experiences considerable trauma, possibly more from "strategic frustration" than involvement in violent action.

Some ordinary people even revel in violence and brutality. Nazi Germany is a revealing case study. In the 1940s, a large proportion of the German people were knowingly involved, either directly or indirectly, in discrimination against, and mass extermination of, Jews, Gypsies, communists, dissenting intellectuals, and other "undesirables". Why? Because the bulk of the German people profited from Hitler's conquest strategy and the dispossession and slavery of hated ethnic minorities. It needs to be emphasised that Germany is not uniquely insensitive to brutality; any society that found itself in Germany's situation would have behaved in a similar way. It is characteristic human behaviour in these circumstances.

Yet, as Figure 8.1 suggests, there is always a small minority who are unable to contemplate life in such an openly brutal society, owing to their "existential sensitivity". They are always quick to protest and to attempt to protect targeted ethnic groups. Less so, of course, when the costs of doing so are high. In totalitarian regimes, those who protest in this manner are brutally swept aside. This was the case with about a quarter of a million "good Germans", who were murdered during the twelve years of Nazi rule.

In our modern technological world—apart from periods of intense global crisis—we grow rich not through brutality *per se*, but through the application of new ideas to the exploitation of the world's resources. Greed, of course, is still at the centre of this drive for prosperity, and it results in a more subtle exploitation of those around us. Here too, "existential schizophrenia" is an essential coping mechanism. Particularly as the perceived need to defend our technological strategy, often leads to the prosecution of brutal military action against countries that constrain our access to strategic resources, such as Middle Eastern oil. Accordingly, we concoct stories about the evil nature of these regimes and their "weapons of mass destruction", and we see ourselves as morally justified in destroying less powerful societies. As discovered in chapter 6 on truth, we tell the truth to our enemies and lies to our own people.

The interesting question here is: How are the majority of those who participate or acquiesce in strategic brutality able to look themselves in the mirror each day? The answer is, as raised earlier in chapter 5 on the question of evil, by the mechanism of existential schizophrenia, which will not be discussed in detail here. Existential schizophrenia, which clearly works best in those who are relatively insensitive to the grossness of existence (or *vice versa*), has enabled human society to survive and progress in the face of the greatest moral outrages. But for the minority of any population, this mechanism is considerably less effective and, as a result, they experience considerable psychological distress. These sensitised people are the ones most likely to seek freedom from the dictates of the strategic *logos*. The rest are slaves to the *logos*.

GREED IN MODERN TECHNOLOGICAL SOCIETIES

While the dark side of the *logos* is easily recognised in societies pursuing the conquest strategy, it is just as pervasive, albeit more subtly, in modern technological societies. Greed is never far from the surface. Even in societies where average living standards are high, the distribution of income is very highly skewed, reflecting the unlimited appetite for riches. In the world's richest nation, the USA, (2014) the top 0.1 percent of families own the same share of wealth—about 22 percent—as the bottom 90 percent, which is no better than the situation existing in the early twentieth century. While the massive disparity in wealth distribution declined for a generation after the Second World War, it began to widen again from the late 1970s. A similar skewness exists (2012) in the distribution of income, with the top 0.1 percent of families taking home over 20 percent of total household income; a percentage that has doubled since the late 1970s. The situation is even worse in the rest of the world. Clearly, more than enough is never enough.

Greed of the Business Elite

How does greed work in the upper quartile of wealth receivers? Essentially, there is a "pact of greed" operating within this group of leading strategists at both the financial and social levels. At the financial level, a "pact of greed" exists between the CEOs of large public companies and the shareholders of those companies. This "pact" consists of an agreement that shareholders will pay obscenely large salaries and bonuses to CEOs—running into tens of millions of dollars each year—if the company executive successfully increases share prices so that shareholders can make extraordinary *speculative* returns. In 2012 the top 200 CEOs in the USA received an average annual remuneration of $15.1 million, with the greediest CEO receiving $96.2 million. It is not called a salary, but rather "executive compensation". **Compensation for selling their chance for ultimate freedom!** The traditional idea that the owners and management of companies should receive ordinary profits and salaries for providing goods and services to their clients has been all but abandoned. This is an outcome of greed run rampant. The real productive services provided by even the most talented CEOs are worth no more than a very small fraction of the "executive compensation" currently paid. **These CEOs are the conquistadors of the modern era—just as ruthless and just as greedy as the sixteenth-century Spanish Conquistadors that destroyed the civilizations of the New World for a few ship-loads of gold.** In contrast, the strategic leader (the President) of the USA—the world's most powerful country—receives a modest salary of \$400,000, with a further \$170,000 to cover expenses. Is there little wonder that the strategic leadership of modern strategic societies has failed?

At the social level, there is—among the political, business, public service, and academic elite—a trafficking in lucrative positions on government committees, business boards, public quangos, and university departments and councils. Politicians, for example, select eager participants from business, universities, and the public service (after retirement) to sit on tax-payer funded committees—such as central bank boards, quangos, committees of enquiry—very few of which serve any useful purpose. Governments also grant prestigious honours—including knighthoods, lordships, and a range of other "gongs"—to those who play well the "pact of greed" game. In turn, university senior managers provide selected retired politicians, business people, and public servants with university titles—honorary doctorates and professorships—and undeserved university positions. And big business offers obscenely well-paid directorships—in 2011 more than a dozen public companies in the USA paid their directors in excess of \$500,000 for 250 to 300 hours "work" per year—to retired politicians, public servants, and even serving academics. These payments, which are equivalent to the salary of the President of the USA, are all part of the "pact of greed". This pact of greed has little to do with enhancing the prospects of society but much to do with enhancing the wealth and power of the selected few. Also there is a growing army of consultants, who are also paid exorbitant sums by governments and business, in return for largely worthless, out-of-date reports. In 2014 the annual revenues of the world's four largest management consulting firms ranged from 10 to 15 billion dollars in an industry receiving 125 billion dollars annually. Management consulting is part of the post-Second World War growth in the belief that government, business, and even academia requires a top-heavy management structure to ensure success. The problem is that while managers *may* understand how to organise social structures, they are unable to appreciate the nature of strategic leadership or the necessary creative response to the demands of the strategic *logos*. **In reality, heavy expenditure on managers and managerial advice is all about oiling the greed machine.**

Greed in modern society is also reflected in illegal and corrupt activities in government, business, organised labour, and international sporting bodies. There was a time when it was assumed that political corruption only occurred in poor countries, but closer surveillance shows that it pervades all societies. Special anti-corruption organisations have made it clear that some politicians exploit their special knowledge and connections to enhance the financial position of themselves and their families; some business people use illegal means to further their economic interests (e.g. the News Limited police corruption charges in 2011 and phone hacking scandal from 2005 to 2011, together with many examples of corporate corruption); some union organisers extort and misappropriate funds from employers and contributing members; while some world sporting bodies indulge in corrupt activities. The list of international sporting bodies involved in match-fixing and corruption seems to grow on a daily basis, with match-fixing in world cricket, soccer, and tennis; drug cheating in the Olympics, world athletics, international cycling, and a multitude of professional team sports; and the corruption of officials in the International Olympic Committee, in FIFA the world soccer body, and in IAAF the world athletics organisation. And at lower levels in these organisations, deception and cheating for material reasons is pervasive, involving large numbers of people. Corruption is clearly widespread and seemingly impossible to eradicate, owing to the nature of human nature. Greed is deeply embedded in modern technological societies as well as the rest of the world struggling to achieve strategic success.

Greed of the Masses

While strategic elites plunder the rest of society, those in the bottom 80 percent of the population are no different in terms of their aspirations. It is just that their opportunities, abilities, and luck are significantly less. They are all enthusiastic supporters of the strategic *logos* without understanding the dynamics of the process in which they are enmeshed. Only a very, very small proportion of mankind has turned its face away from this gross materialism, for what could be truly regarded as ethical reasons. The bottom 80 percent are constantly involved in a rear-guard action against the wealthy and powerful. They employ the few levers available to them—their large numbers and their assumption of the high moral ground—whenever economic conditions allow. Trade unions have, since the late nineteenth century, been the traditional way in which the mass of "workers" have attempted to make modest inroads into the wealth of their employers. But the truth is that the improving living standards of the working classes owed more to the unfolding of the industrial technological paradigm than to union activity. Without the material progress of technological societies, there would have been no advance in the living standards of the masses. Union activity merely helped to expedite a change that was in the process of occurring. Nevertheless, there was a great deal of moral rhetoric associated with these changes. Even the improved share of wealth captured by the bottom 80 percent between the 1940s and the 1970s had more to do with forces affecting the demand and supply of labour than the power of unions. Yet throughout much of the twentieth century, workers and their unions were portrayed as morally superior to the wealthy bosses and their organisations. But the truth is that workers were no less greedy than their bosses; just less rich.

From the 1970s, advanced technological societies began to change in significant ways. Technology displaced workers from traditional factory roles and generated demands for contractors rather than a waged workforce. This shifted some of the risk of capitalism from owners (who were increasingly shareholders) to former workers, now operating as small businesspeople. The risks to former workers were higher, but so also were the financial rewards for the successful. This structural change in US society coincided with a sharp relative fall in the incomes of the bottom 80 percent, with the share of the top 20 percent doubling from the late 1970s to the 2010s. It also coincided with a sharp fall in union membership and in the power of unions as small businessmen had no need of union support. The fortunes of the war between big unions and big business, which from the 1950s to the 1960s flowed in favour of the unions, were dramatically reversed after the 1970s.

Unions, like all other human organisations, have always indulged in dubious practices, including corruption and selling out their membership. These practices are being exposed more regularly these days, now that the power of unions has been broken. In Australia during the 2010s there were a number of judicial enquiries into union practices that exposed stand-over tactics by union officials, the massive illegal use of union funds for personal expenditure by leading officials, and even the betrayal of worker interests in exchange for pay-offs from employers. This dubious and illegal activity, which is coming before the courts, even reaches into the highest level of politics, as unions have always been powerful backers of the Australian Labor Party, and the union movement has always been a stepping stone for ambitious Labor political hopefuls.

Greed, however, is not confined to political, business, union, or other organisational groups. The ordinary citizen enthusiastically pursues self-interest, often under the guise of social reform, moral correctness, or some vague notion of human entitlements. These attempts at rationalisation have no real validity, and are employed to serve the material interests of the individuals concerned. There are in reality no rights of birth in life. The only "rights"—or self-styled entitlements—we possess are those which we are able to persuade the rest of the community we should have. There is no valid system of moral rights, as no higher moral authority (such as God) exists to grant them, only a system of strategic gains. And "social reform" is merely social change that favours those making this type of unsupported argument.

This is so obvious that I will provide only a list of a number of current examples of this form of greed and mindlessness. And I do so in a way that the classical Cynics, such as Diogenes, would approve. First, no matter how worthy, the call for affirmative action—whether gender, race, or disability based—is a call to support the self-interest of self-nominated disadvantaged groups by making inroads into the establishment. Opponents are usually abused as being sexist, racist, homophobic, unfeeling, immoral, etc. Abuse and appeal to the high moral ground are ploys used when rational argument would expose the material self-interest involved.

Second, the support for "unofficial" immigrants is also based on "moral" assertion rather than rational argument, by sections of the community which have found a way to gain materially or politically from voicing this support. Third, some indigenous groups attack research that threatens to undermine their material support. For example, some indigenous groups have opposed the *National Geographic*'s "genographic project", which is attempting to trace the geographical movements of ancient peoples around the globe, through the collection and study of DNA material. The opposing self-interested argument is that this research will challenge long-held cultural beliefs and undermine indigenous claims to land rights and other economic resources. Material benefit is more important here than knowledge. As usual, desires trump ideas. This opposition to human knowledge is euphemistically called "human rights criticism". The basic approach is similar to that of the Christian Church in the past, when it took a self-interested stand against scientists like Galileo (1564–1642) and Darwin (1809–1882), and even executed some such as Giordano Bruno (1548–1600). And it is the way some communist and Islamist countries respond to criticism today (2016): China imprisoning outspoken supporters of democracy from Hong Kong; and Saudi Arabia beheading outspoken Shiite clerics. The only valid criticism of this research should concern its scientific standing and credibility.

Fourth, there is the example of taxpayer-funded IVF treatment—as if the world needs more people—where some couples who get more children than they desire, opt to sue the medical system to cover the cost and trauma of the unwanted extra child or children! A growing proportion of the current pampered generation—a product of the rampant materialism of advanced technological societies—must have exactly what they want, and, if it is not forthcoming, someone other than themselves is to blame and must be held financially accountable. Fifth, there is the very recent example of womb transplants. Couples today seem unable to accept life as it is and to just make the best of it. They feel they have a right to re-engineer themselves in their own image (sorry God!), and science is at hand to assist them, usually at taxpayer expense. They must have what they believe other people have. In the case of womb transplants, this self-obsession raises the disturbing possibility—as indeed all other organ transplants do— of poverty-stricken women in the Third World selling their healthy wombs to wealthy entitlement-seekers. A wealthy individual can only gain an organ like this by depriving someone else. As usual, the wealthy entitlement-seekers exploit the poor and vulnerable.

A sixth example is professional sport, which is plagued by sophisticated attempts to win unfairly, owing to the large sums of money at stake, in the form of prizes, lucrative sponsorship, and bribes. Drug cheating is rampant throughout professional sport. So much so that the viewing public is becoming increasingly sceptical about commercialised sporting activities, ranging from the Olympics, cycling, and a multitude of team events at both the national and international levels. Sport is now a warring arena between the sport cheats and their supporting scientists on the one hand, and the drug investigators and their scientists on the other. It is a war that resembles the genetic battles between bacteria and antibiotics; where each side is constantly upgrading the effectiveness of their tactics. Sport is also used by high-stake gamblers to fraudulently increase their winnings by bribing individuals and teams to deliberately lose a forthcoming contest. Very large sums of money are involved, and sports supervising bodies seem unable or unwilling to eradicate the problem. International sport is also used by unscrupulous sports administrators to massively increase their material wealth by accepting bribes from countries wanting to stage prestigious international events. The Olympics and international soccer are prime examples.

Greed of the Educated Elite

This open-ended list will be closed with examples of flagrant cheating among the educated elite in science and universities. There are some scientists who readily falsify their research results in an effort to obtain large research grants, prestigious prizes, and higher-paid research positions. While the amount of cheating in science may not be large, it is significant, potentially costly to a gullible public, and highly damaging to the prestige of science in the modern world. It has been estimated that between 1973 and 2013, of the 21 million papers published, over 1,000 were retracted because of intellectual fraud. This is an average of 25 retracted papers a year, which affects the leading science journals as well as the average and mediocre ones. Some individual scientists have established an impressive track record for fraudulent publications. In 2002 and 2003, the leading science journals *Science* and *Nature* retracted as many as 16 fraudulent papers co-authored by an award-winning German physicist; and in 2011, 69 papers by a German clinician and 28 papers by a Japanese virologist were also retracted for fraud.

What is particularly disturbing is that this is only the tip of the fraudulent science iceberg. Most scientific results are never subjected to replication tests as scientists are generally more interested in pursuing their own research than reworking that of others. Replication is only undertaken in what are considered to be the most important and exciting research areas. The vast bulk of research publications in science is neither important nor interesting, but this does not mean that second- and third-rate scientists are not as greedy (or even more so in an effort to compensate for lack of ability in a competitive arena) as the first–rate ones. There are some surveys that seek answers from scientists anonymously about cheating. These surveys show that 2 percent of all scientists surveyed admitted to fabricating and falsifying data, and 14 percent said they knew of colleagues who did so; an interesting asymmetry, reflecting considerable self-delusion. Needless to say, this will be a gross underestimate of cheating in science, because even in anonymous surveys, most cheats would be reluctant to admit to themselves that they are frauds—another example of "existential schizophrenia"—let alone to outsiders wanting to publish their responses. Of course, cheating in science involves more than just fabricating or falsifying data. One of the anonymous surveys also revealed that a large proportion of respondents admitted that they had indulged in "low-level" cheating. One-third of the scientists who filled out the questionnaire, revealed that they had deliberately failed to report data that contradicted their hypotheses; or they excluded inconvenient data because they felt these data were atypical. This involves a deliberate distortion of our understanding of reality in favour of personal gain.

And there are regular cases of book advisors and journal editors and their referees refusing to publish scientific work that fails to conform to the conventional wisdom, or that undermines their own published work. This is done to protect the reputations and academic positions of scholars who are part of the establishment; and to further their ideological causes. These biased and untruthful assessments also take place within organisations distributing research funds. Grants bodies and their referees favour those researchers who are part of the old-boy/old-girl network, who are well within the boundaries of the conventional wisdom, and who support the prevailing scientific ideology. Owing to the lack of transparency in these deliberations, hard data on this form of abuse are difficult to obtain, and when critics raise suggestions of fraud, the various mainstream scientific bodies are quick to exonerate any of their colleagues under fire. One famous example concerns the thousands of leaked emails from the Climate Research Unit (CRU) at the University of East Anglia in 2009. While charges of data manipulation (dubbed "climategate") were not upheld by orthodox reviews of the email evidence, it is clear that the academics concerned were unwilling to make their detailed data and calculations readily available. They wanted to maintain the lack of transparency that characterises scholarly practices. And, from time to time since then, there have been reported cases in the media of scientists, who challenge detailed parts of the climate-change program, having their papers rejected on the grounds that they are "unhelpful", "less than helpful", or even "harmful" to the work of the international climate-mitigation lobby. This seems to miss the point of science. It is not funded by the tax-payer to be "helpful" to particular ideologies, but to support the requirements of the strategic *logos*.

The degree to which the suppression of unorthodox papers on climate change occurs—and even a superficial acquaintance with human nature would tell us that there is a reasonable probability that it does occur—should be of concern not only to academic institutions, but also to taxpayers and their political representatives, because the implications for society of biased research into climate change and climate mitigation could be dire. This type of activity is usually undertaken by editors and referees behind closed doors, where there is no oversight of this critical process. It is not possible to "replicate" editorial and grant-giving decision making. As radically new ideas are a threat to the academic establishment and its ideology, there is a very strong temptation to suppress them. Academics and researchers are no less prone to exploiting material opportunities than are sportspeople. **If drugs helped intellectual performance, then a significant number of scholars would consume them.**

Cheating in universities is not limited to research staff. There has always been a small proportion of students who have cheated rather than worked hard to achieve the results expected of them. In the past, this has often been among the ranks of rich "entitled" students, who were accustomed to getting what they wanted without having to work for it. Probably the most famous example of this was Edward Kennedy (1932–2009), later US senator, who was expelled from Harvard University for paying a fellow student to take his Spanish exam. Today, universities have been transformed from finishing schools for the wealthy into degree factories for the masses. In this brave new world, mediocre students are under considerable pressure from their parents to achieve results higher than can be reasonably expected, so an increasing number are resorting to cheating. This has been made easier by universities substituting essays for exams, by essay material being readily available on the internet, and by the establishment of companies openly offering to sell custom-made essay papers to students, particularly foreign students with poor language skills. It is amusing to hear academics asking themselves why students are resorting to cheating, and suggesting that universities need to make intellectual work more interesting than cheating!

University management has contributed to the problem of both staff and student cheating by pursuing ruthlessly their own policies of greed. In Australian universities, the size of management salaries has increased rapidly in the past generation both absolutely and in relation to academic salaries. There was a time when a university vice-chancellor was paid a professorial salary together with a modest administrative allowance; but today (2015–16) the salary of vice-chancellors (topping $1,300,000, not including perks like free housing, private motor vehicles, and paid travel) is equivalent to the total cost of hiring 7 to 8 full professors (with salaries of about $170,000). In addition, university management has become notoriously top-heavy, with a bevy of highly paid deputy vice-chancellors and pro-vice-chancellors cluttering up well-appointed chancellery buildings. In order to fund management greed, universities attempt to give the impression that their institutions sit high on the ladder of international university rankings, and strive to maximise the number of students funded through the Commonwealth government's student loans scheme (HECS). To raise the market's perception of research excellence, academic staff are forced (under threat of expulsion) to complete PhD's, to obtain outside research funding, and to publish prolifically, even when their strengths reside in teaching rather than research. Managers do so because they can grab higher salaries if their university rises in the rankings; a situation very similar to the business sector where CEOs attempt to engineer increases in share prices to obtain extra bonuses. Not surprisingly, this managerial pressure increases the temptation of academic staff to falsify research results and claim credit for work that is not their own. And the attempt by management to increase their revenues has led to universities secretly admitting large numbers of students who fall well below the much trumpeted minimum matriculation (ATAR) scores for admission to degree courses.

A recent (27th January 2016) expose by Fairfax Media of the actual admission standards in NSW, graphically illustrates the extent of this abuse of taxpayer funds and the undermining of public confidence in the professional standards of university graduates. It was revealed that about 50 percent of students currently admitted by NSW's four leading universities do not meet minimum course standards; with the range between worst and least-worst performer being 64 to 27 percent. Some matriculation scores are as low as just 30 out of a possible 100, and are up to 40 matriculation (ATAR) points below the professed cut-off level for business, teaching, and engineering degrees. Even in disciplines such as law (with 91 percent and 40 percent failing to make the grade at NSW's top two universities), medical science (scores as low as 46 out of 100 at one institution), and science (with 13 percent of students admitted to one institution having scores that are more than 20 points below minimum standards). The responses to this expose are interesting. Academics generally agreed with the media's implied criticism of their managers; and one researcher into university management confirmed that many university students are "semi-literate". The knee-jerk reaction of university managers was along the lines that (all of a sudden) they didn't think ATAR scores were appropriate measures of scholastic ability, and they wanted to abandon them; despite having used high ATAR cut-off levels as proof of their university's high academic standards and their effective management. In other words, they are now proposing that objective and transparent processes concerning student admissions to their institutions be abandoned; that future university admissions be beyond outside scrutiny. Needless to say, the reckless pursuit of greed by university management on this scale has serious implications for the standards of professional conduct and for the performance of Australian society in the future.

To sum up: These focused examples of fraudulent behaviour by ordinary citizens, who are not regarded as criminals, shows just how widespread and pervasive greed and mindlessness in society really are. While the catalogue of such cases is endless, any attempt to be more comprehensive would just be boring. Enough has been said to show that this grossness is the outcome of the nature of mankind. It is what we are, and there are no exceptions, just degrees of excessiveness. It is a fact that we are more interested in material gain than in truthful ideas or truthful actions and outcomes. Yet, through the mechanism of "existential schizophrenia", we see ourselves quite falsely as truthful, altruistic, intelligent, and honourable. Life is all about survival and prosperity, not about virtue.

ULTIMATE FREEDOM AND THE EXISTENTIAL SENSITIVITY CURVE

The existential sensitivity curve introduced earlier in this chapter to examine our responses to the grossness of life also reflects the likely freedom that humans experience from the dictates of the strategic *logos*. As shown, the vast majority of humanity is relatively insensitive to the grossness and brutality of life, except when they are on the receiving end. Then it is all tears and self-pity. Yet even adverse personal experience does not modify our attitude to the difficulties of others when there is a conflict with our desire for survival and prosperity. Only when survival and prosperity for oneself and family have been secured do we extend a hand to others, in order to be able to live with ourselves. If it were otherwise, the *logos* would stagnate and eventually disintegrate; and life on Earth would be endangered. The vast majority of humanity, who are relatively insensitive to the grossness of life, have a well-developed existential schizophrenia mechanism, and find it relatively easy to delude themselves into believing they are honourable and altruistic, despite happily exploiting others. This vast majority of humanity will never experience "ultimate freedom"—freedom from the *logos*. They will live out their lives as slaves to the *logos*; and will fail to even realise that they are slaves.

Those more sensitive to the grossness of the world are uncomfortable with their role in life. They are aware that their comfortable lives are due, in some degree, to their active involvement in the exploitation of others. High salaries and large profits for the minority in advanced societies can only be achieved by making consumers pay higher prices and receive lower wages. As I argue above, the ridiculously high remuneration of CEOs and upper management cannot be justified in terms of their real contribution to value added. They are paid well above their marginal productivity. The same is true of the differences in living standards between First World and Third World countries. The high living standards of the West depend to a significant degree on being able to take advantage of lower costs of production, which reflect lower standards of living, in the Third World. While reality is more complex than this brief sketch suggests—differences in per capita income between disparate regions of the world depends fundamentally on the variable success in pursuing the industrial technological paradigm—the exploitation of the weak by the strong also plays an important part. And a small proportion of the population of rich societies is sensitive to this fact and uncomfortable with it.

Being more sensitive to the inequalities of life, some of this small minority indulge in "good works" of varying significance. They are, in effect, attempting to compensate for their inadequate mechanism of existential schizophrenia by redistributing a small proportion of their own good fortune to the less fortunate, or arranging to do so, for those more reluctant to surrender any of their wealth, through reformist social organisations and "progressive" political movements. This is an attempt to make the *logos* more accountable for the large number of people who fall by the wayside. It is a way of saving the goose who lays the golden egg, enjoying their good fortune, and reducing their feelings of guilt. But, of course, the real impact of such action is marginal. If it were otherwise, the *logos* would be endangered, and the insensitive majority would sweep the guilty reformers away.

What is of interest here is that the guilty reformers have no intention of defying the dictates of the *logos*. They want to have it all—a wealthy, guilt-free lifestyle. But, they fail to have it all—they fail to experience ultimate freedom. They remain slaves to the strategic *logos*. What this means is that *almost* 100 percent of humanity has no interest in striving for real freedom—for ultimate freedom.

Can this be true? What about those people seeking solutions to the grossness of life through religion and/or philosophy? With some exceptions, most religious people in advanced societies are not hugely wealthy. They are religious because they have no other way to face the difficulties of life. They are trapped by an inadequate response to life either individually or societally and seek release through fantasy. The smaller group, which is both religious and wealthy, consists of indulgent individuals looking to ease their guilty consciences. And large religious organisations have a history of mobilizing the meagre funds of the gullible poor for the benefit of the clergy, and of abusing their children. Of course, there are always exceptions to these general outcomes, but they are not sufficiently powerful to reform them. Religion—as shown in my book *Dead God Rising* (2010)—has been a supporter of the strategic *logos*.

What of philosophers? In the West today there are two main traditions of academic philosophy: Anglo-American analytical philosophy and continental (mainly French) deconstructionist philosophy. Analytical philosophy traces its roots to Bertrand Russell (1872–1970), his fellow student at the University of Cambridge, G.E. Moore (1873–1958), and the German philosopher Gottlob Frege (1848–1925). They attempted to displace the idealist philosophy of the nineteenth century, mainly German, by employing the rigour, precision, and mathematical orientation of the natural sciences. Critics of this approach to philosophy regard it as trivial, sterile, and a total failure in elucidating reality. In retrospect, a more effective way of countering the idealist element in nineteenth century philosophy would have been to adopt a realist empirical approach rather than a deductive mathematical approach that employs a metaphysical methodology.

The continental approach to philosophy was developed by Martin Heideggar (1889–1976), Jean Paul Sartre (1905–1980), Roland Barthes (1915–1980), Michel Foucault (1926–1984), Jacques Derrida (1930–2004), and Jacques Lacan (1901–1981). Both Heideggar and Sartre criticised the customs and institutions of Western Society and wanted to replace them with more meaningful social systems, such as the *Volk* (people) and its leader, which Hitler and Nazism seemed to initially offer Heideggar; and the communist systems of the USSR and China, which initially attracted Sartre. These allegiances were disastrous because, whatever the faults of the strategic systems of the West, these totalitarian systems were (are) antistrategic (anti-*logos*) and were (are) bound not only to offer much less strategic freedom, but also to fail. Herein lies the danger of metaphysical philosophy—not in creating antistrategic societies (desires drive, ideas merely facilitate), but in accepting them when they come along. In this respect, metaphysical philosophers are not only foolish, but by providing role models they are guilty by association for the resulting suppression of freedom and loss of life. But true to form, they absolve themselves of blame through the exercise of that remarkable defence mechanism of "existential schizophrenia", and, without explanation, move on to their next metaphysically inspired blunder.

The continental deconstructionists are convinced that freedom can only occur if we unravel, or "deconstruct", existing reality, language, and power structures. Foucault claims we are all held back by impersonal and invisible networks of power relationships. Concepts such as male and female sexuality, crime and punishment, and madness are merely social and historical constructs that have no basis in reality. The very idea of "normality" is seen as a false construct. True, social conventions are not an outcome of human nature—that is a false supply-side argument—but they are a response to the strategic demands of the *logos*; something that Foucault with his metaphysical philosophy has been unable to detect, let alone fathom. Jacques Derrida, on the other hand, appears unable to get beyond language to the meaning of reality; accordingly he gets bogged-down in the deconstruction of "texts". Deconstruction is a form of nihilism arising from a failure to look beneath the superficial structures of language and the institutions of society, which are the ephemeral responses to the demands of the *logos*. It constitutes a failure to discern and understand the strategic *logos*—ultimate reality—and to find the freedom they desire. Like the rest of the community, philosophers remain slaves to the *logos*. They are wrong in claiming that life has no meaning; life has meaning, but its meaning is trivial and gross. We need to be able to transcend this triviality and grossness by reaching out for a new freedom.

A NEW FREEDOM

Ultimate freedom is to be found not in antistrategic systems or new and novel forms of language or institutional structure, but in recognising and wrestling the universal life system—the strategic *logos* or ultimate reality. It is the *logos* that underlies all strategic systems, institutions, and man-made structures. Replacing one societal system or structure with another may increase strategic freedom—and then only if it is an outcome of logosian demand—but it does not free us from the *logos*, which will continue to assert its oppressive control. There is no escaping the *logos*, except through death. Some seem to believe that by turning away from conventional society and establishing a small ideal community in the wilderness somewhere that they can make good their escape. But in fact, all they are doing is substituting a new version of the *logos* for an old version, usually of a less successful kind. Most new colonies established in the past by ideological radicals have failed, and the few that succeeded (such as some of those in North America) did so by servicing the "vices" (smoking tobacco) of the wealthy from the societies they fled, using slaves from Africa. Ultimate freedom can only be approached by fully recognising the nature of the *logos*, and by challenging its dictates on its own ground.

Ultimate freedom comes not from attempting to destroy the *logos*, or any of its life-giving systems—such a stance would be antistrategic or anti-life—but rather in challenging and defying the dictates of the *logos*. The aim of the ultimate-freedom seeker is to accept the world as it is without being overwhelmed by its materialist demands, and to live within it with as much dignity as is possible. To enjoy the best that life has to offer without indulging in the grossest aspects of its materialism and lust for worldly pleasures. Such indulgence merely leads to the unnecessary exploitation of others and to an unaesthetic lifestyle.

To wrestle the *logos* means to take a stand in one's own life against the forces driving life—greed and naked self-interest—together with all those excesses of the senses—lust, gluttony, intoxication, brutality, etc. These excesses are encouraged and promoted by those greedy, unscrupulous individuals and organisations that have thrown in their lot with the strategic *logos*. Most things can and should be enjoyed, but in moderation. This requires discipline and resolve in the face of the *logos*. Needless to say, there is nothing novel about this approach to life. It is shared with many individuals and organisations that are unsettled by the gross materialism of the world. What is not shared is an understanding of the source of this materialism and how to challenge it effectively. The only way to find ultimate freedom is to wrestle the *logos*; and the only way to wrestle the logos is to understand this life-giving system.

There is a paradox here. The more successful the *logos*, the less ultimate freedom we are likely to experience. To live sustainably in a society characterised by limited strategic success requires a highly disciplined and frugal approach to life. Such a lifestyle requires a leanness and a thriftiness that endows life with a sense of achievement and meaning; a sense of freedom from the grossness of life. But when a society enjoys a highly successful *logos*, it is characterised by excess and grossness; consumption for the sake of consumption. Its citizens become fat and lazy, even slothful; and they become even more slave-like in their relation to the *logos*. While the strategic freedom of successful societies increases over time, their experience of ultimate freedom diminishes. We need to reverse this relationship, but it can only be done by recognising and understanding the strategic *logos*.

Chapter Nine

Is Life Worth the Effort?

It is with a profound sense of relief that one approaches the end of a long, eventful, and fascinating journey. One begins with feelings of excitement and enthusiasm, possibly leavened with a degree of trepidation: where will this journey lead; what will we see and experience on the way; who will we meet and share this journey with; how will we negotiate the many challenges on the way; will we be able to see it through to a satisfactory conclusion; will we be able to fathom the deeper currents driving us along; will the experience be meaningful; will life be worth the effort? These and many questions more fill our minds, while our emotions drive us forward. It is now time to consider some of these questions as a longer-than-anticipated journey nears its end.

DOES LIFE HAVE MEANING?

From what I have written over the past half-century—2016 is the 50th anniversary of the beginning of my intellectual odyssey—it will come as no surprise when I conclude that, in my opinion, there is no transcendent meaning in life. There is no reality beyond that which can be found in the dynamic materialist system underlying the emergence and sustenance of life and human society. Needless to say, this cannot be demonstrated directly, only indirectly by empirically establishing the operation of a universal life-system—the strategic *logos*—which is the prime mover of all forms of life including humanity. **What is man? Man is the strategic agent of the *logos*.**

The strategic *logos* is the ultimate reality in life. It is the discovery of a life-time of passionate truth-seeking. It is the meaning of life. While this was an exciting discovery—I remember clearly the euphoria of that moment in the winter of 2003 in a downtown café (the ***BGE***?) as I was making notes for my book *The Death of Zarathustra*—it was also disillusioning. The meaning of life was bound up with a life-system driven by base desires with the sole objective of ensuring the immediate survival and prosperity of ephemeral biological life-forms—Shakespeare's "quintessence of dust". While the intellectual effort required in making this discovery—at least as significant as the discovery of the dynamic physical system we call the cosmos—was challenging—taking the best part of five decades to achieve—the implications were, and are, disappointing. But then, my general dynamic theory predicted they would be. The dualistic nature of man that has enabled human society to negotiate an accelerating dynamic process of technological paradigm shifts, has also led to our intellectual expectations exceeding our biological needs. And it is our biological needs—our drives, instincts, and emotions—that provide life with whatever meaning it possesses. Man's mind has outgrown his material reason for existence.

IS THAT ALL THERE IS?

Life, which is "mean" rather than "meaningful", might be considered a great intellectual disappointment, and an excuse to indulge mindlessly in the senses. To live out life as a hedonist. Most members of my generation in the English-speaking world will remember the popular Leiber and Stoller song of the 1960s—particularly the 1969 version by the American singer Peggy Lee—entitled "Is that all there is?" The song's narrator relates a string of happenings in her life that fail to meet her expectations: a fire that destroys her parent's house, a trip to the circus (ironically called "the greatest show on Earth"), unrequited first love, and even the prospect of suicide. Following the telling of each big life event, the narrator repeats the following chorus:

Is that all there is?
Is that all there is?
If that's all there is my friends
Then let's keep on dancing
Let's break out the booze and have a ball
If that's all there is.

Because this song had an unusually profound set of lyrics for a popular song, even the impressive version by the great Peggy Lee (1920–2002)—which has a very 1920s German cabaret feel to it—advanced only as far as number eleven on the US pop singles chart; although it resonated more with adults, who had experienced life's disappointments, than with young people, who were only beginning life's journey. At 25 years of age, it was a favourite of mine, at a time when the "top of the pops" included songs such as "Sugar Sugar", "Oh Happy Days", and "Boom Bang a Bang"!

The real interest of this remembrance of things past is that the Leiber and Stoller song was inspired by the short story "Disillusionment" written by a very young Thomas Mann (1875–1955) and published in 1896. While the 1960s song closely follows the story told by Mann's narrator—including the refrain "is that all there is?"—it substitutes a hedonistic gloss for the much more interesting and profound viewpoint of the original. What the song writers leave out is the most interesting part of the story, which carries the deeper meaning of the Mann original. The omission concerns man's (as well as Mann's) quest for ultimate freedom. In "Disillusionment", we are told that Mann's narrator "gazed for the first time at the sea. The sea is vast, and the sea is wide, my eyes roved far and wide and longed to be free. But there was the horizon. Why a horizon when I wanted the infinite from life?"

Mann's unnamed narrator outlines the disappointments in his life, and claims that he had tried to be like other men and "make myself appear happy", but now he was "alone, unhappy, and a little odd". He goes on to say:

> It is my favourite occupation to gaze at the starry heavens at night—that being the best way to turn my eyes away from Earth and from life. And perhaps it may be pardoned in me that I still cling to my distant hopes. That I dream of a freer life, where the actuality of my fondest anticipations is revealed to be without any torturing residue of disillusionment. Of a life where there are no more horizons. So I dream and wait for death.

Mann's narrator rejects the hedonism of everyman and pines for the experience of ultimate freedom, which he believes can only be found in a metaphysical world without limits. While the life journey of Mann's narrator is far more complex and interesting than that of everyman, he also fails to understand the real meaning of life—of the nature of ultimate reality and the source of ultimate freedom. To understand life, we need to turn our gaze back from the "starry heavens" to the "earth and life" from which the narrator is fleeing. Freedom can only be found in the here and now.

The strategic *logos* is all that there is, and we need to make the best of it. But how should we go about this? First, we need to recognise the centrality of the *logos* to life, and to understand how it operates and exercises control over us, its strategic agents. Essentially, we should not be overwhelmed by the demands of the *logos*. To capitulate to these demands will turn us into slaves of the *logos*; creatures who are mindless followers of its dictates and seductive inducements. This means avoiding being sucked into the vortex of strategic organisations involved in the rapacious exploitation of natural resources and defenceless people within our own and other poorer societies. Failure to do so can lead us into evil actions if these organisations are controlled by antistrategists, such as occurred in Germany during the 1930s and 1940s, or in rogue financial institutions during the Global Financial Crisis (GFC) in 2007–08. We should also be concerned about the recent emergence of self-satisfied communities of educated (but strategically ignorant), well-paid, electronically incestuous inner-city professionals, who demand special attention for their communities, because they have been encouraged by indulgent families to believe they are "entitled". Paradoxically, the "entitled ones" are unaware that their self-indulgent lifestyle is in danger of killing the goose that lays the golden egg, as they have become breeding grounds for the promotion of antistrategic ideologies such as climate mitigation. Increasingly they are returning to parliament, members of antistrategic Green parties that are exercising a growing influence over the leadership of Western strategic societies, which, if it continues, could lead to global disaster—to "the coming eclipse". Ignorance about the nature and role of the strategic *logos* can lead societies into great danger. While submitting to the *logos* is to abandon everything that is worthwhile in life, to strike at its heart is to endanger life itself.

Second, we need to accept ourselves as we are, as no amount of will power can change a human nature that has been shaped by our interaction with the *logos* over the past 2 million years. We need to accept that, like all other life forms, we are inescapably driven by strategic desire. This is a reality we cannot change. If we could, it would destroy our lives and, if it occurred on a widespread scale, would also destroy the strategic *logos*, the well-springs of life. Those philosophers and religious thinkers who aim to eliminate desire as the source of humanity's suffering, are living in fantasy land. And, worse, they are anti-life. We also need to accept that we possess a wide range of instincts and emotions that influence our behaviour. While we are able to moderate and redirect these biological impulses into constructive and creative activities—such as the arts, crafts, literature, and formalised thinking—we cannot eliminate them. Nor should we want to, as they are the source of any joy we might experience in life. We need to accept and embrace our human nature, which is neither good nor evil, but has the capacity to be both. Yet, while we should not attempt to suppress these impulses, nor should we indulge them. This is a trap laid for us by the *logos*. Moderation is the motto of the "supralogosian" individual. Most people fail to realise that the only freedom worth experiencing arises from a life-long struggle against domination by the *logos,* the giver of life.

WHAT ARE THE CORE SUPRALOGOSIAN VIRTUES?

Virtues esteemed by philosophers arise from metaphysical systems of thought, whereas those valued by the supralogosian thinker emerge from an understanding of the strategic *logos*—the ultimate reality. There are six main "supralogosian" virtues—virtues found in reaching "beyond the *logos*": a steady determination to wrestle the *logos* and to challenge its gross demands on individual members of society; a life-long devotion to truth-seeking; a steadfast loyalty to fellow travellers; honesty to oneself and those that matter; courage to face the truth and last the distance; and moderation in the exercise of innate natural impulses. These values are not subjectively, or personally, based; they arise from the interrogation of the strategic *logos* by the truth-seeker employing the realist tool of strategic thinking. **And these values, which are not anti-*logos* but supra-*logos*, are instrumental in resolving the paradox at the heart of life.**

The first of these—**wrestling the logos**—is the foundation on which all other supralogosian virtues are based. It is essential to resist the dictates of the *logos*, despite the fact that most other people in society are clamouring to obey them. This includes refusing to accept those not so subtle awards and honours (knighthoods, lordships, etc.) for services to the *logos*, much sought after by the chattering classes. Only in this way is it possible to ensure that one doesn't get enmeshed in strategic organisations involved in compromising, even evil, activities. It is not enough to assume that because an organisation seems to have widespread community support that one should drop one's guard. This is exactly what happened to many ordinary people in antistrategic societies such as Nazi Germany and Soviet Russia; and is happening today in other totalitarian countries like China and North Korea. In a similar way, many people get caught up in corrupt activities in organisations that have power and influence over others. As we have seen, organisations in business, labour, sport, religion, public service, higher education, and charitable activity are open to the exchange of favours for large amounts of money or prestigious positions. No matter how often this corruption and abuse is exposed, new cases continue to emerge. Greed and mindlessness are unending.

The second virtue of **truth-seeking** provides meaning and (nonstrategic) direction in an otherwise meaningless world. What does it mean to be a truth-seeker? It might help to begin with what it doesn't mean.

• It doesn't mean that one will always want to know the truth, because the truth is often painful, and dangerous. Truth can be a vivisector. Many times we will want to gloss over matters that come too close to ourselves. It is always easier to see the truth in relation to others than to oneself. This is an outcome of our human nature, which is geared to ensure survival and prosperity, not moral rectitude. What it does mean is that even in these natural circumstances, the truth-seeker will keep revisiting problematic issues, despite the personal pain it may cause, until they are resolved with honour. The thing that separates the truth-seeker from the truth-avoider is that the former genuinely wants to get to the truth, whereas the latter wants to side-step the truth. It is a matter of intention and degree, rather than achievement. There are no absolutes in this life. The truth-seeker sometimes succeeds, and sometimes fails.

- It doesn't mean that one will always publish the truth about oneself or those we care most about. Even the truth-seeker has a right to privacy; and the public doesn't have a right to know everything the truth-seeker knows. Thinkers are not a free public resource, despite the fact that they provide their best ideas, which are based on decades of hard intellectual effort, usually free of charge (as I have done since my retirement).

- It doesn't mean that one will always *tell* the truth. Few will thank you for that, and it may well place the truth-teller in a dangerous position. Ask any whistle blower. The truth-seeker has no responsibility to the oppressive *logos*. Under pressure, one may even lie to prevent getting into personal difficulties. Once again this is an outcome of human nature. The difference between a truth-teller and a truth-distorter is that the former wants to tell the truth, whereas the truth-distorter lies habitually as a way of life. Most people lie (pun!) somewhere in between.

While truth-seeking is a passion, one must be aware of the dangers. It is because truth is a vivisector, that mankind developed the art of existential schizophrenia. Hence, it is essential for the truth-seeker to understand this defence mechanism against truth's double-edged sword. Those who failed to realise this essential truth, such as Friedrich Nietzsche, were destroyed by the truth so fearlessly sought. Truth-seeking is a delicate balancing act between exposing oneself to the ferocity of the truth, and seeking shelter in comforting delusions. Both extremes are deadly: unprotected exposure (the choice of the very few) can lead to insanity and death, whereas total protection (the choice of the very many) leads inescapably to a life of self-deception and lies. The former life is short; the latter is not worth living for the truth-seeker. Truth for the strategist is dispensable; truth for the supralogosian individual is both deliverer and dispatcher. The *logos*-wrestler lives an exhilarating yet, dangerous, life.

The third virtue, **loyalty,** is central to the life of the supralogosian truth-seeker, because it ensures a balanced, loving existence in a greedy and brutal world. Disloyal people, who ruthlessly pursue self-interest to the detriment of personal relationships, live empty, sterile, and lonely lives. Also, one cannot wrestle the *logos* alone; one needs the closeness of a supportive family and a few good friends to help provide the stability required to face the truth of existence. Like truth, loyalty is also a double-edged instrument. Unwavering loyalty will always bring strategists down, as it reduces flexibility in the face of constantly changing circumstances. We have seen how, in the sketch of the Australian 2015 leadership coup, persistent loyalty by the Old Leader to close colleagues and support staff helped in his undoing. This is unusual, because, in general, loyalty to colleagues and friends exercised by strategists usually evaporates whenever self-interest is endangered. But for the *logos*-wrestler, loyalty to relatives and friends is a central virtue. It is upheld despite the challenge to self-interest and the danger to survival. But, let it be clear, the loyalty exercised is for fellow travellers not followers of the *logos*.

The fourth virtue, **honesty**, is also a difficult virtue for the strategist. Conscientious strategists in societies that are wealthy and progressive will usually attempt to be as honest as possible. But if there is a conflict between honesty and strategic success, standards of honesty and straight dealing fall dramatically. Of course, in less wealthy and less progressive societies, little pretence to honesty prevails and corruption and double-dealing are endemic. This is a function of the need to survive, not of culture. Yet even in materially progressive societies, where the pressure for dishonest dealing is less intense, and the probability of being exposed is much greater, major lapses do occur. Company management regularly fails to disclose information that could damage their bottom line, and habitually covers up major problems for the community arising from oil spills, radiation leaks, toxic materials like asbestos, together with outbreaks of food, water, and air pollution. And in a significant number of cases, large corporations deliberately map out business strategies designed to deceive the public in order to increase their profitability. The most notorious example is the action of cigarette companies designing a product that maximised consumer dependency, while having a significant impact on consumer health, despite being promoted as having no health implications. Similarly, large international companies promoted asbestos products as safe, when they were in possession of long-standing evidence to show that it caused serious lung problems and death. Even more surprising was the recent (September 2015) revelation that a major international motor vehicle manufacturer had deliberately installed software in their diesel engine vehicles to provide false regulatory test results concerning pollution. In these and many other cases distributed throughout society, dishonesty rather than honesty is a central strategic virtue. In contrast, honesty is a major supralogosian virtue, even if it is difficult to achieve owing to the nature of human nature.

The fifth virtue for the *logos*-wrestler is **courage**. It is essential for the truth-seeker to be true to oneself, which in turn requires courage. This requires supralogosians to resist the desire, no matter how strong, to appear to be more than one was born to be. It is important to be able to achieve the most one can as a person, without employing artificial and dishonest means. The truth-seeker will refuse to cheat in exams or sporting events; will reject the use of false credentials; will avoid having inessential cosmetic surgery; will want to grow old gracefully without using artificial means (usually unsuccessful) to disguise the fact; and to die a natural, unprolonged, death.

The sixth virtue, **moderation**, is a necessary brake on the run-away vice of indulgence. It is natural, and important, for the supralogosian to satisfy his or her desires in a balanced and moderate way. To deny this is to deny the essential nature of man. Yet unchecked indulgence can drive one back into the embrace of the *logos*. It is essential, therefore, that the natural desire for survival and prosperity does not lead to greed; that physical love does not end in lust; that the natural desire for prestige and reputation does not lead to envy and unhealthy competition with others; that interest in food, drink, and stimulants does not lead to gluttony and substance abuse; that essential recreation does not lead to sloth; that pleasure in one's work does not lead to excessive pride; that the accumulation instinct necessary for survival does not lead to a compulsion to own the world (a bonsai garden in a courtyard or on a balcony can be as pleasurable as a private forest or a large estate); that the desire for control over one's own life does not lead to the control over others; that one's demand for justice does not lead to vengeance; and so on. It is all a matter of degree, informed by an understanding of the existential *logos*, not of absolute standards imposed by the metaphysical concepts of philosophers about the Absolute; or the personal preference of the philosopher raised to an absolute level.

Of course, given the unchanging nature of human nature, all supralogosian warriors will invariably fall short in their own eyes, and no doubt in the eyes of uncomprehending critics. But it is entirely a personal matter and not a matter of censuring others. The central issue is one of persistence in both the struggle with the *logos*, and the pursuit of truth; everything else will follow in time. There are no accusations, no recriminations in the fellowship of *logos*-wrestlers and truth-seekers.

WHAT VALUE LIFE?

Life is a fascinating experience, provided one is able to resist the grossness of its materialist demands. Yet, the *logos* should be recognised and respected for the life-giving entity that it is. While it should be treated as a worthy and impressive adversary, it should also be kept at arm's length. Life is certainly an experience not to be missed. But then, if one did miss out on life, it wouldn't be missed! After death, nothing that happened in life will matter at all; life only matters in the here and now.

What is most difficult to grasp is why I am I, and not someone else who is thinking the same thing. The biological explanation is clear enough: each self-conscious human being is unique, because no two people have the same cerebral make-up (neurons) and connections (synapses)—not even identical twins—owing to everyone's unique relationship with the *logos*, filtered through various layers of strategic organisations. Owing to the remarkable fact that the human brain consists of some 100 billion neurons, the possible cerebral combinations are infinitely large. Each individual is exposed to different aspects of strategic demand generated by their common life-system and is, therefore, unique. But, that said, it is still remarkable that each individual sees itself in such a distinctively personal manner; of all the human beings that have existed, and will exist, each individual sees itself as "me". This is the great lottery of life. This is why life should be experienced as meaningfully as possible. Certainly it should be experienced as a thing in itself, and not as a stepping stone to a "better" existence as envisaged by metaphysical snake-oil salesmen.

Having worked out what life is all about, and experienced the *best*—not the *most*—life has to offer, it is time to move on; to return once more to nothingness. That life doesn't last forever is a consoling thought. Unlike Friedrich Nietzsche, I'm unable to find comfort in the idea of the "eternal recurrence"; in the idea that one should be prepared to live one's life down to the last detail, over and over again. It would not only be unbearable—even Nietzsche retreated into insanity at the age of only 45 years from the horror of such a thought—but would destroy the joyous ephemerality of life. And, unlike the advisor to the Anglo-Saxon king Edwin of Northumbria (584-633)—who was contemplating changing the allegiance of his kingdom from the old pagan gods to the trendy new Christian God—one should not be disturbed by the ephemerality of life. Edwin's advisor is reported by Bede (*The English People*, 731 AD) to have said:

> The present life of man, O king, seems to me, in comparison of that time which is unknown to us, like to a swift flight of a sparrow through the room wherein you sit at supper in winter, with your commanders and ministers, and a good fire in the midst, whilst the storms of rain and snow prevail abroad; the sparrow, I say, flying in at one door, and immediately out at another, whilst he is within, is safe from the wintry storm; but after a short space of fair weather, he immediately vanishes out of your sight, into the dark winter from which he had emerged. So this life of man appears for a short space, but of what went before, or what is to follow, we are utterly ignorant.

This is an elegant metaphor for the ephemerality of life: a sparrow flying briefly through a lighted room on its journey from darkness to darkness. While the great king's clerical advisor was more concerned with the "dark winter" outside the lighted room, my focus in this book is on how we can fly most freely through this ephemeral space.

"Alpine Heights", © G.D. Snooks

Ultimate Reality

References

This list of books and selected papers, published by G.D. Snooks between 1974 and 2015, provides the empirical and theoretical basis for *Ultimate Reality*.

Snooks, G.D. (1974), *Depression and Recovery in Western Australia, 1928/29—1938/39. A Study in Cyclical and Structural Change.* Nedlands: UWA Press.

Snooks, G.D. (1993a). *Economics Without Time.* London: Macmillan

Snooks, G.D., ed. (1993b), *Historical Analysis in Economics.* London & New York: Routledge.

Snooks, G.D. (1994a), *Portrait of the Family within the Total Economy. A Study in Longrun Dynamics: Australia, 1788–1990.* Cambridge: Cambridge University Press.

Snooks, G.D., ed. (1994b), *Was the Industrial Revolution Necessary?* London & New York: Routledge.

Snooks, G.D. (1996). *The Dynamic Society.* London & New York: Routledge.

Snooks, G.D. (1997). *The Ephemeral Civilization.* London & New York: Routledge.

Snooks, G.D. (1998a). *The Laws of History.* London & New York: Routledge.

Snooks, G.D. (1998b). *Longrun Dynamics: A General Economic and Political Theory. London:* Macmillan.

Snooks, G. D. (1999). *Global Transition. A general Theory of Economic Development.* London: Macmillan.

Snooks, G.D. (2000). *The Global Crisis Makers.* London: Macmillan.

Snooks, G.D. (2003). *The Collapse of Darwinism; or The Rise of a Realist Theory of Life.* Lanham, MD and Oxford: Lexington Books, Roman & Littlefield.

Snooks, G.D. (2005). "The origin of life on Earth: A new general dynamic theory", *Advances in Space Research,* 36: 226–234.

Snooks, G.D. (2006). *The Selfcreating Mind.* Lanham, MD and Oxford: University Press of America, Roman & Littlefield.

Snooks, G.D. (2007). "Self-organisation or selfcreation? From social physics to realist dynamics". *Social Evolution & History* 6 (March): 118–144.

Snooks, G.D. (2008a). "A general theory of complex living systems: Exploring the demand side of dynamics", *Complexity,* 13 (July/August): 12–20.

Snooks, G.D. (2008b). "The Neanderthal enigma: A new theoretical approach", Global Dynamic Systems Centre (RSSS, ANU), *Working Papers,* No. 5 (August): 1–42.

Snooks, G.D. (2010a). *The Coming Eclipse, or the Triumph of Climate Mitigation over Solar Revolution.* Canberra: IGDS Books.

Snooks, G.D. (2010b). *Dead God Rising. The Role of Religion and Science in the Universal Life-System.* Canberra: IGDS Books.

Snooks, G.D. (2011). *The Death of Zarathustra. Note on Truth for the Risk-Taker.* Canberra: IGDS Books.

Snooks, G.D. (2013), "The Cosmos & the Logos (I)", Institute of Global Dynamic Systems (Canberra), *Working Papers*, no. 11, July 2013 (1st version, May 2009): 1–32.

Snooks, G.D. (2015a), "The Cosmos and the Logos (II): A Realist Theory of Life's Emergence, Evolution and Future", Ch. 8 in B. Rodrigue, L. Grinnin & A. Korotayev (eds), *From the Big Bang to Galactic Civilization: A Big History Anthology. Volume I.* Delhi: Primus Books.

Snooks, G.D. (2015b), *Ark of the Sun. The Improbable Voyage of Life.* Canberra: IGDS Books.

Snooks, G.D. and J. McDonald (1986), *Domesday economy. A new approach to Anglo-Norman history.* Oxford: Clarendon Press.

About the Author

Graeme Donald Snooks is the Executive Director of the Institute of Global Dynamic Systems (IGDS) in Canberra. For twenty-one years between 1989 and 2010 he was the foundation Coghlan Research Professor in Economics & History in the Institute of Advanced Studies at the Australian National University. Some three decades ago he embarked on an ambitious research program to develop a realist dynamic theory of the changing fortunes of human society and life from their beginnings. This has given rise to the widely acclaimed dynamic-strategy theory (published in *Advances in Space Research,* and in *Complexity* the journal of the Santa Fe Institute), which Professor Snooks is employing to rethink all aspects of the life sciences. This is the first general dynamic theory in the history of human thought to employ an effective demand-side approach. The dynamic-strategy theory is unique in a world of unworkable supply-side theories.

The results of this research have been published in a number of well-received trilogies, including the global history trilogy (*The Dynamic Society, The Ephemeral Civilization,* and *The Laws of History*), the social dynamics trilogy (*Longrun Dynamics, Global Transition,* and *The Global Crisis Makers*), and the dynamics of life trilogy (*The Collapse of Darwinism, The Selfcreating Mind,* and *Dead God Rising*). More recently, Professor Snooks has published books on: the role of truth in human society—*The Death of Zarathustra*; an overview of the entire research program —*Ark of the Sun*; and a realist philosophy of life—*Ultimate Reality and its Dissidents.* The core discovery of this research program is the universal life system, called the strategic *logos*, which was analyzed for the first time in *Dead God Rising* and *The Death of Zarathustra,* and developed further in *Ark of the Sun* and *Ultimate Reality.*

About IGDS Books

IGDS Books is the imprint of the publishing activities of the Institute of Global Dynamic Systems in Canberra. It is the mission of IGDS Books to publish innovative work that pushes beyond the existing frontiers of knowledge—a challenge that major scholarly publishers have abandoned in this electronic era. As Executive Director of the Institute, Professor Graeme Snooks oversees the activities of IGDS Books.

For information about the Institute or **IGDS Books,** see the Institute's website, or contact Professor Snooks at seouenaca@gmail.com.

IGDS Books include:

G.D. Snooks, *THE COMING ECLIPSE – or The Triumph of Climate Mitigation Over Solar Revolution* (March 2010)

G.D. Snooks, *DEAD GOD RISING. Religion & Science in the Universal Life-System* (November 2010)

G.D. Snooks, *THE DEATH OF ZARATHUSTRA. Notes on Truth for the Risk-taker* (March 2011).

G.D. Snooks, *ARK OF THE SUN. The Improbable Voyage of Life* (November 2015).

G.D. Snooks, *ULTIMATE REALITY AND ITS DISSIDENTS. A Philosophy of Life* (March 2015).

For information about and orders for the Institute's publications—books and working papers—please contact the Institute Administrator at institutegds@gmail.com.

www.ingramcontent.com/pod-product-compliance
Lightning Source LLC
Chambersburg PA
CBHW060301100426
42742CB00011B/1827